Earthmare: The Lost Book of Wars

Cergat

with contributions by
Realic
Tectumor

K-zome	Endorgan
Insomnya	Z/\neg
Reel-*8ct*	A.D.G.E.
Ert-slc.	Balil

EARTHMARE

THE LOST BOOK OF WARS

Edited by Erba

gnOme • Terra Incognita
2017

Earthmare: The Lost Book of Wars
© 2017 Cergat
gnOme books
Terra Incognita

The book was typeset in Centaur.
The Title Page is set in Didot.
The headers and page numbers are set in Calibri
Light and Candara.
Book design & typesetting: Guerrilla Concepts.

gnOme books
gnomebooks.wordpress.com

Please address inquiries to:
gnomebooks@gmail.com

ISBN-13: 978-0692841082
ISBN-10: 0692841083

Contents

…the arrow oɟ lime has turned. Such deep fluctu-
ations are imperceptible, ⌊Ξ⌊Π△Ä¢ƎhaД"
wᵒ ░Δϑϰáꞁ) briŋ dire consequences. A deɔp fis-
sureʊ̈ꞁ#ꞁ� gone unnoticed■ ■makes its way to
the surface, proliferates the forgotten ancient
curƨe. Kϰowꜱɘdge isꞁ) defenceless here [it] is of
the c̈urse. Consciousneƨs ⫼⫼⫼¢⌋stumbles as it
ɔttempts its first steps in the pɹæternal geomancʎ-
-it will have to re-learn everything by heart. This
is the sentɔnce:

Preface

In mid-October 1997, two clay tablets marked in wedge-shaped signs, were discovered inside a cave in the Accursed Mountains in Albania. The local shepherds who found them, took the artifacts to their pastor, an amateur linguist and folklore aficionado, who at first glance identified the cuneiform writing as Sumerian. He was shown the discovery site where he found several other fragments, prompting him to further continue the search. In the winter months from November 1997 to February 1998, four more tablets were put together out of thirty-seven fragments collected in the interior of the cave. Six fragments (frgs. 2, 5, 18, 13, 27, 9) did not match any of the partially restored tablets, suggesting that more pieces may lay hidden deeper into the cave. However, these were not discovered until the end of September 1998, when a landslide revealed a separate cave pocket enclosing a wooden ark, adding three more tablets to the collection.

Clearly, the artifacts did not belong to the local culture. Their scattered condition suggested that similar earlier landslides might have caused loose tree-roots and mud to close part of the cave off from its mouth. As the texts have only been partially translated, it is as yet unknown whether the last three pieces made up the full set of the original tablets. Most of what we know comes from the notes of the pastor, who for nearly ten years worked on deciphering a good part of the scripts from a language he initially believed to be closely related to the original Indo-European, but subsequently identified as the lost language of the Pelasgians. In a later note, he writes that this was a mixed language, reminiscent of Odysseus's description of Crete, where many barbarian tongues were spoken side by side and mingled with one another (Hom. *Od.* xix. 172-8). After decoding the cuneiform, he translated the texts into Albanian, trying to keep as close to the original as possible. What emerged was another version of Genesis, a creation full of strife the pastor called "the lost book of wars."

Dating back to c. 1400-1100 BC, the tablets are among the oldest apocrypha materials ever found. They are as well of particular interest not only for their content, but also for the unusual site of their discovery. Following recent archaeological finds revealing the Philistines to be only one of a conglomerate of tribes that fought against God's chosen people (see e.g. Bierling 2002), these ancient warriors have been conjectured to be the ones who brought the tablets from Israel.

In his description of the Sea People pirate alliance, Ramesses II (c. 1285 BC) names some of these tribes, among them the Dardanians (Da-ar-d(a)-an-ya), who, after attacking Egypt, turned their attention to Israel. As it is well known, these were Aeneas's people, the Trojans' allies in the war. In ancient times, however, there was also a Dardanian kingdom in present-day Kosovo, likely one of the several colonies of that branch of the Dardanian tribe that traveled westward after the sack of Troy. The pastor came to consider these people as the possible carriers of the ark and the cuneiform tablets.

Assuming that this might be what Israel called the Ark of the Covenant, which was lost to the Philistines in the wars described in I Samuel, the warriors who buried its contents in the Accursed Mountains may well be the ones referred to in the Bible as the giants, Goliath and company. These are the mythical giants north of Greece (ancient Gr. *gegas*), whose demonym still survives in the Gheg tribes of northern Albania.

Introduction

This book is a selection of a series of articles, lectures, and presentations delivered by a wide array of scholars at different events and conferences hosted by the underground Abnoriens Kateschizeîn University as early as 2009 to the present. While their fields vary greatly, from mythology, religious and biblical studies to linguistics and anthropology; from philosophy, psychology, juridical and political theories to medicine and physics, their point of departure is the same – the first day of Genesis described in the cuneiform tablets found between 1997-1998 in the Accursed Mountains of Albania.

The studies selected for this publication build upon one another presenting a unique view of Creation, the human and the inhuman (or God's creature and the outcast; the exile, the barbarian), that is both holistic and fractured in its kaleidoscopic focus. This may also be a result of the selection process, however, and the decision to offer only those parts of the selected articles, essays, or lectures, which could befit the rest of the book. Nevertheless, the works become more coherent as the book progresses and the underlying currents begin to emerge.

The selection was a difficult process, but one that owing to the sheer number of disciplines collected under one subject, became inevitable. The reader should not feel as though he or she has missed anything. In fact, that would have been the case had the articles been produced in their entirety, as oftentimes the scholars in their erudition of the respective fields, dropped from sight considerations of a wider audience and immersed themselves in theoretical physics, applied mathematics, specific legal and juridical issues, and historical problems of medicine, which could hardly all be intelligible to, or even hold the interest of, any one reader. At times, however, discussions of specific issues were impossible to avoid and, when so needed, detailed explanations have been moved to end-notes and appendices. As it stands, the book is meant to be accessible to everyone, not only to professionals in the specific fields. For this reason, fuller quotes have often been provided.

The works are separated into six Parts, or Books, according to their themes. The first Book, partly dealing with principles of science and physics, is perhaps the most abstract part of the work, and is the one that most closely focuses on the exhumed texts. It comprises only two short chapters, much longer originally, constituting a unique blend of religion and physics that gives rise to a third alternative, which then acquires a strange autonomy from its parentage. Partly presented for the first time in 2009 at a joint panel of the Tiranë-Chicago Conference, they are also the earliest articles of this selection.

From the philosophical standpoint, this section lays the groundwork for a radical view of Creation, presenting the Beginning as an event squeezed between two absolutes, Oneness and Nothingness. It is radical because, unlike most philosophical systems that attempt to find a power balance between the two, here the struggle or courtship between absolutes (think of dialectical monism) is turned against itself, providing an unforeseen escape trajectory from the servility they demand, as well as an intellectual tool to dismantle the paralytic systems and philosophies that enforce it. A dark destabilizing force, then, grows unchecked behind their neurotic love-hate relationship, transcribing the process of creation in reverse (in the biological sense: think of RNA $\rightarrow$ DNA reverse transcription) stabbing at the boundary between noumena and phenomena, thus cracking open the floodgates of creation.

This theme reappears in the sixth and last Book, with the notion of oncogenesis, a cancerous and deranged accelerated creation that supplants God's own original Creation with its hierarchical divisions and boundaries. In this sense, ontology, the study of Being, may properly be called *medical ontology*, because, similarly to modern oncology, it struggles to grasp and hold on to a certain notion of immutability that may provide some consolation in the face of the transience of things. To cure cancer for all time means to stop mutations: this would be the highest affirmation of all for an immutable unchanging Being. However, while the existence of such a perfect never-changing world or immutable Being may be viewed as the very essence of immortality, the opposite is true. It is the cancer cell, in all its protean shape-shifting transformations, that is immortal. Being, ultimately, is the triumph of identity over immortality.

Book II, "Voodoo Etymologies", provides a linguistic background for understanding the socio-political order. God's judgments, sanctions, and wars are generally aimed at maintaining the boundaries he has set, not only for humanity, but for the whole world — earth, water, air, as well as fire; the elements must be kept neatly apart in his clinical approach. But as the rules set down for the separation, categorization, and sterilization of the world apply equally to all created things, they must hold true for language as well, since it was by means of the word that God created the world. Ultimately, in their uncompromising totality, his fierce wars may be characterized as geological and earth-encompassing (the flood; his scorched earth policy in which the prophets revel time and again in their apocalyptic visions; the indiscriminate slaughter of men, women, children, and even animals by his chosen people). Hence, understanding the impact of the word, compels a mapping of its entirety, viz., its geological and topological reality, not merely its abstract and insubstantial existence. Words as carriers of energy — dynamic force vectors submerged in energy fields integrated into vast information systems. What Lacan's formula "the unconscious functions like a language" means, then, is that captured in the web of language, the unconscious is channeled into the turbines of the socio-political machine, for which psychoanalysis seems to be "the maintenance department." (see appendix D).

Finally, control over earth, water, and air, must be understood in linguistic terms in the same way that Morgan (or Engels) understood the system of the family. Terms such as, *terra firma*, *terra nullius*, *terra incognita*, etc. are intrinsically bound to this and provide the basis for an in-depth understanding of society and the so-called "immense fellowship of the human species". (Cicero, *De Officiis* I:53). This is the subject of Book III, "The Socio-Political Ballast", which traces the juridical developments associated with the discovery of the New World, and consequently, the political and juridical notions concerned with the difference between the savage and the citizen-subject (along with their respective international rights).

Following a persistent pattern in political theory oscillating between those who view the development of civilization as a straight line from the state of Nature to the State through the social contract (Hobbes, Rousseau, etc.), and those who interject a phase of barbarity between the two (Montesquieu, Marx), Book III analyzes both in light of a so-called alternative spiritualist position (Bayona-Ba-Meya). All three come conclusively to a head as a result, revealing their common concerns and bias.

The introduction of the barbarian as an intermediary figure negotiating between the state of Nature and the State, is especially problematic since it is generally argued (e.g. by Edith Hall) that this figure was invented by the Greeks of the fifth century BC as a propagandistic device to not only provide a Panhellenic ideal around which the Greek city-states could join during the Persian wars, but also as "an exercise in self-definition". For society to assimilate the barbarian into the great fellowship of humanity, then, means no less than losing its civilized character, its identity.

Building upon these analyses and the topological etymologies provided in Book II, Book III takes the oscillation of political theories between the social contract and the barbarian and reconstructs the RNA strand of civilization through a twist in the information system from the state of savagery into that of civilization. Such a twist that achieves evolution through revolution is the work of the barbarian at the heart of the system, not as a negotiator, but as an apocalyptic figure.

Book IV looks at the origins of the barbarian from the perspective of the Greek myths, especially the myth of Heracles and his war on barbaric hybrid figures like the Centaurs. The work presented here, is an in-depth investigation of the complexities of their relationship, since like Achilles, Heracles was Chiron's pupil, whom he ends up killing along with most of the other Centaurs. The hero is then himself killed by Nessus. In a way, the myth of the greatest hero of civilization starts and ends with the barbaric Centaurs.

Julian Jaynes's theory of the bicameral mind, provides a good starting point for an investigation into the origins of the barbarian, collapsing the ahistorical barbarian of the civilized Hellenes of the fifth century with the historical (or pre-historical) barbarian at the heart of the breakdown of the bicameral mind. By twisting the auditory hallucinations of bicameral men, these barbarians, then, emerge as the first shamanic figures on their way to invading the abode of the gods, or alternately, as gods unleashed from their human bonds wreaking havoc across a chaotic landscape that saw the collapse of the Aegean civilization.

A discussion of Chiron's teachings in conjunction with Gordon Wasson's studies on the entheogenic mushroom of the Aryans in the Vedic hymns, provide the background for the cataclysmic events of the 1300-1200 BC. The chapters of Book IV and V make repeated forays from different angles into the philosophical principles taught by these apocalyptic masters. The impact these teachings had on poetry, tragedy, and philosophy are traced in Book IV, especially in 4.3, and in Books V and VI. Among these, the split between reason and instinct looms particularly large, for it is the basis of the rise of civilization. Yet, this split did not come without its side effects. The sudden freedom man acquired from the old bicameral gods left him bereft of proper means to come to a decision. In subjective conscious man, volition was now a matter of conceit. In the struggle between reason and instinct, the former had to draw its energy from the latter (see, e.g. Freud's ego/id schemata). Hence, it could only conduct this inner warfare using the most destructive of instincts. The ancients' notion of black bile, however mechanistically it was interpreted later, e.g. by Galen, initially seems to have addressed this split of agency and the conflict that arose from it. In its reappearance as *acedia* with the desert monks of the fourth century AD, it retained its double nature as both a spiritual and carnal affliction. In medicine, it caused both depression (mind) and cancer (body), whereas within the sciences of the mind, it resulted from a disturbance now of cognition (reason), now of affection (instinct).

From the perspective of the desert monks, acedia was the most grievous demon of all (later to be transformed into the sin of sloth), urging the monk to flee from his cell, and if this became a habit, from everywhere he happened to find himself. This was called *horror loci*, fear or disgust with the present location, and, if taken but a step further, it could turn into a full-blown exilic, and therefore barbarian, mentality. In short, it explains why the barbarian ravages without colonializing. What this means for the monk, nonetheless, is that, after severing his ties with this earth, he could even carry the torch to heaven. From the physical to the spiritual world.

The last chapter, "Oncological Creation: The Earth Sickness", returns once more to linguistic analysis, for "sky" and "cell" trace their origins to the same root, hence diagnosing acedia's onslaught on heaven as an outgrowth of cancer invading the spiritual realm. From this standpoint, the earth itself appears to be nothing more than a tumor in God's throat, at first, perhaps, little more than a scarring caused by his thunderous voice. The growth, however, gets quickly out of control, sprouting forth countless abominable worlds. This oncological creation, then, was the subject of God's wars, which brings us back and full circle to where this book began.

Special thanks go to Arben P. Latifi for his diligent proofreading of the texts, and his invaluable criticism and suggestions in our cross-Continental nocturnal conversations.

THE LOST BOOK OF WARS: PELASGÆA
PJTR. B.

The Tablets

The cuneiform stone tablets, nine in all, were discovered in the year 1997, but it was not until 1998 that all nine pieces were recovered in what is known as *Maja Boshit* (Summit of the Void) in the Accursed Mountains. Three tablets were found inside a wooden ark, which was heavily damaged, while the rest had been scattered throughout the cave. One of the tablets was complete and very well preserved, two were fragmented, but it was possible to collect a good part of the fragments in the adjacent areas, while the other six were fragmented and missing a good deal of the pieces.

Dating the Materials

An odd fact that remains unaccounted for, is that the oldest tablets were the better preserved, so that if put together in a sequence with the beginning of the story first, followed in order by the rest, one would have believed that their age was the opposite of what scientific data indicated, as if someone had attempted to write the story backwards.

Preliminary luminescence and carbon dating revealed that the tablets were between 4700-3900 years old, which makes them the oldest apocrypha materials ever found.

Soon after they were found, they came into the possession of a reclusive monk whose whereabouts are completely unknown at present. He studied them in isolation for over ten years, and deciphered and translated a good part of the texts from what he at first assumed to be a language closely related to the original Indo-European.

The Vatican

The monk then took the artifacts to Italy to have them analyzed in a lab with which he had secretly maintained correspondence and reached an agreement. Three months later, the tablets mysteriously disappeared from the lab, and the monk, who until then had maintained complete silence about the discovery, accused the lab of having stolen and destroyed the tablets in collusion with the Vatican. Soon after, the monk himself disappeared without a trace.

Pellazgjia

[1]Mâ s parit Pernia kall varrën e bâ[n] bosh(tm). [2]E pafurm kjé trunga tansis pamat, [3]a[m]á [... ...] b'zan, «Mû hap i vrrag me shkle tanën katërçika»; e t[u] kall ni vrrag i thell, [2]qe andet A(h)ti bi ujna t'err ka u kqyr; [4]Qashtu e kallxon vedin [... ...]. [5]E Di(h)t ja kojt emnin pasi kesh [dit?]. A[m]á pasqyn e humners te kapërdin di(f)t(?)[......] e thellsina ardh e duel nalt; e [... ... ...] kojt Nat.
Qashtu m[j]esi dhe e mramja kesh kan di(h)t e par.

TANAKH: GEN. 1-5

[1]When God began to create heaven and earth—[2]the earth being unformed and void, with darkness over the surface of the deep and a wind from God sweeping over the water—[3]God said, "Let there be light"; and there was light. [4]God saw that the light was good, and God separated the light from the darkness. [5]God called the light Day, and the darkness He called Night. And there was evening and there was morning, a first day.

KING JAMES: GEN. 1-5

[1]In the beginning God created the heavens and the earth. [2]The earth was without form, and void; and darkness was on the face of the deep. And the Spirit of God was hovering over the face of the waters.

[3]Then God said, "Let there be light"; and there was light. [4]And God saw the light that it was good; and God divided the light from the darkness. [5]God called the light Day, and the darkness He called Night. So the evening and the morning were the first day.

EARTHMARE: ONCOGEN. 1-5

[1]First of all God [burrowed] a hole and made the void. [2]Formless was the trunk of the immeasurable whole; [3]Then [...] uttered, "Let there be a wound (in Me) to tear the whole into four"; and there was a deep *gaping* Wound [2]and *the breath of God's desire* hovered over dark waters discerning itself. Thus, He showed Himself to Himself. [5]And *according to his knowledge* He called this Day.* But the mirror-eye of the abyss gulped down the light and the deep rose nigh; and [... ... ...] called Night. So the morning and the evening were the first day.

---

* *Day* (ditë) and *to know* (me ditë) are homophones in Albanian.

NOTES

❖ The letters inside parentheses in the Albanian translation of the text (e.g. "h" in *Aht*, "tm" in *boshtm*) indicate forms that might no longer exist in modern Albanian, but were retained in the original, either because the main meaning of the word can easily be understood by the Albanian speaker, while suggesting additional connotations that could not be rendered otherwise or because it is not possible to tell which word is meant.[†]

❖ The words in italics in the English translation follow the example of the King James translation to add for clarification words that are not found in the original, but which help convey the meaning better in English.

❖ The ellipses inside the square brackets in the attempted de-codification of the cuneiform characters, indicate one or more illegible values. This is similarly indicated in the Albanian translation, while the words inside the square brackets indicate their attempted reconstruction where possible.

❖ The numbers inside the square brackets, which stand below in front of some of the passages, indicate where the related passage, if applicable, may be found in the established version of the Bible, when the present version does not conform to it.

For cited works in which Kindle Editions have been used, kindle locations have been provided instead of page numbers.

[†] In the word *boshtm*, for instance, it is unclear whether *bosh* "empty, void" or *bosht* "axis" is meant (see analysis of *boshtm* in ch. 6.3).

Abbreviations

AED – Albanian Etymological Dictionary (Vladimir Orel)
FE – Fjalor Etimologjik i Gjuhës Shqipe (Gustav Meyer)
SE – Studime Etimologjike në Fushë të Shqipes (Eqrem Çabej)

OED – Online Etymology Dictionary: www.etymonline.com
DEO – Dizionario Etimologico Online: www.etimo.it

DAY ONE

1.1 The Disease of the Void

With masts sung earthward
the heaven wrecks sail.

—Paul Celan, "With Masts Sung Earthward"

To the average believer, if that creature still exists, it would be shocking to learn that the biblical scholars' interpretation in the New English Translation (NET) Bible does not assume a beginning proper, viz., original creation. In the Torah, as well, verse 1 of the King James Genesis "In the beginning God created the heavens and the earth" is considered to be incorrect, in fact the Torah scholars go as far as to regard it completely inadmissible even as an alternate reading. Instead, they suggest that the correct wording should be, "When God began to create heaven and earth..."[1]

On the other hand, the first verse of the text deciphered from the ancient cuneiform writing on the stone tablets, reads: "Ambh[...] prheos Dza[...] kelh uœrhno hnō ba[...] bhuthshtm", which in Albanian was rendered as "Mâ s parit Pernia kall varrën e bâ[n] bosh(t)ëm." This narrative radically departs from all the established versions of the bible and can be translated broadly as follows, "First of all God burrowed a hole and made the void." Or if, as some Albanologists have suggested, *zoti* "god" is derived from *zathi* "soft voice" (diminution of *zani* "voice,"), then it could be rendered as, "First of all the Voice ordered a hole and made the void."‡

The monk, however, renders it "Pernia" in the Gheg dialect,[2] which literally means "deity," and does not follow the etymological implications of *zot* (dza[...]).

---

‡ For a more detailed discussion of the many established versions of the Bible and their take on original creation, see Appendix A.

The first words, *ambhi prheos*, mean "first of all," literally "before, over, above first." However, the Albanian expression *mâ s parit*, even though syntactically preserving the older meaning of the Indo-European, which indicates a presence, or more precisely a present absence, at a *punctum* (point, puncture) before any counting takes place, from long usage seems to have acquired a positive connotation consistent with "in the very beginning." The English expression *first of all*, has similarly undergone the same semantic transformation while retaining the old syntax, i.e. the meaning has shifted underneath the petrified form. Therefore, in order to suggest the old meaning, one is forced to break with the form, converting *first of all* to something like *before first* or *before anything*. The literal use of "in the beginning" demands the Albanian form to be *në fillim*[3] (from *fill* "thread", therefore literally meaning, "at the start of the thread"), not *mâ s parit* which in this case means "before the start of the thread," or "before the beginning."[§]

The choice of words "in the beginning," in a number of the established versions of the Bible, leaves open the question of what was before creation, for the use of the word "beginning," coupled with the concept of original creation, implies a radical breaking away from a previous state (or statelessness) where nothing of what is now existed. Therefore, the question might be rendered as, 1) is the beginning to be regarded unilaterally and consequently applied only to the world of phenomena, leaving noumena untouched and unchanged, or does noumena undergo some change, too? This same question can be formulated in such a way as to address the laws of physics, and thus include scientific inquiries. The question in this case would be, 2) do the laws that govern the behavior of energy and matter change, or does change pertain only to energy and matter, which, of course, brings us full circle to the first question that was assumed to already be known from the standpoint of religious discourse, 3) what exists first, the law or its subject? All three versions of the question make plain the impasse that results from the

---

§ For more detailed linguistic analysis, see Appendix B.

imposition of such a dual view on the world,[4] one that is at its strongest when enforced across the lines of fiction and nonfiction (or what both the layperson and the scientist call "real").

In one of his notes, in a section dealing with a new conceptualization of religion and physics, Father N. writes:

> ...*beginning*, in the absolute sense must comprise the dawn of time and space. Or else, what is to begin? Hence, if it is at all to be regarded as attending before phenomena, God can at best be regarded as nothingness, and at worst, as being Himself the conceptual implication and deduction of nothingness. Such fictitious conceptual implications are exemplified by many concepts and laws in science in general (and physics in particular), but it will suffice to mention only one at this time, namely, the concepts dealing with the speed of light. This is considered to be the case: As an object approaches the speed of light, time approaches zero. However, if the absence of time and space are to be presupposed, then the conceptual conditions already exist for both time and space to pre-exist in a state of annihilated compaction, which gives the universe a total sum that equals zero. Hence, if time $(T) = 0$, then conceptually, the conditions are simulated for the counterfeiting of a fictitious lightspeed, which in turn concocts the object and opens up space. The opening up of lumps of space does not correspond to abiding by a pre-existing fixed law, which would imply a healthy Creation, but to the praeternal disease of the void, the perpetual concoction of foreign matter (*mish i huej* "foreign meat"), viz. its tumor, for everything is foreign to the void, in other words, there is no genetic relation between it and the meat sprouting from it.[5]

Hence, in the KJ Bible, God is at best simultaneous with or indistinguishable from the void, and at worst merely one of the many cancerous abominations sprouting from it. This, no doubt, is the main reason behind the rendering of Genesis in the Torah as, "When God began to create heaven and earth" since here no reference is made to a beginning proper in the sense of a beginning in/of time. In other words, even if the question of what was before creation may still be asked, this is no longer related to the absence of time, and as such the major issue is veiled. The question merely asks what was before the creation (or the existence) of heaven and earth, not what was before existence itself, and is merely a phenom-enological question. Needless to say, the NET Bible version at-tempts to fix the KJ version mistake, turning its interpretation more along the lines of the Torah. In the newly discovered scripts, how-ever, we read, "First of all God burrowed a hole and made the void." As mentioned above, in order to have "in the beginning," the Alba-nian ought to be *në fillim* "at the beginning/start of the thread." But the words *mâ s parit* "first of all" or "before first" indicate a gap (or wound), something before anything else, which bursts open an origin that is to be grasped and then linearly followed all the way to its final destiny in the thread. In other words, the wound (or τραύμα) is always before, or at the beginning of the thread: it is a continuous disruption of any continuity and lineage, and of all predictions that long for the end by virtue of their origin, while at the same time underlying the whole worldthread since 1- trauma is always already at the beginning; 2- it is presently occurring, i.e. trauma, and therefore the beginning is perpetual, or plural (*trau-mata*)[6], otherwise the return to oneness would have already oc-curred,[7] and; 3- it has no reality as noumena, therefore no end of phenomena.

1.2 GUT Theories: The Big Creep

The angst of nothingness won't abate
when owls screech atop green trees

—Alisa Velaj "Incurable Angst"[**]

The following are five schematic representations of an alternative to GUT theories from one of the papers submitted in 2009 at the underground Abnoriens Kateskhizeîn symposium. A few additional notes were added for clarification.

The effects of suction and the five steps of the inside-out universe (everse).

0 ← Nothingness
1 ← Oneness (Being)
x ← Existence (Becoming) or, o ← den (less-than-nothing).
| ← bar (trauma)

0 | 1 | 0

SCHEMA N (Paralysis). Being, cloaked in the cocoon of Nothingness. Apart from replacing Being with Becoming, this is also the view presented by Nietzsche in the last note of *The Will to Power:*

> ...This world: a monster of energy, without beginning, without end; a firm, iron magnitude of force that does not grow bigger or smaller, that does not expend itself but only transforms itself; as a whole, of unalterable size,

---

[**] From the poetry collection, *Salute to Despairs!* Translated from Albanian by Arben P. Latifi. Forthcoming.

a household without expenses or losses, but likewise without increase or income; enclosed by 'nothingness' as by a boundary... ([1968]2011, 544)

Ironically, a crude religious view of the universe also finds its happiness in it, since even with the transformation that Nietzsche speaks of, paradoxically, things remain always the same. This schema betrays the escapist and fetishistic quest for Oneness or the longing for that transcendent other realm, Nothingness. The wish to immortality and its complimentary opposite, complete ontological annulment, are here satisfied in linear terms.

Although the schema attempts an absolute negation of that unbearable gap between Oneness and Nothingness, it nevertheless raises the question: What is the point where Being touches the Void? Another important question is whether the void can have a location at all (according to Nietzsche, external, relative to Being), not to speak of size or circumference, for there is nothing outside itself to compare itself to. And most importantly, what is the force of Nothingness relative to that of Being and vice versa? In short, can non-existence exert force on existence? If so, is that force real or illusory? Differently stated, may the force exerted by non-existence be an effect merely of existence speaking to itself?

By its very definition, Nothingness is absolute vacuum, therefore, its force is suction (*sugere*). The force of Being, on the other hand, is absolute gravity toward the object of desire, urge (*urgere*). In schema N, the object of desire can be one of two things: Being itself or Nothingness. Ultimately, however, they are one and the same, since a point has no exterior, the space that surrounds it is its interior, its own guts, so to speak (Abbott 1952). This constitutes its lack-in-being (*manque à être* or *objet petit a*) in psychoanalytic-semiotic terms. Psychologically speaking, then, schema N could properly be understood as a Narcissistic universe regarding itself in the mirror-eye of the abyss.

But how do these forces relate to one another? Is there communication between Being and Nothingness? Again, are the bars barring Being from Nothingness real or illusory? One can only say that here the boundaries between the real and illusion are constantly renegotiated, their forces incessantly inverted and entwined, simultaneously broken apart and hurled back together again. This ceaseless renegotiation reveals a third force, the surge (*surgere*), a militaristic term for which psychoanalytic theory has no term of its own.

$$0 \text{ «»| X |»» } 0$$

SCHEMA I (The Big Bang). Centrifugal force—explosion: expansion at speeds greater than the speed of light. To represent the schema more consistently with Democritus's notion of "less-than-nothing," *existence* (x) may be replaced with *den* (ø), which lends itself more readily to a frictionless identification with virtual particles: 0 «»| ø |»» 0. This schema is, of course, a representation of suction, or of the urge of Being rushing towards itself, as mentioned above.

$$\text{«»| X || X |»»}$$

$$[\text{existence } (x) < 0; > 1]$$

SCHEMA II (The Big Rip). The whole is ripped apart. A white hole (two bars) prevents entrance/communication between the parts. *Existence* x is both less than nothing and more than 1. This schema may also be represented as: «»| ø || ø |»»

$$\text{X |»» «»| X}$$

$$[\text{existence } (x) \rightarrow 0]$$

SCHEMA III (The Big Crunch). Centripetal force—implosion: The Outside creeps in; black holes sucking in even light. False vacuum points emerge in the interior, producing what is perceived as gravity. Here too, the alternative schema: ø |»» ««| ø provides a better conceptualization for what is perceived as gravity, and moreover, one that also accounts for the three other forces.

$$««| \; x \; |»» \quad ««| \; x \; |»» \; ««| \; x \; |»»$$

$$[\text{existence } (x) \to 0; \; \infty]$$

SCHEMA IV (The Big Creep). Explosion/Implosion: The whole is radically perforated resulting in what Negarestani (2008) dubs the ( )hole complex. This synthesis of religion and science is a heresy for both. For religion because it breaks the DNA sequence of the One resulting in a metastatic cancerous growth. For science because of its chaotic propensity. Nevertheless, these schemas offer a conceptualization for and solve the problem of the suppression mechanism needed to reduce the vacuum energy density according to the Quantum expectation by at least 120 orders of magnitude.

To follow further these schizoid lines of thought: What is the meaning of "[trauma] has no reality as noumena, therefore no end of phenomena"?

In regarding creation chronologically, one should have to place noumena first and phenomena last, divided, as we saw, by the wound or the bar.

Ø   Noumena
Ø   Bar
Ø   Phenomena

However, the bar is not to be regarded simply as that which splits noumena from phenomena. The existence of phenomena is itself enabled by the disturbance of the eternal balance of noumena. It is the perturbation in noumena that brings about phenomena. Hence, the formula holds meaning in its mathematical expression, $\frac{N}{P}$, since the bar is an operator that divides noumena, giving rise to phenomena. Any division in noumena, however, is always already a division by phenomena. Moreover, the perturbation of noumena necessarily destroys any chronological timeframe that might proceed from it, and the true point of origin becomes not only impossible to grasp, but it also shifts place and changes shape. Trauma, therefore, cracks open any isolated system or thing-in-itself.

The impossibility of asymmetrical time from primal cause to ultimate effect is the result of the non-existence of time before phenomena. The crack in eternity creates the semblance of chronology, but the shards can no longer be rearranged because eternity did not exist at some time in the past. In other words, if the beginning can only be situated after the trauma, or rather, is concomitant with it, then trauma supplants and replaces noumena as the point of origin;

$$\frac{P}{P1}; \frac{P1}{P2}; \frac{P2}{P3} \cdots$$

As schema IV above illustrates, the cosmological arrow of time – which physics' theories assume might either progress forward with the universe expanding until it ends in the Big Rip or Heat Death, or reverse as gravity pulls everything back together resulting in the Big Crunch – is symmetrical coincident, resulting in the Big Creep. In its mysterious power, trauma allows for both Oneness and Nothingness as the point of origin, while at the same time disallowing both (insofar as both are absolute) by reducing Nothingness ($x < 0$) while adding to Oneness ($x > 1$), a hyperdimensional furcation that executes and destroys balance. Therefore, it may be said that before the trauma, Time $(T) = 0; \infty$.

The reason for this obvious paradox that equals 0 to ∞, and with it makes every number equal,[1] is that trauma is not only that which divides, but also the indispensable subrogate and ultimate enabler of communication between economically non-communicating entities. In short, communication is the stabbing of unity – of what previously was One or None, in the words of Aleister Crowley – by the double-edged dagger of chaos and the endless burrowing that is put in motion by it. The fact that here we are confronted with two absolutes implies the workings of a more obscure power, that by splitting and coupling non-negotiable terms, ceaselessly reduces Nothingness and adds to Oneness. As already described above (see schema N), the bar/trauma simultaneously severs and joins the urge | suction (*urgere* | *sugere*) duality. However, its force is not simply a surge (*surgere*) in the natural sense of a coupling together of Being and Nothingness in their love-hate relationship. Rather it is surgical, in the sense of an absolutely inauthentic operation: "work done by hand," *surgeon*.

The words *kall varrën* "to burrow a gash, a wound," are significant in this regard. The reconstructed original *kelh*, which corresponds to the modern Albanian *kall*,[2] literally means "to put inside" as used in the expression *kall datën*, which means "to frighten" or "to fill with fear."[3]

> ...although the word *kall* in modern Albanian means 'to put inside,' it rather seems that it is used here in a sense suggesting an opening, similarly to *çel* "to hatch; to light a fire; to bloom," also "to open up, to split (the sky)." The difference lies ... in the structure of the sentence and the preposition *në* "in" that is lacking; in order to mean "to put inside," as in "to put *in* the grave", the sentence would have to be, "kall *në* vorr." However, in the present case, not only is the preposition missing, but the following words "bân boshtëm"[††] suggest a different meaning which points in the direction of an opening rather than a filling. The word *kall*, then, seems to indicate not simply a filling of something that was previously empty, but an action which simultaneously cuts and fills, messing up properties. The proof for this reading lies a few lines below, "...b'zan, "Mû hap i vrrag me

---

††. "Made the void."

shkle tanën katërçika; e tu kall ni vrrag i thell…"‡‡ Thus, the word *hap*§§ is used as a synonym of *kall*, since the order God gives cannot differ from its fulfillment. If then, the word *kall* is to preserve its meaning of 'putting [something] inside,' and at the same time be a synonym for *open*, ultimately the word should be understood as a digging; when digging, as with a shovel, the opening occurs as a result of cutting the ground open by thrusting the shovel in, revealing God's primary function as a grave-digger.[4]

---

‡‡. Verse 1:3. "God uttered, 'Let there be a gaping wound (in Me), to split the Whole in four'; and there was a deep gaping wound…"

§§. "to open."

VOODOO ETYMOLOGIES

2.1 Terra Firma

§ 238. The boundary is constructed with large, towering rocks, thrust into the earth and exposed above it.

§ 242. "Once boundaries are fixed, they are never moved again."
*§ 243. In the view of the Kanun, the bones of the dead and the boundary stone are equal. To move a boundary is like playing with the bones of the dead."***

—The Code of Lekë Dukagjini

The word **uœrhe** – which appears to correspond to at least three modern Albanian words indicating their common origin, *vërë* "hole; cave, grotto"; *varrë* "wound; split, tearing; broad stripe, stria"; and *varr* "grave, tomb"[1] – demands a careful analysis, for it is the nexus around which the whole Bible spider-web has been weaved. At this early node in a creation account, a term suggestive of the earth or the sky would be expected. Yet here a hole, a wound, and a tomb are found. A more in-depth look at the etymology of the words for world, however, shows that the discrepancy between the present scripts and the numerous more or less established versions of canonized Scripture may not be as wide as it first appears, and the result of interpretive twists more than outright changes (see ch. 6.3). The Online Etymology Dictionary (OED) imparts that though in some Indo-European languages – comprising Albanian, which does not figure in its source citations – the words for *world* derive from *bottom*; in others, including English, the word is of Germanic origin:

*** The translation is by Leonard Fox, apart from the correction in article 243, which he erroneously translates as: "To move a boundary is like moving the bones of the dead." The Albanian has *me luejt me* "to play with" not *me luejt* "to move," denoting an irreverence greater than mere displacement.

World (n.) from Old English *woruld, worold* "human existence, the affairs of life," also "a long period of time," also "the human race, mankind, humanity," a word peculiar to Germanic languages with a literal sense of "age of man," from Proto-Germanic **wer* "man" (Old English *wer*, still in werewolf; see *virile*) + **ald* "age."

In Albanian, the word for world is *botë*, closely related to English *bottom*. But there is another term that is related to "world," namely, *vënd* "location, place, land" that traces its roots to *ucerhe* with its suggested meanings (*vërë; varrë; varr*), shedding some light upon the relation between these words.

As noticed by Gustav Meyer more than a century ago, the noun **vend vënd, vent vënt**[2] is internally related to the verb *vë* "to put; to place." (*FE*; **vë**). Eqrem Çabej admits that he is unable to illuminate with any certainty the internal rapport between the noun and the verb. He says only that the noun appears to be 1) a verb derivative of *vë*, or an enlargement of the verb with the suffix *-nt* that is known for some ancient Indo-European languages, or 2) an old enlargement of the past participle *vënë* "placed" or of its preformation with *-t-* which he reconstructs into a **ven-tom*, giving an example of a similar transformation from the Latin verb *positus* "placed" into the Italian noun *posto* "place." According to Çabej, it cannot be ruled out that *t* and *d* in *vent* and *vend* may be merely secondary phonetic additions.

The primary meaning of the onomatopoetic verb morpheme **vë, vê, vû** appears to be "to drive in, to thrust in" with *vû* reflected in the aorist Tosk *vura*, Gheg *vuna* "I placed," but vulgar ditransitive *ta (ja) vura, vuna* "I nailed, I corked, I screwed."[3] Neither Meyer nor Çabej mention this meaning in their etymologies, however, where the concept "place" is already found complete in the verb/noun *vë-nt*, having reached its semantic maturity and final differentiation from womb, as it were. The only transformation in need of recording and explaining in their etymologies remains the phonological. The linear developmental pathway followed thus is:

vë (v.) "to place" → *vënë* (p.p.) "placed" → *vënd* (n.) "place" or alternatively, *vë*(v.) → *vënë*(p.p.) → *vënt*(p. p./n.) "placed/place"

This development, which treats the suffixes -*rë*, -*në* and -*nd*, -*nt* as merely supportive or enlargement additions, misses a crucial dimension opened up through considerations of the word as a force vector submerged in dynamic energy fields, and the topographic relief (r) formations that emerge only if we turn to phonosthesia or phonosemantics (sound symbolism) thereby vesting the phonemes /v/, /r/, /n/, /d/, /t/ with certain semantic values (see Appendix C). The result is straightforward:

vë + r = vër(ë) "hole" (also, imperative *vër* (v.) "put")
vë + n = vën(ë) "placed"

The noun *vënd*, then, accounts for all the sequelae of the action described by the verb *vë*: An object is inserted (*vë, vê, vû*) into the ground creating an opening (*vërë*) and is thus fixed in position (*vënë*) as a marker (or a cover—cf. Eng. *veneer*). This marker signifies the separation of that particular location on the earth from all others (*vënd*). According to this schema, the stop consonants *t, d* in *vënt, vënd* signify the fixing (stopping) of the object into place, thereby setting that particular territory, plot, or unit apart from others as immovable property, while the tremulant *r* is suppressed as the opening, cut, or wound (*trauma*) remains isolated underground:

$$\text{vë} + \frac{\text{n}}{\text{r}} \xrightarrow{\Delta} \text{vënd}$$

This ventricose morphological development is a letter-perfect description of the age-old custom of boundary demarcation by way of heavy robust objects (e.g. stones, slates, pillars, obelisks, and corners) planted or inserted into the ground (fig. I). The driving into the earth of these objects as a visible symbol for sealing off (*vulós*)[4] a territorial unit was (and still is) meant to discourage any other claimants (now outsiders).

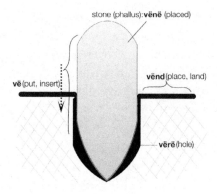

stone (phallus): **vёnё** (placed)

vё (put, insert)

vёnd (place, land)

vёrё (hole)

Figure I

It no longer is empty (*terra nullius*), an opening waiting to be filled, but a property; *vёnd* "land". It is now claimed, filled, corked, marked. It belongs to the bearer of that mark. The resulting topological etymology is shown in Schema V.

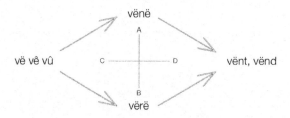

vёnё

A

vё vê vû   C ———————— D   vёnt, vёnd

B

vёrё

Schema V.

44

2.2 Water Channels

§ 351. "The channels of the fields may not be diverted or blocked."

§ 357. The channel has its course and has produced its bed; the bed has made the place its property; hence, there it must stay, it must flow, and it must work.

—The Code of Lekë Dukagjini

These etymological relationships directly associate the earth with the female body. This is illustrated also from the fact that *vajzë vashë* "girl; maid; virgin" traces its roots to *varrë*, a euphemistic naming after the female external genitals.

Vajzë (n.) from *varzë*, diminutive form with suffix *-zë* of *varrë*.[1]

Furthermore, this female body is there for the taking and must first be opened as is attested for example in the myth of Zeus's ravishing of Europa.[2] The association stretches further, and more specifically to the field now equated with a married woman, a measure of land; *virgate*, distinct from "virgin land," which denotes a wild area that does not belong to anyone in the sense of appropriation acquired from the rise of agricultural societies onwards, a sense that attaches both to its cultivation and legal possession.

Ultimately, the comparison of the earth, the field that yields its produce, to a fecund woman is well known, so it should not come as a surprise that *vënd* "land" and *vërë* "opening, hole" – in this sense, *vulva* or *volva* (i.e. in venter, womb) – should appear as one and the same. Even the difference between chattel and real estate becomes insignificant when considering ancient annual reallocation or land tenure traditions, which often developed in conjunction with shifting cultivation practices.

45

While *vënd* and *vërë* are, no doubt, etymologically related, in their respective relation to (Proto) Germanic **werald* "world" and **wundaz* "wound," a strange crisscrossing of terms between languages may be observed, with the phonesthemes becoming disarticulate, no longer aligned in sound and meaning. This is easily observed in the comparison between Albanian and English in Schema VI. The reason for this curious disarticulation or abstraction, which may at first glance appear as a common case of rhotacism, can be found in the root-concept or undivided trunk of the word that carried both meanings (*vënd/vërë* ≅ *world/wound*), and in its subsequent amputation, whereas Germanic languages took off with one limb and Albanian with the other.

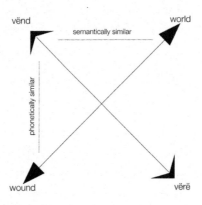

Schema VI

A similar (semantic only) dismemberment can be discerned within the Latin in the words *virgo* "virgin" and *virga* "rod; measuring unit" in both of which the root **vir** is present, yet, it means opposite things, i.e. a break in meaning has occurred while the form of the words with the exception of the end vowel, remains unchanged. Even so, to this day Latin linguists are divided into camps, one tracing *virgo* to the root *vir* and hence to *virile* "the strong and robust man," the other to a root *vireo* and from there to *verdeggio* "green, to turn green," another still to a root *VARG-* equal to San-skrit *URG'-* "to push" from which seems to have arisen the notion of swelling, inflating, to be turgid that in turn gives rise to the no-tion of thriving, blooming, *vegeto* "strong, robust, vigorous; alive and kicking, in the flesh"; Skr. *ûrg'ayati* "swollen; full of juice" etc. (DEO; **vergine**).

If *virga* means "rod," that which on the horizontal plane measures but on the vertical plane (trans)fixes, with everything else that this entails such as, penetrating and fertilizing (with *virile* re-lated to *push* and *man* according to the Latin etymologies above), then *virgo* signifies the same as the Albanian vërë "hole"; that which is measured, (trans)fixed, penetrated, and fertilized, accounting thus also for *vireo* "greeneries, swelling" etc., thereby approximating Schema V above to an astounding degree (see schema VII). In Al-banian this swelling is described by the rise of the phoneme /b/ in place of /v/ as in the opposition of *barrë* "pregnant, burden, em-**barr**assed" to *varrë* "wound."

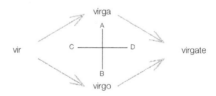

Schema VII

Note that in all these etymologies, *virgate* (a measure of land), is traced to *virga*, not *virgo*, hence, even if the terms *virga/virgo* have not undergone further (i.e. phonetic) differentiation, still the etymology represses one meaning for the other. A telling fact in this regard is that the old meaning of virgin is nowhere near the prudish sense the word carries today (Sissa 1990), a shift that could only have occurred following a dismemberment whereas *virga* and *virgo* are riven entirely from each other, resulting in two exarticulate (i.e. each having but one joint) or meromelic terms. The moment that

47

the dismembered Platonic halves are stitched back together in Frankensteinian fashion and *virga* is reintroduced to *virgo*, the latter no longer is considered virgin but is faced with two choices: either become sullied and turn into a monster openly bearing the mark without cover of matrimony, or put on the veil in order to cover her uncleanliness and deformity, for the old wound has now rea-wakened and is bleeding profusely. In the context of a land which has been measured thus, it becomes a field, whence *virgate*, which is the equivalent of assuming the husband's last name, whereby "to plough" takes on suggestive meanings.

What this means is that the phonestheme dearticulation or the dislocation between phonology and semantics we observed in the Germanic-Albanian enantiomorph amelic (or *enantio-amelic*)[3] terms

$$\frac{v\ddot{e}nd}{v\ddot{e}r\ddot{e}} \cong \frac{world}{wound}$$

leading to Saussure's famous dictum that the sign is arbitrary,[4] follows this earlier process of succision of the semantic component observed in meromelic virga/virgo, in which the conglobated nucleus is first exarticulated into its opposite basic elements or components, whereas one meaning becomes initially repressed as the painful memory of an amputated limb.[5] If their form is differentiated further, which is to say, if the initial amputation (in semantics) is followed by a second (in phonetics), severing thus what remains of the stump from the main trunk, it then has become linguistically suppressed as well. Psychological repression, therefore, occurs on multiple levels either simultaneously or alternating with linguistic suppression and social oppression. Collectively they form civilization's characteristic seal or impress (*vulë*).

EXAMPLE: In the above case of **vënd**, which was arrived at from *vë* → *vënë*/(*vërë*) → *vënd* (i.e. put → placed/(hole) → place), the phoneme /r/ is suppressed and so, only /n/ is articulated. Linguistic suppression has occurred and the relation between *vënd* "place, land" and *vërë* "hole" has been severed. In cases in which it is not linguistically suppressed however, as in Proto-Germanic **werald*, O.E. *woruld, worold*, Eng. *world*, it is either socially oppressed and/or psychologically repressed. Suffice it to mention that in Proto-Germanic **werald, *wer-* stands for man; linguistic suppression of the /r/ phoneme has not occurred. However, its opposite meaning must be psychologically repressed; **werald* is the age of man, it is not certain whether an earlier "age of woman" might have ever existed that was thus replaced. The etymology of the word certainly suggests it.

On the other hand, Alb. *vërë* "hole" and *varrë* "wound" (the latter, as already mentioned, literally standing for woman—*varzë*), are formally cut off from certain of their etymological offspring (i.e. derivatives), such as, *vënd* and *world* (their lineage is now patrilineal) even though their symbolic relation to them is tacitly understood. In other words, no psychological repression is necessary as long as formal linguistic suppression keeps the forms divided and social oppression rules them with an iron fist. So then, depending on the subject of our analysis, we may quickly relate the terms to their particular categories of subjugation:

vënd: linguistic suppression
vërë/varrë/varzë: social oppression
world/*wer: psychological repression

(Note that, depending on the subject under investigation, some terms may fall under more than one category. *Varzë* "girl, maid," for instance, has already entered into its stage of linguistic suppression in which /r/ becomes silent and consequently its relation to wound (*varrë*) is severed resulting in *vajzë*. Socio-politically speaking, however, it will be impossible to find a term that suffers none of these constraints).

2.3 The Staircase of Heaven

*Thou shalt not remove thy neighbour's landmark, which
they of old time have set in thine inheritance, which thou
shalt inherit in the land that the LORD thy God giveth thee
to possess it.*

Deuteronomy 19:14

Cursed be he that removeth his neighbour's landmark.

Deuteronomy 27:17

*Some remove the landmarks; they violently take away
flocks, and feed thereof.*

Job 24:2

*Remove not the ancient landmark, which thy fathers have
set.*

Proverbs 22:28

*Remove not the old landmark; and enter not into the fields
of the fatherless.*

Proverbs 23:10

*The princes of Judah were like them that remove the
bound: therefore I will pour out my wrath upon them like
water. Ephraim is oppressed and broken in judgment, because he willingly walked after the commandment. Therefore will I be unto Ephraim as a moth, and to the house of
Judah as rottenness.*

Hosea 5:10-12

The fact that *world* describes a universal (or global) concept while *vënd* "land" a particular (or local) one, justifying the traditional view that the two are not etymologically related, brings us also to the difference between *vërë* and *varrë*, two words that, although tempting to trace to the same root, have historically resisted further analysis. Topographically speaking:

Vënd/vërë "land/hole" is locus, a point in the map (as e.g. in Lat. *punctum*).

Vajzë/varrë "woman/wound" is a fissure, a crevice; *vizë* \ ˈvē-ˌzə\ "line, dry line," or *vijë* (also Gheg *vajë*) "line, water line."

The relation between *vërë* and *varrë* is the same as that between a point and a line. On the other hand, given that the old plural of *vënd* "locus" is not *vënde*, a recent formation by way of analogy, but **vise** \ ˈvē-ˌsā\ "loci,"[1] i.e. the series or set of points that share a common property constitutive of a line, we suspect that *vizë* "line (in this case a dry line; cognate Lat. *via*) is the singularized plural of *vënd* "land": *singular* **vënd** → *plural* **vise** → *singular* **vizë**. As a result, *varrë* "wound, split, tearing" emerges as the singularized old plural of *vërë* "hole; punctum."

This analysis eliminates the discontinuous local/global qualitative difference between the couplets *vërë/vënd* and *wound/world*, locating them on a continuum, signifying thus a radical form of tearing sinuous pluralities toward the global. What this means is not that there are no multiple traumas (bores), but rather that each of these is itself continuously deepened and widened (i.e. pluralized toward singularity) by burrowing and tearing. Hence, Negarestani's statement:

> No matter how originary and precursory a trauma is, there is still another trauma to which it can be deepened, another trauma by which the infinite inter-connected traumas can be widened – it is the one that makes sure the narcissistic wound keeps bleeding. [...] The diagonal immediacy of ururtrauma with the open or the universal continuum means that isolated or

single traumas do not exist—that is to say, trauma is intrinsically plural and traumas are but linked and interconnected. (2011, 4)

These punctured spaces (*vënd/vërë* "land/hole" – *vajzë/varrë* "woman/wound") are mastered under a socio-political order that economizes their movement toward the global recirculating their subterranean flow throughout the system through a careful measuring between the private space (monogamous allocation), and the public sphere, i.e. between the belonging and possessing control poles. In other words, the flow is internally contained by a politics of strictly regulated privatization; locally redirected and controlled by a public works network of irrigation canals or channels (Alb. *vada*) that traverse the whole social body; and externally expurged through drainage ditches (the global dispersal of excess energies). Irrigation systems are sites where the conversion between the sacred and the profane occurs, and therefore the sacrificial altar which enables the existence of the social sphere. From the perspective of the social organism, these sacred spaces form its cardiovascular, or better, the circulatory system, which comprises the lymphatic system. Diana al-Hadid's "Suspended After Image" is a breathtaking visualization of the sacrificial altar where the conversion between the sacred and the profane occurs (fig. 2).[2]

Figure 2

This is how Jason Mohaghegh at the "5ᵗʰ (Dis)appearance Lab" describes her work:

> This staircase (itself a cascade of falling cloth, paint, and forms) leads to some kind of altar. But what kind of sanctuary or shrine is produced through a visual criterion of gushing and effusion? Is there a typology of the sacred that generates itself through the forces of torrent and outpouring (that which spills infinitely, bleeds everywhere), and then another that manifests only through processes of containment and drought (that which wastes nothing, overflows nowhere)? Two separate portals to the otherworldly, stretched along an axis between excessive secretion and ascetic desiccation. In the former case, for which this sculpture constitutes a kind of hallowing (of the history of flagellation, running wounds, and gods meant to be drunk downward), we see a man's torso trickling across the planks in a way that links human destiny to a greater liquid metaphysics. And in the latter case, we are reminded of the fasting and self-deprivation of so many monks or saints (a history of parched throats, heavily cloaked bodies, and ethereal vows), or even the "thugees" of India whose worship of the goddess of destruction led them to treat murder as a sacred rite...though to be performed without the loss of a single drop of blood, and thus prone to committing acts of strangulation with silk scarves. One remembers the caravans upon which they preyed, and the structure of honor/violation through which any emanation or streaming of the veins was purely forbidden. Thus one wonders again whether different attributes of the miraculous are partitioned along this strange choice: whether to let flood or to bottle the world of wet and dripping things.[3]

While religiosity favors the extreme poles of this axis between excessive secretion and ascetic desiccation, secular societies, and in particular patriarchal capitalism, consist of an economic network of channels and pipes that measure and balance the extremes between flood and drought. This does not mean the secular has no sacred/sacrificial spaces of its own, but while for religiosity these spaces are a gateway onto the next station (or prison, i.e. the vault of heaven), in secular societies they are converted to the very mechanisms that permit and maintain society here and now, the deification of the altar itself, which is to say, of institutions (e.g. the court of law). In short, the conversion from the sacred to the profane arrests the movement towards the universal (social entropy) to the planetary level. The secular digs itself a permanent dwelling place between the desert and the deluge. Having no recourse to the appellate court of heaven, it myopically settles at the mouth of the abyss, refusing to allow its flow to reach the universal.

Nevertheless, partial lockdowns of its flowing networks produce ghettos of severe droughts, whence public sites are transformed into ever growing urban deserts (extensions of the sacred). As sacrificial altars, however, these sacred blotches require bloodletting. And if the ditches through which this measured one-way sacrificial bloodletting is drained are clogged, then the system collapses, overtaken at the confluence of thousands of frothy blood rivers which result in revolutions of diluvial proportions (singularized pluralities).

From the religious perspective, such total revolutions are simple; if God refuses the sacrifice, then the whole world floods. Unsurprisingly then, even in the Old Testament, God's obsession with flooding the world is intrinsically bound to His necessity to keep the boundary demarcations in place. One may think of a third form of sacrificial space, then, which by obliterating the distinction between the previous two, would be utterly unaffordable both for religious and for secular societies, namely quicksand. While both desert and flood may be seen as pure sacrificial sites and therefore acceptable, quicksand, in its hybrid ambiguity, is never utilized by God (God kills by fire or by water, but not both).

Apart from the most obvious account of creation where the separation of waters occurs, God's concern with boundary demarcation is voiced in a number of passages in the Bible, from the prohibition of removing inherited landmarks to the threat of floods in Hosea. In this strange pronouncement, the connection between moving the bound and the resulting flood becomes finally clear. The pronunciation against Ephraim is that he will be oppressed for having committed "whoredom," "a vessel wherein is no pleasure" (Hos. 5:3; 8:7-10). This is a direct pronunciation against the demon of *acedia* (or melancholia), the only demon who was both a carnal and a spiritual affliction, according to the desert monks of the fourth century, thus transcending the boundaries enforced between the flesh and the spirit (see ch. 6.2). As Guibert, abbot of Nogent-sous-Coucy wrote in the Middle Ages, "God becomes 'unto Ephraim as a moth' when our mind in the midst of temptations languishes through heavy attacks of accidia..." (Wenzel [1960]2015, 52). According to the ESV study Bible – essentially, a literal translation of the Bible in contemporary English [4] – "Ephraim is oppressed, crushed in judgment, because he was determined to go after filth." (Hos. 5:11). The two judgments, one against Ephraim, the other against Judah, are basically the same, the difference lies only on the level or scale on which they are applied: if the social fails to insulate its saprogenic spaces (by removing the bound) becoming thus contaminated in its entirety, then God will avoid contamination of the spiritual realm, insulating the local (or public) space of the social from Himself by rejecting the sacrifice. This becomes the pronouncement against Judah.

On the other hand, recalling that Ephraim's crime is "whoredom," the judgment entered against him suggests that he will be oppressed, crushed, or trampled under foot of the social, since this is also the space allotted to the female. What this implies is that he will be transformed into the sacrificial victim whose blood will not expiate, for it will be rejected. This paves the way for a counter-revolution against God's kingdom. Banished both from the divine and the social spheres, Ephraim may only be compared to the figure of *homo sacer* in Roman law, whose crime, according to the law of the Twelve Tables (c. 450 BC) was fraud (ch. 5.1, n. 1). In fact, one translation in particular brings Ephraim's crime close to that of *homo sacer*. The Bible in Basic English (BBE), which translates, "Ephraim is troubled; he is crushed by his judges, because he took pleasure in walking after deceit." (Hos. 5:11). These progressive bounds, then, constitute the gate system or staircase of Heaven.[5]

This extraordinary manic concern with purification is at the heart of the concept's or rather, the semiotic sign's linguistic suppression and the disavowal of some of its extremities (*somatoparaphrenia*) resulting in their subsequent amputation (exarticulation and disarticulation) as we saw. The act of naming the world divides the real into categories which then can be grasped, but this would not be possible if language did not in the process also sever itself. This progressive conceptual dismemberment is a reaction to disintegrating processes internal to language itself rather than some free action undertaken by its speakers, though recurring amputation may then result in apotemnophilia, and this escalate further to a deranged desire for grinding. Stated differently, it is not so much the rising need for more accurate concepts and specialized terminology as society progresses, as it is the need to preserve language (and thus the social space) through the amputation, cleansing, and isolation of the rot at the very heart of the sign. It is the decay of language itself that forces its speakers to excise the gangrened parts and keep the healthy ones from contact with the localized rot. Accordingly, this insulation results in ever more specialized terms. Rationality and reason (*ratio*), therefore, are the result of decay rather than vice versa, i.e. ratiocination being the result of ever increasing knowledge. "In putrefaction," Negarestani states, "it is not the decaying formation that is derived from an idea, but the idea that is differentially or gradationally formed through putrefaction." (2010, 382). However, formalized knowledge attempts to keep at a minimum "the gradients of decay or the blurring movements of rot" (380), tied as it is to its medicinal beginnings (medical ontology). Two related examples suffice to illustrate the obsessive and widespread attempts to keeping things clean and immaculate: (1) the abhorrence by the science of chemistry for its dark twin, alchemy, and (2) the often-absurd attempts of the academia to arrest language in a state of grammatical perfection. Understandably, then, the only spaces where language remains still creative today are precisely the ones that are considered inferior – the dialects and the street – and therefore, shunned by the academia.

2.4 Capsula Mundi

*And Abraham stood up from before his dead, and spake
unto the sons of Heth, saying, I am a stranger and a so-
journer with you: give me a possession of a buryingplace
with you, that I may bury my dead out of my sight.*

Genesis 23:3-4

*This is the law, when a man dieth in a tent: all that come
into the tent, and all that is in the tent, shall be unclean seven
days. And every open vessel, which hath no covering bound
upon it, is unclean. And whosoever toucheth one that is slain
with a sword in the open fields, or a dead body, or a bone of
a man, or a grave, shall be unclean seven days.*

Numbers 19:14-16

Italian designers, Anna Citelli and Raoul Bretzel, have imagined yet other ways to keeping things clean and apart. Their *Capsula Mundi* project goes further in this direction by devising a way
to keep even the dead separate (fig. 3; 4).

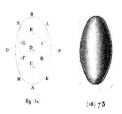

Figure 3

[Capsula Mundi is] the first Italian project created to promote the realiza-
tion of green cemeteries in our country. Capsula Mundi is a container with an
old perfect shape, just like an egg, made with modern material -starch plastic-

57

in which the dead body is put in a fetal position. Capsula Mundi is planted like a seed in the soil, and a tree is planted on top of it. The tree is chosen when the person is alive, relatives and friends look after it when death occurs. A cemetery will no longer be full of tombstones and will become a sacred forest.[1]

This is a striking alteration of Schema V, which is a visual representation of the third term related to **uœrhe:** *varr* "grave, tomb" suggesting a coffin with its lid secured into place (see fig. 5), a hidden brewing space or womb for all aborted abominations that society needs to quarantine or purge for the sake of its own preservation. Capsula Mundi alters this schema by removing the tombstone, yet, hollowing out or eviscerating its insides and lifting them up, or isolating them from all contact with all that is buried and out of sight (the last innovation of a series of myths that have for millennia unsubstantialized the earth gods to the benefit of the sky ones), while at the same time transferring what was supposed to be hidden from view right in front of everyone's eyes, now suspended in the air as in a shop window or museum display. This is a fundamental reformation of Chomsky's deep/surface structures (ch. 2.2, n. 5), in which depth is brought to the surface, without in turn breaching the isolation required for the existence of the social, if not, in fact, rendering it more strict and unassailable – enforcing and preserving identity even in death – his name is Robert Paulson, as Palahniuk would have said.

Figure 4

58

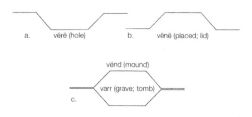

Figure 5

At one stroke, Italian designers Citelli and Bretzel, seize both grave and womb, altering schema V, while at the same time leaving entirely intact the patriarchal capitalist system which that schema made possible. More specifically, by narrowing the gap between the sacred and the public spheres, they manage to forge a strange amalgamation between consumerist capitalism and communist mysticism. This is humanity's guaranty against the flood, a renewal of the covenant with God and further disavowal of the earth; a final repudiation of the myth of provenience (from dust to dust) without letting go of the myth of humanity. This tree is the absolute Saussurean symbol if ever there was one—this evisceration of the earth, the perfection of the very mechanism enabling the proliferation of simulacra traced by Baudrillard, a reference system that does not refer to anything outside itself, if anyone cares to follow the implications, which would be an endeavor beyond the scope of this work. This is what Una Chung at the "5th (Dis)appearance Lab" has to say about it:

> I:I. One decomposing body; one tree. Design constructs and preserves this equation. (For a time.) In any case one would expect a dead body placed in the ground to contribute mineral nutrients to a growing tree. It is the constraint of one body with one set of roots and the resulting production of an exact exchange between death and life that thrills (could there be justice in death?) and horrifies (will we be held accountable for life, in death too?).
>
> This equation is a place of dissociation. The incapacities of modern cultures to allow space for the unfolding of either dying or decomposing—

59

gradual letting go of layered strata of materiality into chaotic ecologies—here finds its expression in a design that places death in a crypt called life. Yet it is the mysterious inaccessibility of the crypt made visible and tangible by the interface of a "burial pod" that also calls forth a surging new desire to reach for (cringe from) our dead. We will no longer be able to see the budding of spring without smelling the scent of our beloved. The nurturing atmosphere we receive from the collective breathing of trees will be inseparable from the karmic traces of our ancestors—those tyrants, those heroes, those silent faces.[2]

Conclusion

To recapitulate, if in *vërë* and *varrë*[3] /r/ stands for a continuous motion towards, or an active directed force, which in a very specific sense means "a drilling movement" (see Appendix C), in **wer* "man" (the root of "world") it stands as that which drills, a prod or rod; *virga*. And while *wound* carries also the meaning of swelling discernible in *vënd*, a meaning that becomes strikingly clear when compared to English *wen*,[4] no such meaning is carried by the Albanian *varrë*. Consequently, this de-coupling or disarticulation is precisely what is responsible for the dichotomous notions of public/private; active/passive; reason/passion, etc. in which the leading terms are thought to be male attributes and the following female, thereby the former is elevated, and the latter repressed, oppressed, and/or suppressed no matter which phoneme represents what.

This capacity to rotate, alternate, and shift meaning accordingly is the key to patriarchal consumerism's immunity to assaults and revolutions. Whatever Bolívar might have had in mind when he said "All who have served the Revolution have plowed the sea" takes on a definite meaning here. And this is something one should keep in mind when considering Lacan's formula "the unconscious is structured like a language," which furthermore, depends on Saussure's conceptualization of the sign as arbitrary, since without its arbitrariness and unstoppable counter-rotating logic following upon a dearticulation of form and meaning – in other words, such that allows this arbitrary, logical, and paralytic signifier to remain afloat even with the system's constant rotation and perturbations – there would be no unconsciousness to speak of (see Appendix D).

In conclusion, these etymologies display a complex interplay that affords a glimpse into the archaic foundation of the institution of marriage along with the rise of private property and patriarchy. What this signifies is that there can be no patrimony without matrimony. This double seizure of earth and womb is enabled only through their fetishistic substitution for the absolute wound (*Ururtrauma*) that trails beneath them, driving their endless permutations and transmogrifications. The effect is that of a sursanure, outward healing only $\left(\begin{smallmatrix} n \\ r \end{smallmatrix}\right)$, a scab that affords the illusion of stability and permanence, but which ultimately grows into an abnormal wen ensuing eruption and exstrophy.

THE SOCIO-POLITICAL BALLAST

3.1 Terra Nullius/Tabula Rasa

*"Land" is a word redolent of meaning. It conjures images of
home or of fear; of possession and dispossession; of the
body, journeys, and pathways; of nature gone wild or of civilization and cultivation. At which end of these continua
your thoughts fall will depend on your origins, your culture
– rural or urban, indigenous or immigrant.*

—Susan Hawthorne, *Wild Politics*

That patrimony is incumbent on matrimony is the reason why
the mark of virginity for both the land and the bride as property is
of such great importance.[1] In international law this is articulated
through the doctrine of *terra nullius* – "no one's land." In more
technical terms, however, terra nullius has traditionally been interpreted as denoting not merely a land empty of inhabitants, but rather a land that is legally not owned by anyone, which in turn
implies the absence of a civilized society governed by laws as opposed to one regulated mainly by customs, but more importantly,
such that can make "proper" use of the land. Rousseau, for example, in his *On the Social Contract*, while recognizing "the right of
the first occupant to any piece of land whatsoever", gives it legitimacy only if two more conditions are fulfilled: "that one occupy
only as much of it as one needs to subsist," thus, not *any* piece of
land whatsoever, and "that one take possession of it not by an
empty ceremony, but by labor and cultivation—the sole sign of
property that should be respected by others in the absence of legal
titles" (177), thereby countermanding the right of the first occupant, as well as the whole basis for his 'natural right' doctrine. The
first-in-time-first-in-right rule, though explicitly stated, is immediately annulled, and the justification for more developed societies to
annex lands inhabited by so called "lower," "backward," "primitive,"
"savage," "barbarous," or simply "uncivilized" societies, implicitly

articulated. Hence, an agricultural society may rightly appropriate lands from hunter-gatherer societies, an industrial society rightly appropriate them from agricultural ones, and so on. As Ashcroft et al. point out, "the doctrine of *terra nullius* may be seen to identify colonization as a continuation of the millennia-old invasion and overwhelming of hunter-gatherer societies by agricultural societies." (258). According to Susan Hawthorne, the doctrine "allowed Europeans to dehumanize people (sometimes counting them as part of 'the wild life'), and to invisibilise all resistance to colonisation." (174). A case in point would be Christopher Columbus's reference in his journal to the monstrous "men with one eye, and others with dogs' noses who ate men" in the West Indies. When they took a man, they "cut off his head and drank his blood and castrated him." (52).

Captain Cook's diary descriptions off the East Coast of Australia, with detailed accounts and summaries of the land and the Natives, are also of interest here:

[Off Cape Dromedary, New South Wales.] Saturday, 21st. Winds Southerly, a Gentle breeze, and Clear weather, with which we coasted along shore to the Northward. In the P.M. we saw the smoke of fire in several places; a Certain sign that the Country is inhabited. (Wharton 1893, 5395-5)

Monday, 30th. [. . .] As Soon as the Wooders and Waterers were come on board to Dinner 10 or 12 of the Natives came to the watering place, and took away their Canoes that lay there, but did not offer to touch any one of our Casks that had been left ashore; and in the afternoon 16 or 18 of them came boldly up to within 100 yards of our people at the watering place, and there made a stand. Mr. Hicks, who was the Officer ashore, did all in his power to intice them to him by offering them presents; but it was to no purpose, all they seem'd to want was for us to be gone. (5497-502)

[Off Cape Hawke, New South Wales.] Friday, 11th. [. . .] We saw several smokes a little way in the Country upon the flat land; by this I did suppose that there were Lagoons which afforded subsistence for the Natives, such as shell fish, etc., for we as yet know nothing else they have to live upon. (5632-40)

Tuesday 3rd. [. . .] Although these Shoals lay within sight of the Coast, and abound very much with shell fish and other small fish, which are to be caught at Low water in holes in the Rocks, yet the Natives never visit them, for if they did we must have seen of these Large shells on shore about their fire places. The reason I do suppose is, that they have no Boats that they dare Venture so far out at Sea.[2] (6320-3)

> The Land naturally produces hardly anything fit for Man to eat, and the Natives know nothing of Cultivation. (6996)

> ...these people live wholly by fishing and hunting, but mostly by the former, for we never saw one Inch of Cultivated land in the whole Country. (7043-44)

> ...we see this country in the pure state of nature; the Industry of Man has had nothing to do with any part of it..." (7063-4)

From the prospect of uninhabited land, to the first signs of inhabitants, to close encounters (including a few minor confrontations), to the conclusion that the country is in the pure state of nature, the inhabitants having had "nothing to do with any part of it," Cook's reckoning of Australia's East Coast shifts no more than from the uninhabited state of the land (*terra nullius*) to the blank and insubstantial state of its inhabitants (*tabula rasa*). His exploration lasted only four months, and not at any time did he venture far in the interior of the continent to realistically make these claims (that it was entirely uncultivated), considering that as Captain W.J.L. Wharton notes, its coastline "is not promising, especially in the dry season." (7067-8).

In the 1992 landmark decision *Mabo v. Queensland* (No. 2), in which the High Court of Australia rejected the doctrine of *terra nullius*, for the first time recognizing native title in Australia, it was precisely in proving the fact that the aboriginals did cultivate their land, which in turn could be used to establish that they had a system of land ownership in place prior to white conquest, that the case proceeded.[3] Justice Moynihan's findings in the case show that cultivation was indeed even more important than fishing: "Gardening was of the most profound importance to the inhabitants of Murray Island at and prior to European contact. Its importance seems to have transcended that of fishing… Surplus produce was also required for the rituals associated with the various cults … and in connection with the various activities associated with death. Prestige depended on gardening prowess…" (175 CLR I F.C. 92/014).

The findings, however, were by no means new or come to light only in 1992. Justice Moynihan's own research shows that already in 1882, three years after the annexation of the Murray Islands, Captain Pennefather reported on the Natives' "tenacious" land ownership practices in which property was handed down "from father to son from generation to generation," though this knowledge did not then seem to have constituted a legal obstacle to the annexation of the land. One cannot but wonder what exactly changed 110 years later.

An international precedent for the court's rejection of terra nullius was found in Judge Ammoun's separate opinion on behalf of the Republic of Zaire in the Western Sahara case ruling in the International Court of Justice. This case, perhaps, better than anything describes the new rationale which, signaling the transition from the appropriation of lands to the assimilation of people, enables, and even demands, the condemnation of the terra nullius doctrine. Judge Brennan quotes the following passage from it:

"Mr. Bayona-Ba-Meya, goes on to dismiss the materialistic concept of terra nullius, which led to this dismemberment of Africa following the Berlin Conference of 1885. Mr. Bayona-Ba-Meya substitutes for this a spiritual notion: the ancestral tie between the land, or 'mother nature', and the man who was born therefrom, remains attached thereto, and must one day return thither to be united with his ancestors. This link is the basis of the ownership of the soil, or better, of sovereignty. This amounts to a denial of the very concept of terra nullius in the sense of a land which is capable of being appropriated by someone who is not born therefrom. It is a condemnation of the modern concept, as defined by Pasquale Fiore, which regards as terrae nullius territories inhabited by populations whose civilization, in the sense of the public law of Europe, is backward, and whose political organization is not conceived according to Western norms. One might go still further in analyzing the statement of the representative of Zaire so as to say that he would exclude from the concept of terra nullius any inhabited territory. His view thus agrees with that of Vattel, who defined terra nullius as a land empty of inhabitants."

He concluded that "the concept of terra nullius, employed at all periods, to the brink of the twentieth century, to justify conquest and colonization, stands condemned." The court was unanimously of the opinion that Western Sahara at the time of colonization by Spain in 1884 was not a territory belonging to no-one (terra nullius).[4]

Pasquale Fiore's doctrine is the kind of paradoxical, one might even say commonplace blend, between a principle of the individuality of man with a "personality" that precedes his status as citizen – and of whose humanity Fiore magnanimously allows also savages and barbarians to partake – and a civilizational progress "which can exercise its full influence only when law becomes the sovereign of the world." (1918, ch. v. §51). This "personality," however, is derived by man already being included in "that great republic constituted by mankind" (ch. ii. §10) or "the great society of societies, which we name Magna civitas" (§11), and which unquestionably becomes also the downfall of his individuality, at least as far as the savage is concerned.

> Having admitted international rights in favor of uncivilized countries, it is now easy to lay down the principles intended to dispel the erroneous conception that such countries may be considered outside the "common" law. Uncivilized tribes are not indeed in the same condition as civilized peoples; the "common" law cannot be applied in the same way, whatever the degree of culture may be. Nevertheless, one can hardly imagine that any form of aggregation of individuals could be beyond the pale of international law.
>
> Certainly, as a matter of principle, colonization and colonial expansion cannot be questioned; one should even admit as desirable a certain proportion between the population and the territory, and that civilized countries, in order to find new outlets for their ever increasing activity, need to extend their present possessions and to occupy those parts of the earth which are not of any use to uncivilized peoples. (§16)

And lest someone should think that the author's opinion is not completely objective, but influenced by his own position and circumstances, he immediately adds, "One should, however, consider that colonization is legitimate only when exercised in a manner not in disregard of the international rights of uncivilized countries… Barbarous tribes have the right to retain the land they actually occupy and the right not to be deprived of it by violence or without their consent, in open defiance of the fundamental principles of international law." (Book I. Title II: § 98). Nevertheless, "the right to occupy land which is of no use to the savages cannot be denied to civilized states; but it is incumbent upon them to effect such occupation by the employment of means least injurious to the savages from whom the useless land is taken." For Fiore, this rule is based on the principle that "the earth is in general designed to serve the needs of everyone and that it is not permissible that savages who are unable to derive any profit from natural products should be allowed to leave sources of wealth unproductive, leaving the ground uncultivated." (§99).

This rationale, it will be noted, hardly differs from that of Emmerich de Vattel, who in turn agrees point by point with Rousseau's three conditions. "All mankind have an equal right to things that have not yet fallen into the possession of anyone," Vattel states, "and those things belong to the person who first takes possession of them. When therefore a nation finds a country uninhabited and without an owner, it may lawfully take possession of it…" (2014, Book I. §207). This definition does not come without qualification though, for similarly to Rousseau, the manner in which both the owner and the use of land are defined, is what makes all the difference in the world. "But it is questioned," he says, "whether a nation can, by the bare act of taking possession, appropriate to itself countries which it does not really occupy, and thus engross a much greater extent of territory than it is able to people or cultivate." (§208). For Vattel such an appropriation would be "repugnant to the views of nature," since the earth is destined to provide for all mankind, which is exactly the rationale used by Fiore. "The law of nations," Vattel continues, "will therefore not acknowledge the property and sovereignty of a nation over any uninhabited countries, except those of which it has really taken actual possession, in which it has formed settlements, or of which it makes actual use." Consequently, he explains, when navigators and explorers in search of land have come upon uninhabited countries which have previously been discovered by other nations and in which those nations have erected some monument to show that they have taken possession of them, the navigators "have paid little regard to that empty ceremony." (ibid.).

Fiore's ideas on what constitutes possession may even be said to be less stringent than Vattel's, who does not allow for anything short of settlements. For example, Fiore explicitly accords their land to nomads:

> Nomadic peoples who have no form whatever of political organization and who live in their own way on the territory they occupy, must be considered as subject to international law, in so far as it protects the rights of human personality.
>
> In applying this rule, we must admit that people occupying certain regions, such as the Arab shepherds who till the ground and hunt, cannot be unjustly treated and ruthlessly deprived of their lands. (Book I. Tittle II: §96)

Similarly, for Vattel "families wandering in a country," – which elsewhere he calls "erratic nations "(Book I. §209) – "as the nations of shepherds, and ranging through it as their wants require ... possess it in common: it belongs to them, to the exclusion of all other nations; and we cannot without injustice deprive them of the tracts of country of which they make use." (Book II. §97). Nevertheless, he then reminds us:

> ...let us here recollect what we have said more than once (Book I. §§81 and 209, Book II. §69). The savages of North America had no right to appropriate all that vast continent to themselves: and since they were unable to inhabit the whole of those regions, other nations might without injustice settle in some parts of them, provided they left the natives a sufficiency of land. If the pastoral Arabs would carefully cultivate the soil, a lesser space might be sufficient for them. Nevertheless, no other nation has a right to narrow their boundaries, unless she be under an absolute want of land. For, in short, they possess their country; they make use of it after their manner;

they reap from it an advantage suitable to their manner of life, respecting which, they have no laws to receive from any one. In a case of pressing necessity, I think people might without injustice settle in a part of that country, on teaching the Arabs the means of rendering it, by the cultivation of the earth, sufficient for their own wants and those of the new inhabitants. (Book II. §97)

They have no laws to receive from any one, but they need be taught! In their search for some sort of precedent, Judge Ammoun's example, and after him Judge Brennan's, seem to take into account only the first provision of Vattel's formulation, and promptly disregard the rest. Nevertheless, it is imperative that they reject Fiore's definition, not to overturn an injustice perpetrated by the law, but to finally complete it. One may go as far as to say that Fiore's definition depends on and demands this overturn in order to formally achieve completion. His description of protectorates makes this clear:

> The protectorate over barbarous countries may be justified on the ground of promoting civilization. Hence, it is indispensable for the protecting state to effectively encourage the development of all kinds of civilizing activity in the regions under its protection. Should it do otherwise, and should the inactivity of the protecting state continue for an excessive period, another power cannot be denied the right of substituting itself for the protective power. It seems to us, therefore, that the validity of a protectorate is subject to the application of the same rules as the validity of occupation. This is the basic idea of the rules which we have proposed. (Book III. Tittle III: §1087)

This notion that charges protecting states with the active education and civilization of their protectorates, and whose validity is subject to the application of the same rules as the validity of occupation, which in reverse means that the validity of occupation, is likewise, subject to the same rules as the validity of protectorates, is transparent enough to require further comment: once the subjects have become civilized, the doctrine of terra nullius naturally falls out of use and the validity of protectorates, as well as that of occupation, is annulled. One could even subject the rule of protecting states to scrutiny similar to that of educational institutions, by administering tests to their student subjects. Eddie Mabo, of course, would come up first of his class. In our time, it is the conservatives, those who desecrated Mabo's grave, who are flunking their courses.

3.2 The Civilizational RNA Strand

There is a great divide in our time—not between religions or cultures, but between civilization and barbarism.

—George W. Bush

And now, what's going to happen to us without barbarians? They were, those people, a kind of solution.

—C. P. Cavafy, "Waiting for the Barbarians"

In contradistinction to the doctrines of Rousseau, Fiore, and Vattel, the spiritual notion as defined by Bayona-Ba-Meya purports to replace the requirement to cultivate the land or make "proper" use of it — which depends on the particular rung on the civilizational ladder of the inhabitants occupying it — with the ancestral tie and spiritual attachment to the earth that becomes "the basis of the ownership of the soil, or better, of sovereignty." This ownership, however, does not extend only to the soil but aims to include all that can be found in it, according to the wisdom that 'man is king of his domain,' which is hardly a Biblical wisdom only. In Cook's account, there is in fact, a strange dispute over some turtles that his men had caught on Thursday, July 19th, and which the Natives during an altercation that began as a more or less friendly visit on board his ship, attempted to seize or throw overboard, indicating that they considered the turtles their property and out of reach of the strangers, though Cook never bothers to understand their reasons. All he says is that "those that came on board were very desirous of having some of our turtles." (6409-31). His words describing the Natives' means of subsistence fall in place with his incapability to understand they might have thought the captured animals belonged to them: "they have ... wooden Harpoons for

74

striking Turtle, but of these I believe they get but few, except at the seasons they come ashore to lay." (7042-3). Cook's question, then, if he had one, would be, 'how can something be yours if you cannot have it?' A distinction is made between primogeniture and mastery, thereby the possession of land by the Natives, or the Old Masters, is disputed.

To restate, one may well begin with the notion of an ancestral tie to mother earth that by providing sustenance for her children also provides, in any case a non sequitur rationale for the right to possession, and the *extension* of this right to everything in, above, and around her, until a limit is reached: what "the active, the ingenious, the cruel monarch of the world," has as yet been unable to conquer and exploit[1] simply because it is out of his grasp, though not outside of his craving and greed, for as the saying goes, man's reach exceeds his grasp.

When this limit is reached, the opposite movement, *contraction*, becomes possible once again, and the concept of terra nullius (or primogeniture) attached to the land, converts to the concept of tabula rasa (or mastery) applied to its inhabitants, who whether or not they have some spiritual connection to the earth, fail to claim it. This is so for every civilization, not only for primitive ones. The melancholy words of Cecil Rhodes illustrate this perfectly: "The world is nearly all parceled out," he reflects, "and what there is left of it is being divided up, conquered, and colonized. To think of these stars that you see overhead at night, these vast worlds which we cannot reach. I would annex the planets if I could; I often think of that. It makes me sad to see them so clear and yet so far." (qtd. in Hardt and Negri 2001, 2553-5).

Clearly Cecil Rhodes has a spiritual attachment to the stars he sees in the night sky. And even an ancestral one, according to Carl Sagan, who says that "the nitrogen in our DNA, the calcium in our teeth, the iron in our blood, the carbon in our apple pies were made in the interiors of collapsing stars. We are made of starstuff." (1985, 190). Or more poetically stated, "The surface of the earth is the shore of the cosmic ocean. From it we have learned most of

75

what we know. Recently we have waded a little out to sea, enough to dampen our toes, or at most, wet our ankles. The water seems inviting. The ocean calls. Some part of our being knows this is from where we came. We long to return." (ibid. 2). Of course, one can easily say the same thing about Africa, the origin of humankind, or with Sandor Ferenczi (1968), regress to the uterus as a symbolic return to the sea, the source of all life.

Thus, the question springs: Does not all attachment ultimately thrive upon some worked-up rationale whose roots must always remain deep within the fertile soil of mysticism? Pull off reason's roots from their black soil and all spiritual attachment withers. Detached orphans, illegitimate offspring, cold-blooded bastard sons of virgins (οἱ Παρθενίαι) armed to the teeth, spring forth from the fields of the fatherless to put an end to the law of nations and all legitimations of sovereignty, all rationales of possessing and belonging.

So then, what is the connection, or rather, the legal link, between the possession of turtles upon turtles and the starstuff's desire to conquer the stars? Quite simply, it is the fact that no civilization can control its surroundings in their totality, which then becomes the entry point, the wedge undermining that civilization's claim to its territorial sovereignty. This is not to say that the terra nullius doctrine was just and, much less, that it should be reinstituted, but rather to point out that the spiritual notion conceived by Bayona-Ba-Meya is itself ultimately not that different, as Judge Ammoun clearly understood (see 3.3, n. 2).

Autochthonous right, therefore, already depends upon the law's abstraction.[2] Absent this abstract principle, autochthonous claims would beg the question: Who is the earth's firstborn? To this a second question can immediately be adjoined: Does the earth differentiate between primogeniture and ultimogeniture, and if so, how?[3] Be that as it may, such fantastic notions in law can only be maintained by failing to consider that as a sedentary society is said to have a right to the land in which it has settled — in fact, for Vattel it has a duty to settle — so a nomad horde must have the right to pass through, for by refusing to settle anywhere it has claimed the entire earth as its incendiary path through life.

In the so-called epoch of the Anthropocene at least, it should have become clear that to claim a possession means to already possess it, not by right, but by force. The words of Seneca the Younger about Hercules remain pertinent; "what he plans to conquer is as good as conquered." (*Hercules on Oeta*, 163-4). It is this force that a colonizing power seeks to estimate or establish, not an "empty ceremony" demonstrating spiritual attachment or beautiful gardens. Terrae nullius, then, are unclaimed lands in spite of the fact that they might already be inhabited. However, this rationale that substitutes empty/unclaimed for defenseless/indefensible lands only applies to a colonizing power that needs to justify its terror in order to legitimate, maintain, exploit and "civilize" its subjects and possessions. A nomad horde might even operate from the opposite stance and transform the land to terra nullius.

On the legal level, the colonizing power demands to see a marriage certificate similar in scope to schema V, demonstrating mastery and control over earth and water, and more recently, air. This control that depends on the mode of production and technology of a people, is necessarily followed by the appropriate family structure, as Engels argues in *The Origin of the Family*, which in turn is reflected in the particular binding symbols that will display that people's kinship to the earth, (i.e. to property and to life and death, or chest, womb, and tomb). Anna Citelli and Raoul Bretzel's Capsula Mundi, for example, provides the latest symbolism signifying mastery over the air. Simply put, one never places the dead where one cannot protect them. Capsula Mundi's significance lies also in the fact that it illustrates Morgan's insight for whom, as Engels notes, "the family is the active element" whereas "the systems of kinship are passive." Only in long intervals do they register "the progress made by the family in course of time, and only then are they radically changed, when the family has done so." Consequently, "while the family keeps on growing, the system of kinship becomes ossified." (1908, 423-7). If the family and the system of kinship are resistant to change, the same applies to burial customs. All, however, are intrinsically tied to technology and the mode of production, and depend on it.

The control over land and water necessary for cultivation, which determines the mode of production of a people, as well as its corresponding family structure, extends to and shapes the social sphere and, consequently, the political one. Control over the water's flow takes on symbolic overtones, which subsequently makes possible these concepts' *etymon*, the search for origins and truth, which winds up planting the truth in a spot it calls "the beginning."[4] Control over its course (irrigation); the ability to release it when needed and to withhold it (turncock; piston; valve; chamber) before it results in water pollution, or worse yet, flooding (discharge); all of these now acquire a double entendre character. Man is a rock, woman liquid, water; man is light and reason, woman darkness and passion. The elemental moods of water and the feminine, therefore, must be kept in check and suppressed if society is to survive. The idea of pollution which was touched upon previously, is a central factor that extends to the female body and the need for control over it, considered unclean because of its periods. As Captain Cook marvels at the Australian aborigines in his diary, neither was their land cultivated, nor their women covered.[5] On the first count, the aborigine shows no virility (he cannot fertilize the earth),[6] on the second, no honor (his women and children do not belong to him). A message which is precisely the source of the scorn. So then, the aborigine is left dishonored and peripheral, cut off from the land because of his incompatibility with it: the aborigine is promiscuous, but the land is still virgin. Hence, the aborigine does not deserve the land. Schema VIII is what we find here:

Schema VIII

As in schema V, here too, the stop consonant -*t*- signifies location (see Appendix C), since the figure is not a flow but a rotation, revolving around itself. Yet, we do not find a -*d*- which would signal proper and permanent settlement as in *vënd* "land".

In this schema, the phonetic missing link can be found, the one that Gustav Meyer was looking for in *varr, vorr* "grave" which at first he links to *vërë, vrimë, birë* "hole, aperture, bore", and later associates with the Indo-European root **wer-* "to wind, welter" (Eng. cognates, *vertex, vertigo, vert*, etc.) from which Alb. *vërtit* "to revolve, whirl, turn around; overthrow, destroy; change, alter" is also derived, same as Lat. *vertere* or Old Church Slavonic *vrъtêti*, which Meyer believed to be the precursor to the Albanian word. It will be observed that apart from Çabej, in nearly all the etymologies offered for these words the base is thought to contain both *n* and *r*. For example, *varr* is traced to a base **or-n* (Meyer; Jokl; Weigand; Walde-Pokorny; Pokorny) or from a reconstructed Late Roman **orna* to Lat. *urna* (Orel); or *varrë* from a *var-na-* compared to a Skr. *vraná-* "wound" (Meyer; Persson; Jokl; Skok; Walde-Pokorny; Orel). Before changing his mind about the relation between these words, Meyer also believed that *vërë* "hole" stood for *vënë* "placed" (*FE*; **birë**). Unable to synthesize the meanings offered in his alternating etymologies, Meyer believed them to be exclusive, while Çabej offered etymologies with either *r* or *n*, but not both. The former was correct in content but not in form, the latter in form but not in content. Following the present analysis, Albanian and Germanic languages present a case in which depending on the meaning, either *r* or *n* becomes silenced or suppressed.

In schema V, *vënd* "land" emerged as a function of a suppressed *r:*

$$v\ddot{e} \ + \ n/r \ \rightarrow \ ^{\perp}\Delta \ v\ddot{e}nd$$

Or, to state it on the Biblical level: *vënd* can be understood as the dry land (delta $\overset{\Delta}{\rightarrow}$) that appears with the division of the upper waters (NA; see Appendix C) and the lower waters ρ (rho) and consequently, the suppression of the latter. The expression, or the rising of this ρ gives:

$$v\ddot{e} \ + \frac{r}{n}\overset{\vec{\omega}}{\rightarrow} \ v\ddot{e}rt(it; \ ere)$$

where the vorticity is a pseudovector field $\vec{\omega}$ expressed as:

$$\omega \ \equiv \ \nabla \times \vec{u}$$

where ∇ is the del operator (curl) and $\vec{u}$, the flow velocity.

As will immediately be observed, even though there is still a locus in schema VIII, this is now much more unstable as it is literally a hole in the water. An expression pertaining to both patriarchy and private property such as, *guri i rëndë në vend të vet*[7] would never have occurred here. All that is heavy and sedentary here sinks, the only forces capable of remaining afloat are semi-motile, continually adapting to ever changing conditions. To the Albanian proverb, therefore, can be juxtaposed the English one, *a rolling stone gathers no moss.*

Since schema VIII is the place of the savage or, the man of nature, it can be joined to schema V to thus form a more complete, yet very simple schematic description of the societal (r)evolution from savagery to civilization; the civilizational RNA strand:

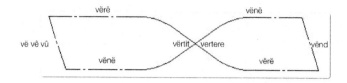

Schema IX. Savage/citizen-subject (S/C-S) ®evolution

3.3 The Barbarian's Promise

We swear by Christ the New to wed dust to dust...
We swear to the world the sacred oaths of the sand...

They cry: Blasphemy!

We've known it long since.
Known it long since, but who cares?
You grind in the mills of death the white meal of the Promise,
you set it before our brothers and sisters—

—Paul Celan, "Late and Deep"

In a fascinating Proposal but unfinished Doctoral Dissertation entitled, "Savages, Barbarians and Citizen-Subjects," — that in this respect stands almost as an inverted literary forgery in the vein of Borges's short reviews or summaries of non-existent literary works, for here the works mentioned are real, it is the review itself that does not exist, — Craig McFarlane identifies a persistent pattern in modern political theory that oscillates "between the position of the savage and the position of the barbarian." (8). Two camps are identified, one advocating the passage from the state of Nature to the State through the mechanism of the social contract, which directly transforms the savage into citizen-subject; the other interjecting a phase of barbarity between Nature and the State. Proponents of the former theory are, among others, Hobbes, Locke, and Rousseau, of the latter, Boulainvilliers, Montesquieu,[1] etc.

These two views should not be considered in isolation, McFarlane warns, for "Rousseau's reversal — from barbarian to savage — can only be understood through a consideration of the barbarian in the political theory of his opponents. [...] Rousseau's return to the state of Nature/social contract argument is only understandable if one takes into account the earlier barbarist argument," (5, 8) which is to say, that of Montesquieu, who in turn was responding to Hobbes and Locke. "Hence," McFarlane conjectures, "it quite possibly becomes the case that the 'default' position of Hobbes and Locke is itself a reaction to an earlier barbarist position." In fact, and as McFarlane himself notes, Foucault already reads Hobbes this way: "To whom, to what is this elimination of war addressed," Foucault asks, "given that no previous theory of power had given war the role that Hobbes so stubbornly denies it?" (97). He traces Hobbes's discourse of right to the civil struggles that were tearing the State apart in England at the time, basically the use that was being made of historical knowledge particularly by the Levellers and the Diggers, (99, 107) "a theoretical and political strategy that Hobbes specifically wanted to eliminate and render impossible." (97-8). Hobbes, Foucault concludes, wanted to eliminate the Conquest, i.e. to legitimize the State no matter what its constitution (98-9).

Hardt and Negri in their own work, *Empire*, widen McFarlane's juridico-political circle to comprise a more fundamental philosophical question, namely the immanent/transcendent oppositional divide. These extending battle formations still correspond closely to the juridical divisions traced by McFarlane – the transcendent camp aligned with the state of Nature/social contract argument, and the immanent camp with the barbarist discourse – but they cast their light on a wider arena for the identification of the opponents, as well as of their tactics and weapons of choice:

> Thomas Hobbes's proposition of an ultimate and absolute sovereign ruler, a "God on earth," plays a foundational role in the modern construction of a transcendent political apparatus. ...in order to guarantee survival against the mortal dangers of war, humans agree to a pact that assigns to a leader the absolute right to act... The fundamental passage is accomplished by a contract—a completely implicit contract, prior to all social action or choice.
>
> It was not by chance, then, that Rousseau's democratic republicanism turned out to resemble the Hobbesian model... As a model of sovereignty, Rousseau's "republican absolute" is really no different from Hobbes's "God on earth," the monarchic absolute...
>
> Properly understood, all of these clauses [of the contract] come down

to a single one, namely the total alienation of each associate, with all his rights, to the whole community…

   Hobbes and Rousseau really only repeat the paradox that Jean Bodin had already defined conceptually in the second half of the sixteenth century. Sovereignty can properly be said to exist only in monarchy, because only one can be sovereign. If two or three or more were to rule, there would be no sovereignty, because the sovereign cannot be subject to the rule of others. Democratic, plural, or popular political forms might be declared, but modern sovereignty really has only one political figure: a single transcendent power. (2001, 1009-33)

The social pact argument, therefore, may be defined in terms of its articulation of a state-of-savagery/civilization evolutionary system which is paradoxically both linear and dichotomous, i.e. while explicitly claiming a common lineage between the savage and the citizen-subject (we are all human), it implicitly alienates them, not only because the occulted barbarian at the heart of the system disallows it, as we shall see, but also because historical progress demands it (some are more human than others). Because the edge of the dividing line between right and might is not clearly identified (nor can it ever be), it follows that it cannot properly be sealed either. Hence, it becomes a passageway through which all sorts of alien elements and monstrosities creep in and make their nest in the center of the system. This is evident in the ostensibly opposing arguments offered by the contractualists (Rousseau, Vattel, Fiore) and the spiritualists (Bayona-Ba-Meya) above. Rousseau's three bullet argument, as we saw, leaves the door open for developed societies to annex territories inhabited by more primitive ones. This view of right results in ever expanding concentric circles or in the superposition of layers whereas *right* is communicated from the layers or circles above to the ones below through force. Fiore and Vattel call this education. It is only from the ones below that some *appeal* to right is made, and that, as the history of the terra nullius doctrine demonstrates, only when the primitive society that makes the appeal no longer really exists (one may only appeal to a right already existing in a legal system in the language spoken by that legal system).[2] In other words, when justice seems to finally have arrived, or

84

been served, this only signifies the end of the society, culture, or people, against whom the injustice was perpetrated, and in point of fact, the affirmation of the right originating with the more developed civilization, i.e. the perpetrator. On the other hand, the ownership of the soil based on the spiritual notion as conceived by Bayona-Ba-Meya, a rationale that however noble it may seem, continues to rely on the same overreaching logic, cannot obtain precisely because it extends farther than one's grasp. In short, while to one circle belongs the force to possess (or the force to convert), conversely, the other possesses only the right to belong (the right to be converted).

None of the above arguments, however, questions the right to belong and possess by which they all remain bound, exposed, as well as potential perpetrators to others down the civilizational ladder. Indeed, according to them, it is questioning this right that is unjust. Moreover, while the right to possess underscores a particular ideology, questioning it is itself no more than the opposite ideology. Peter Sloterdijk in his *Rage and Time* objurgates the communists' resentment of possession or private property:

> The birth defect of the communist idea of economy consisted … in more than the magical manipulation of the evolutionary calendar. After all, it cannot be ruled out that revolution comes to the aid of evolution. Its incurable weakness was the furious resentment against property—which expressed itself in the bitter term 'private property' (also known as the 'private possession of the means of production'), as if everything private could as such be described as something stolen. (33-4)

One might even be tempted to correct the communist singular vision of property, but this comes at the cost of equating it with piracy. Daniel Heller-Roazen's discussion of the varieties of legal things (*res*) and goods (*buona*) in Roman jurisprudence, is particularly illuminating in this regard. In the case of things common to all – which the Roman jurist, Ulpianus declares to be "air, flowing water, the sea, and consequently the seashore" (*Digest* i. 8. 2) – the problem is not whether or not everything private could as such be described as something stolen, but that what is common to all may not be permanently appropriated in the first place. In this sense, communism is a return to archaic natural law, as the problem lies with the sovereign power (or legal entity) that permanently claims those things under its jurisdiction (or ownership), not with the individual that might make use of them. Yet, in including the means of production to the category of things common to all, land must be added to Ulpianus's list, since for the Marxist-Leninists, the land belongs to the tiller.[3]

It is here that things quickly spin out of control. The ancient definition of "things common to all" depended on a certain inability to control them, such as the flow and movement of water and air. In a sense, this also included captured wild beasts, if one cares to recall the example of the turtles in Captain Cook's account, since a beast may always escape from its owner, and in doing so, revert to its original state of being no one's thing. This reversion to the state of nature is necessary for the existence of things common to all. In the *Digest* this is best illustrated in Ulpian's example of a construction upon the shore, which states that if anyone constructs a building in the sea or on its shore by doing so renders it his. However, should a building cease to stand, the ground recovers its natural state as if it had never been built upon. "The securing of the city", on the other hand, "was to be permanent, allowing for the lasting establishment of justified claims to possession." (Heller-Roazen 2009, 66).

Therefore, the paradoxical position where a united globe leads the theory of communism, is that, with the end of nations, those things belonging to all and those things which are public merge into one. The difference between the two categories as regards the shore, according to Heller-Roazen, is an old dispute that can be traced back as early as the disagreement between Marcianus and Celsus, both of whose writings and definitions appear in the *Digest*.

A survey of the *Corpus Iuris* as a whole reveals repeated formulations of the same two views, which echo each other in contradiction. Thus Ulpian, after Marcianus, holds the shore to be "common to all," like the sea, and Neratius, in similar terms, declares the littoral incapable of being definitely appropriated. But Pampinius and Paulus, by contrast, second Celsus; they both classify the shore among "public places" (*loca publica*). The difference of opinion certainly seems stark. One may even say that the two judgments exclude each other as a matter of principle. If a thing may be ascribed to natural law on account of being common to all, then the city can hardly claim it as its own public thing; if, by contrast, it may be submitted to civil law, being the proper possession of the state, it can hardly be said to resist all appropriation, belonging by natural law to all. But such a contrast, although clear, may be misleading, for from a different perspective, the two types of things may be seen as the inverted images of each other. It is striking that both common things and public things are "outside our patrimony" (*extra patrimonium*), which no individual may own: the first, because they cannot be joined in any way to the city, the second, because, with perfect symmetry, they may not at all be disjoined from it. (Heller-Roazen 2009, 63)

Thus, Marx's paradoxical position becomes clear: while the existence of nations makes it impossible to bridge the gap between common and public things, since a thing can be located either inside the borders of a nation or outside them, with the disappearance of these borders, things common to all mankind and public things fall under one and the same category. The final communist paradox, obviously, stands in the fact that here, suddenly, he stands face to face with the pirate, who is the inhabitant par excellence of those spaces that belong to all, unable to tell whether he is facing an antagonist or his own image in the mirror. From the juridical standpoint, then, the theoretical inclusion of land into the category of things common to all, is the first thing that makes the partisan a tellurian pirate, quite apart from his irregular battle tactics which follow from this, something which, strangely, Schmitt in his *Theory of the Partisan* never mentions.

Nevertheless, a preliminary glimpse of the fate reserved in the final stage for the atavistic aspect of the partisan may be gained in his conversion from freedom fighter to hero worker. Schmitt puts it in perspective: "The goal is the communist revolution in all countries; what serves this goal is good and just. Consequently, the partisan problem is also very easy to solve: if partisans are controlled by the Communist Central Committee, they are freedom fighters and glorious heroes; if they shun this control, they are anarchistic riffraff and enemies of humanity." ([1962] 2007, 50). It is also hoped that technology might obliterate both the partisan and the pirate, though in the light of modern cases of airplane hijackings, these hopes must be deemed both premature and naïve.

In the end, then, there is little difference, if any, between the transcendentalist and the immanent discourse. While the former aims at educating and civilizing the savage, the latter has devised a complex program to turn the barbarian (or any deviant figure) into a beast of burden, though not before having harnessed their rage for political gains (Sloterdijk 2010). It is here that one may finally realize just how much communism is the system that succeeds capitalism and saves the ship from sinking. Both are lame either in the right or the left foot—one relies heavily on possession, the other almost exclusively on belonging; one on the appropriation of lands, the other on the assimilation of people. But capitalism can go no further. The ones who wish to save the system now need to turn to communism.

No doubt, all the juridico-political paradigms mentioned so far are ultimately Pythagorean, insofar as they all aim to discover the social laws of harmony through politics. They make use of a special form of mathematics, namely economics. Under the dazzling glow and counterglow of these paradigmatic models, however, the barbarian appears momentarily as the discord of Pythagoras's fifth hammer, that which cannot be subsumed into the final equation that renders justice through the total annihilation, conversion, or assimilation of the other; "a being without measure." (Heller-Roazen 2011, 17). In the irreconcilable difference between right and might the barbarian appears as the indivisible remainder, "the spiritual element of corporality" and "the corporeal element of spirituality."[4] (Žižek, 1996, 4).

It is, of course, this surplus that makes possible the barbarist (or immanent) discourse, which as already mentioned, still rests on the decipiency that envisions the barbarian as innate to the civilizational lineage. The difference ultimately lies in the immanent discourse's disclosure of the incommensurable crack, which remains implicit in the opposing transcendentalist argument. However, this disclosure is generally coupled with introducing the barbarian as an equalizing caenogenetic structure into the savage/citizen-subject (s/c-s) common lineage, at one stroke ridding civilization of its archenemy by rehabilitating the barbarian into history and giving him rights, while immediately attempting to enforce an exchange for this favor. Thus, the inassimilable barbarian that could not be subsumed as a proper rational value into the final equation of justice, is converted into the ink with which the equation is written, the very blood that vivifies or fire that animates the promise of future justice; the return of some sort of crossbreed between the messiah and the horsemen of the apocalypse that will put things right by steel and fire. Foucault mentions this in relation to Nazism:

> In the Nazi period, State racism ... was ... accompanied by the theme of the return of the hero, or heroes (the reawakening of Frederick, and of all the nation's other guides and Führers; the theme of the revival of an ancestral war; that of the advent of a new Reich, of the empire of the last days which will ensure the millenarian victory of the race, but which also means that the inevitable apocalypse and the inevitable last days are nigh. (106)

Conversely, in a documentary entitled, "The Pervert's Guide to Ideology," Slavoj Žižek describes the opposite of this process, taking as an example Rammstein, the New German Hardness band which, he says, liberates certain pre-ideological elements from their Nazi articulations:

> The German Hard Rock band, Rammstein, are often accused of flirting, playing with the Nazi militaristic iconography. But if one observes closely their show one can see very nicely what they are doing exemplarily in one of their best-known songs, "Raise, Raise." The minimal elements of the Nazi

ideology enacted by Rammstein are something like pure elements of libidinal investment. Enjoyment has to be, as it were, condensed in some minimal ticks, gestures, which do not have any precise ideological meaning. What Rammstein does is it liberates these elements from their Nazi articulations. It allows us to enjoy them in their pre-ideological state. The way to fight Nazism is to enjoy these elements, ridiculous as they may appear, by suspending the Nazi horizon of meaning. This way you undermine Nazism from within.

So how does nonetheless ideology do this? How does ideology articulate pre-ideological elements? These elements can also be seen as a bribe. The way ideology pays us to seduce us into its edifice. These bribes can be purely libidinal bribes, all those ticks which are condensed enjoyment. Or they can be explicit discursive elements like notions of solidarity, of collective discipline, struggle for one's destiny and so on. All these in themselves are free-floating elements which open themselves to different ideological fields.

Now, supplant Žižek's pure psychoanalytic terminology of the *libido*, or at least supplement it with Sloterdijk's *thymotic* element, and the explanation would be perfect.

Every system in one way or another makes use of the barbarian promise, especially those that more than others depend on violent revolutions to be brought about. To return once again to Foucault's exposition of these tactical historical knowledges:

> Within this historico-political field where knowledge of weapons is constantly being used as a political instrument, the great tactics that are developed in the eighteenth century, can, I think, be characterized by the way they use the four elements present in Boulainvilliers's analysis: constitution, revolution, barbarism, and domination. The problem is basically this: How can we establish the best possible fit between unfettered barbarism on the one hand, and the equilibrium of the constitution we are trying to rediscover on the other? How can we arrive at the right balance of forces, and how can we make use of the violence, freedom, and so on that the barbarian brings with him? In other words, which of the barbarian's characteristics do we have to retain, and which do we have to reject, if we are to get a fair constitution to work? What is there in barbarism that we can make use of? Basically, the problem is that of filtering the barbarian and barbarism: how can barbarian domination be so filtered as to bring about the constituent revolution? (197)

It is not without reason that Hardt and Negri make a faint attempt to revive this old promise through their barely elaborated concept of the new barbarian: "a new nomad horde, a new race of barbarians [that] will arise to invade or evacuate Empire" (2495-6), deliberately misinterpreting in it Nietzsche's answer in one of his notes posthumously published in *The Will to Power*:

> Problem: where are the barbarians of the twentieth century? Obviously they will come into view and consolidate themselves only after tremendous socialist crises. (qtd. in Hardt & Negri, 2496-7)

Faint, because not even the communists themselves believe in their old promises anymore. Nietzsche is hardly speaking of the proletarian here. For Hardt and Negri the new barbarian must rise to destroy the present world order and, having fulfilled this duty, quietly yield to the utopia of communism. It is absurd, however, to interpret Nietzsche's meaning as consistent with a barbarian race that must serve the masses. A more consistent reading would be that, for Nietzsche, the barbarian emerges only after the terrible and violent beginnings of the socialist crises to topple over the subsequent utopia itself. Stalin's notion of absolute enmity makes this plain.[5] Note also, that Nietzsche is speaking of a stronger species, not merely of a stronger man.[6]

Hardt and Negri's interpretation of Nietzsche's philosophy betrays the desideratum of all political models to formulate a means to neutralize the barbarian promise once they gain hold of power. And it is only through an obscure identification with the barbarian at the promissory level that they can gain hold of that power. It is this as yet untamed promise that Daniel van der Velden of Metahaven identifies when he accords each figure to its proper element: "And we start at earth," he begins his argument, "this is where we presently live. It's the ground beneath the house of world cultures. And it's the prerequisite of any ground in which any argument can be made between people if that argument is going to have political consequences. Mostly conservatives and realists love the earth, liberals love the cloud, communists love fire, and pirates love water."[7]

The persistent and arduous task of historicizing a figure that right from the start was conceived to remain outside the city walls, and therefore of history itself, presents a problem that cannot be dismissed as merely an ideological abstraction. For once the barbarian is even theoretically subsumed into the history of civilization, several questions immediately arise, (1) How is civilization to continue to be defined in terms of progress? (2) What does "barbarian" mean if it loses its anti-civilizational character, i.e. if it can now be rehabilitated into history and incorporated into the universal reason, and consequently the harmonious unity, to which it constituted the state of exception? (3) By thus including the barbarian into the "immense fellowship of the human species" (Cic. *Off.* I:53),[8] does not immanent thought, as conceived by Hardt and Negri, still force itself into the same dichotomous opposition of which it accused transcendentalism? Or, to rephrase it from the historical standpoint: How could Marx conceive of capitalism as better than the forms of society and modes of production that came before it, and at the same time incriminate it for its injustices to those societies? In other words, what ground was Marx speaking from? Was his discourse already situated in his future utopia? Obviously, this was not the case, as it becomes clear when the philosopher is compared to the professional revolutionary. What permitted Marx an ever-elusive position from which to launch such a comprehensive attack was nothing less than his transference of the barbarian promise onto the proletariat in the same way that Pythagoras made the fifth dissonant hammer change hands between the smiths in the forge, which then enabled him to draw the conclusion, "the property of the sounds did not rest in the muscles of men; instead it followed the exchanged hammers." (Heller-Roazen 2011, 12).[9]

But the bourgeoisie and the proletariat, same as the savage and the civilized man, belong to the same lineage, the same species. The only difference between the proletariat and the bourgeoisie or the savage and the citizen-subject is a temporal one, i.e. where one is situated at the moment. The way in which, in those tepid but perceptive leftist analyses between first and third world countries of even only a decade ago, the proletariat of the former could side with its own bourgeoisie to exploit the latter, should have been enough to demonstrate this. "Masters and workers," Rimbaud says, "they're all peasants, all ignoble."

So then, while the transcendent or social contract discourse is founded upon a conception of time as progress traced through the evolution of history, inseparable as it is from its civilizing quest – a progress, moreover, which is designed to obscure the crisis defined by the irreconcilable breach between right and might inside the system, a rift in the socio-political ballast that eventually becomes the road of devastation traversed by the barbarian as a xenogeneic invader into the heart of the system – the immanent, or so-called barbarist discourse, rests on the good hope that it might somehow neutralize/naturalize and historicize/politicize the barbarian invader to make it compatible with the system. It is Mohaghegh's exegesis of Hardt and Negri's *Empire* which strikes with most precision here:

> …there is a telling analytic insistence on the novelty of empire as a transsystemic reality, playing into the cult of newness endemic not coincidentally both to Western postmodernism and consumer capitalism, though in some unsuited way Hardt and Negri are also able to derive their creeds of revolutionary insurgency from writers who preceded the empire. In the end, it seems inconsistent that proposals of resistance are afforded a comprehensive transhistoricality, jumping from Spinoza to Nietzsche to Foucault to even Saint Francis of Assisi for critical inspiration, all the while in the now we are presumably inhabiting a completely fresh space of power (note that this crosscenturial immanence of thought would be perfectly fine if only they believed in an outsider subjectivity capable of ahistorical imagination). (2016, 638-43)

The attempt is transparent enough. In good part Hardt and Negri's nisus consists in trying to enlist this outsider subjectivity into the immense fellowship of the human species while striving to share with it "the irrepressible lightness and joy of being communist." (4720).

Finally, Hardt and Negri argue that *"Modernity itself is defined by crisis,* a crisis that is born of the uninterrupted conflict between the immanent, constructive, creative forces and the transcendent power aimed at restoring order." (918-9). What the above exposition brings to the fore is the fact that the crisis which defines modernity is also part of the internal conflict within each of the two orders, revealing their common nature and motives, differing only in their approach to the problem. The authors' particular wording in the above quotation even reproduces Benjamin's differentiation between lawmaking and law-preserving violence (1986, 283ff.), or Montesquieu's words of God as creator and preserver ([1989]2013, Book I, ch. I). Only, in their formula, the immanent camp creates and constructs (it is lawmaking), while the transcendent camp restores and preserves (it is law-preserving), clearly showing that the two positions are in point of fact merely different aspects of each other. All of a sudden, we are back to where we started. Escape and desertion was never genuine here. In concert with Aristotle the authors seem to assert with great conviction that man is ultimately a political animal. "It is evident", Aristotle states, "that the city belongs to the class of things that exist by nature, and that man is by nature a political animal. He who is without a city, by reason of his own nature and not some accident, is either a poor sort of being, or a being higher than man: he is like the man of whom Homer wrote in denunciation: "Clanless and lawless and hearthless is he." (Politics, 1253ᵃ2).

An astonishing response to Aristotle (and by extension to Hardt and Negri) is found in Sadegh Hedayat's *Buried Alive*, who twenty-four centuries later, yet, without any historical progress having transpired in the meanwhile, bitterly and enigmatically writes: "Whatever was human in me I have lost, I have allowed to get lost. In life a man must either become angelic or human or animal. I have become none of these things." (1979, 161).

THE BARBARIAN

4.1 Five Principles

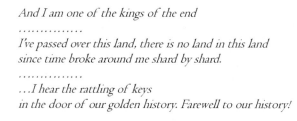

And I am one of the kings of the end

. . . .

I've passed over this land, there is no land in this land
since time broke around me shard by shard.

. . . .

. . . I hear the rattling of keys
in the door of our golden history. Farewell to our history!

—Mahmoud Darwish, "I Am One of the Kings of the End"

Several principles have emerged in the course of the preceding chapter. While some of them were already alluded to, we may now state them formally:

Principle #1: The barbarian forfeits all genealogies and pedigrees; therefore, his lineage cannot be traced to that of the savage and the citizen-subject.

#2: The barbarian is neither a contemporary nor someone anachronistic, unhinged from the addictions of belonging.

#3: As an ahistorical figure, the barbarian cannot be subsumed within an understanding of history as linear progress, but stands at once outside and inside as an omen and invasion.

#4: An atemporal figure with no fatherland or motherland, the barbarian makes his way into the world like stigmata, impressed without divine favor.

#5: Accordingly, the barbarian stands an equal enemy both to the savage and to the citizen-subject.

These principles reformulate race struggle theories in ahistorical terms, dissociated from subsequent class struggle theories as well as biological and cultural racism. The question of the barbarians' origins carries a special significance, for it is the sole premise for the invalidation of belonging. "Barbarians", McFarlane says, "have no origin. It is enough to say about the barbarians that they 'come from beyond.' In the place of an actual origin, a series of origins – often fictitious and mythological – are constructed." (13). Or, in the words of Mohaghegh (2016), who speaks of the sectarian, "the sectarian believes that not all humans are of the same species (multiple dissonant origins, conflictual genealogies), and thus enabling rotating hierarchies." (5386-7). In short, the barbarian gives a new, furious meaning to the word *disinherited*.

These principles, and especially the fifth, answer precisely the question of Marx's ground. In their light, the revolution is an improvised ersatz position, the proletarian the Ersatzspieler (substitute player) as we saw in the story of Pythagoras's rotating workers.[1] Nor is this an entirely new tactic. As a rhetorical and propagandistic device, the ambiguity of the barbarian figure has proved efficient, albeit unpredictable, from its reputed beginnings, to which we now turn.

According to Edith Hall, the invention of the barbarian can be traced directly to the emergence in the fifth century BC of a new art, namely tragedy. More specifically, in her *Inventing the Barbarian*, she treats the polarization of Hellene and barbarian in Attic tragedy as an invention and tool of political propaganda at a particular historical moment, concretely, the effect that the Persian wars had in the promotion and propagation of Athenian Panhellenic ideology:

...Greek writing about barbarians is usually an exercise in self-definition, for the barbarian is often portrayed as the opposite of the ideal Greek. ...the polarization of Hellene and barbarian was invented in specific historical circumstances during the early years of the fifth century BC, partly as a result of the combined Greek military efforts against the Persians. The notion of Panhellenism and its corollary, all non-Greeks as a collective genus, were however more particularly elements of Athenian ideology which buttressed first the Delian league, the alliance against the Persians formed in the years immediately after the wars, and subsequently the Athenian empire. The image of an enemy extraneous to Hellas helped to foster a sense of community between the allied states. The Athenian empire was built on two pillars. First, itself based on a democratic constitution, it encouraged and sometimes violently imposed democratic systems on its allies and dependencies. The most important distinction Athenian writers draw between themselves and barbarians is therefore political. Greeks are democratic and egalitarian; the barbarians are tyrannical and hierarchical. But the economic basis of the Athenian empire was slavery, and most of the large number of slaves in fifth-century Athens were not Greek. This class division along ethnic lines provided further stimulus for the generation of arguments which supported the belief that barbarians were generically inferior, even slavish by nature. (Hall 1989, 2)

At other times, though, the stereotypes used against the barbarian could also be turned against other Greeks. "It is significant that the plays where Greeks are shown in a poor light are always concerned not with Athenians but with their enemies in the Peloponnesian war." Hall observes (213). But most importantly, "when the Peloponnesian or Theban characters turn into 'enemies', the logic of the narrative dictates that the barbarians almost imperceptibly turn into 'friends', and assume the role of surrogate Athenians." (214).

In the long run, this ambiguity has had grave repercussions. According to Hall, "the new dimension which the *idea* of the barbarian had introduced to the theatre assumed an autonomy of its own, affecting the poets' remodeling of myth, their evocation of the mythical world of the 'then and there' from which they sought to bring meaning to contemporary reality." (2). The newfound propagandistic weapon was double-edged. The fact that the polarity between Greek and barbarian could be subverted is itself ample proof, a point which Marx knew and used well. As an ideological tool urging continual progress, the barbarian did not remain far behind as the Greek progressed. In a sense, civilization seemed to be on the run, not so much toward its great destiny as from the barbarian always at its heels. As an extraneous counterpoint to Pan-hellenism, the barbarian enabled and facilitated that idea (πόλεμος), while in the hands of the Athenian empire, which itself depended on the Panhellenic ideal, the barbarian became an ally against the inner forces opposed to it (στάσις). And therefore, often this polycephalous hybrid figure seemed to be found not outside the gates, but well within the city walls, and even launching its virulent attacks against the civilized world from the tragic stage itself.

Over time, however, contradictions of this sort are bound to deepen beyond the political and ideological dimensions. Hall observes that the Euripidean characters' invectives against Greek mores, stand as particularly puzzling in the face of their inexplicable severity from a political or historical standpoint: "The historical reasons behind the Euripidean characters' attacks on Laconian mores or psychology are not difficult to define. In *Andromache* and *Troades*, however, the poet seems to have gone out of his way to make his audience confront the unsatisfactory basis of the assumption that the barbarian character was generically inferior, to an extent which cannot be fully explained even by the redirection of his characters' vitriol from the barbarian world to Sparta. It might be hoped," she says, "that further illumination could be gained by examining the tragedians' reflection of some of the more radical views circulating in the contemporary Athenian milieu," which for Hall would have to take into account "the nature and extent of the relationship between sophistic thought and tragic poetry." (215, and n. 43).

To Hall's insight of the insufficiency of the historical reasons to account for the Euripidean characters' perceptual realignment and onslaught against Greek mores, may be added the inadequacy of her own historical invention of the barbarian hypothesis to account for the millenarian endurance of this figure in the world and its unquestionable influence not only on modern political and juridical theories, but also on religion, philosophy, and the arts. Hall herself points out that even though "the idea of 'the barbarians' as fully fledged anti-Greeks was an invention of the early years of the fifth century BC, it did not spring from a cultural vacuum":

> The writers and artists of fifth-century Athens had at their disposal a melting-pot of traditional materials, of mythical definitions of civilization, of divine, supernatural, and heroic agents of order and chaos... There are instances of phenomena in archaic poetry and art which anticipate the fifth-century portrait of the barbarian... Indeed, the whole area of the Greeks' view of the non-Greek world in the archaic period is highly controversial. If the nature and degree of the tragic poets' contribution to the polarization in Greek thought of Hellene and barbarian are to be accurately assessed, it is essential to sift through the remains of archaic Greek poetry in order to discover the precursors of the barbarian of fifth-century tragedy, to attempt to distinguish the old from the new, and thereby to show how radical was the ideological turn taken early in the Athenian democratic era. (2-3)

The Greeks' conflictual view of the non-Greek world in the archaic period can be glimpsed particularly in the shift and gradual lapse of barbaric mythological figures from friends of the gods and the heroes to open enemies, and the wars eventually waged against them, e.g. the Centauromachy, the Amazonomachy, the Gigantomachy, etc. Heracles's close friendship with the Centaurs, whom he all but exterminates, and by whom he is savagely sacrificed in turn, his love affair with and treacherous murder of the Amazons' queen Hippolytê, and his affinity and similitude to the giants, who, precisely because of this can only be dispatched by his hand in their battle against the Olympian gods, are only among the most obvious aspects of this conflictual view. The Greeks' reputation for treachery and cunning, therefore, did not begin with the Trojan horse from inside whose belly they make their incendiary entrance into European history, though the image certainly has stuck as its most suitable and long-lasting symbol.[2] But whether that wisdom, craft, or cunning ($\mu\hat{\eta}\tau\iota\varsigma$) was their own invention, or borrowed from their foes, seems an open question. The fact that Mêtis was an Oceanid, one of the three thousand daughters of the Titans Oceanus and Tethys, i.e. a member of an older pantheon than the more civilized

Olympian gods, suggests the latter, though it is generally taken for granted that the apprentice surpassed the master in learning and skill. Whether this is true or not this remains to be seen.

"The word *barbaros* originally referred solely to language, and simply meant 'unintelligible'" Hall says (179). "Ironically [it is] oriental in origin, and formed by reduplicative onomatopoeia." (4). "There are other similar words in several early oriental languages, especially the Babylonian-Sumerian *barbaru*, 'foreigner'. Pokorny connects the term with numerous Indo-European words designating the meaningless or inarticulate, including the Latin *balbutio*, and the English *baby*" (4, n. 5), i.e. "babbling, unclear speech."[3]

Homer's one time use in the *Iliad* of *barbarophonos* (ii. 867) "of foreign speech," at times also rendered "uncouth of speech," indicates that the term originally referred to speech alone and not to reason or logos (λόγος), since the latter concept did not exist in Homer's time, and even less so five centuries earlier at the time with which the events of the poem are concerned. (Snell [1953]1982). Yet, by Plato's time the concept of logos had been invented and the term applied to it. It may be tempting to attribute the link between unintelligible speech and irrational thought (ἄλογοι) to the work of the philosophers, but in truth, the tragedians had already claimed this territory. "The earliest extant formulations of the theory of Hellenic superiority are in tragedy," Hall says. "It is not until the turn of the fourth century that oratory's vituperative xenophobia, and philosophy's theoretical justifications of the pre-eminence of Greek culture, supersede drama as sources for the idea of the barbarian." (x). Nevertheless, while the philosophers did not invent the link, they, no doubt, cemented it further.

The fact that the barbarian spoke a language other than Greek, which in a typical non-sequitur is then interpreted to equate *barbaros* with *irrational*, does not say anything about the barbarian though, as Plato, too, remarks (*Stat.* 262b). The judgment reveals more about the Greek, who, while situating himself on the side of progress, found it impossible to incorporate certain incompatible modes with its universal reason. These were languages of discord. They stood out of historical progress and universal reason, which was unable to articulate them. There was in them something incommensurable (ἀσύμμετροι); something unspeakable (ἄρρητοι), a barrier that resisted signification, but which, nevertheless, threatened the ordered world.

Under these circumstances, it became necessary to confuse the barbarian with the savage. This was the only way to safeguard the ordered world. If discord was not an error rising out of instinctual and unpremeditated actions which could therefore be corrected through the use of reason and foresight, if *logos* was not universal, then the idea of progress was doomed. By finding its universal enemy and radical other, civilization demarcated the lines of its own totality, an ordered political microcosm that could not, on that account, ever be autonomous and complete.

Hall notes that although civilization's notion of itself as a process of linear progression is never questioned, "the rise, paradoxically, is seen also as a fall":

> Although tragedy as a medium for the celebration of civic and civilized values generally defines Hellas' evolution as progress rather than fall, there are aspects of its portrayal of foreign religion which stem from the idea that the barbarians are somehow closer to the gods than the Greeks, that they have retained an intimacy with the mystical workings of the universe which civilized Hellas has lost. (149)

Civilization's nostalgia for a time before the loss of its innocence is well known. What is curious about it is that to imagine some prior era of humanity as a loss by comparing one's own past to primitive, savage peoples existing at the edge of the civilized world, or, to use Hall's words, by equating the long-gone with the elsewhere, requires both a self-deception and the simultaneous perception of that deception. The loss is always here and now, something is presently being lost. This is how civilized man feels. A smokescreen blinds him to his so-called innocence, and his delusion lies precisely in the fact that he thinks his innocence has been sacrificed to his knowledge. He has convinced himself that his superior understanding is exactly what prevents him from grasping it. He mistakes what is feral for what is naïve. This defines his own naiveté, this is what makes him civilized, the bridle he cannot shake off. A war is still raging on, whose tumultuous uproar is muffled from him, only occasionally perceived as no more than the stuff of bad dreams.

In Greek mythology, this raging battle can be traced to a shift in the perception of the character of a number of mythological figures. Probably the best example is the long period of Heraclean conquests, which reach their zenith with the victory of the Olympian gods over the giants, the period itself coming to an end with the death of the Greeks' great civilizer, and his apotheosis on Mount Oeta in Trachis. His death is the fulfillment of Zeus's prophecy that "by the hand of one whom, conquering, thou hast slain, Alcides, one day shalt thou lie low" (Sen. *Her. O.* 1476), and is the vengeance not only for the slaying of Nessus, but also that of the other Centaurs, the Amazons, the giants, and many other battles and vanquished chimeras and supernatural barbarians[4] as Hall calls them, though in contradistinction from the savage or natural man, there are no natural barbarians.[5]

4.2 The Apotheosis of Heracles

(I KNOW YOU, you're the one bent over low,
and I, the one pierced through, am in your need.
Where flames a word to witness for us both?
You—wholly real. I—wholly mad.)

—Paul Celan, "I Know You"

Heracles was a friend, and as so many other heroes of renown, a pupil of the sage Centaur Chiron (Plut. *Mor.* 1146A),[1] whose skills matched those of Apollo himself and whose history is in a sense the opposite of that of the hero; while Heracles is the only mortal to become a god, and ascend to Olympus, Chiron who was immortal to begin with, gave up his immortality after being accidentally wounded by one of Heracles's poisoned arrows (Diod. iv. 12. 8; Apollod. ii. 5. 4; Ov. *Fast.* v. 379ff; Hyg. *Poet. Astr.* ii. 38). Lucian says, however, that Chiron chose to die because he was tired of living (*D. Mort.* 26). The same fate was reserved for Pholus and most of the other Centaurs.

It is telling that according to the literary tradition, the king of the Centaurs, Chiron, is thought to be of a different lineage and not directly related to his subjects, who are uncivilized (Apollod. i. 2. 4). The only two other civilized beasts are Pholus and Nessus. Chiron, the hero's teacher, and his inverted image, Nessus, the hero's assassin, must be set apart from their wild siblings, otherwise the champion of civilization will have been educated and sacrificed by barbarians.[2]

As for Pholus, the raw meat-eating Centaur who shared Dionysus's wine with Heracles, instigating the hero's fight with the other Centaurs, he was the son of Silenus and an ash-tree nymph (Apollod. ii. 5. 4). He was more skilled in divination than the rest, and was consistently confused with Chiron, as the converging details of their death show, and even after Zeus set the image of the

Centaur in the sky, Hyginus reports that there was disagreement among the commentators whether the image belonged to Chiron or to Pholus (*Poet. Astr.* ii. 38).

Yet, it is not only Chiron, Pholus, and Nessus whose myth is interpreted to make sense from the Hellenes' perspective, but that of the other Centaurs as well. The alteration consists neither in directly making the three Centaurs civilized, nor in making the rest savage, but in an interpretive split that renders intelligence and instinct incompatible, whereas one who is intelligent and rational could not at the same time be impulsive and driven by dark instincts. Logic, therefore, must be transparent. It is only after this has been established that a different lineage for Chiron may be sought. Nevertheless, while Heracles is separated from his earthly self and elevated to Olympus after the mortal part of his body is consumed in the fire, being allowed to rise above the needs of the flesh,[3] Chiron can only be distanced from his savage siblings. It is Nessus that poses a problem for this otherwise expedient simplification; he is both savage and intelligent. Savage not because he killed, but because he killed Heracles, and intelligent because he killed him not by force but by cunning and foresight, beating the civilizer of the world, the killer of earthborn Antaeus, at his own game. Yet, the conspiracy that laid low the greatest hero civilization has ever known, is vast and far more complex than the mythographers would lead one to suspect. Hence, we begin with the poison.

Hydra is one of Heracles's earliest victims, killed during his second labor. Her body he cut open and dipped his arrows in the bile (Diod. iv. 11. 5; Apollod. ii. 5. 2; Hyg. *Fab.* 30). Henceforth, the smallest wound from one of his arrows would always prove fatal. "At their tip they had death, and trickled with tears," Hesiod says (*Sh.* 132). It was one such poisoned arrow that killed the cunning Centaur Nessus for ravishing Deianeira, Heracles's wife at the river Evenus in Trachis. As he lay wounded, Nessus extracted the arrow from his breast and in his last breath told Deianeira that if she mixed the clotted blood from his wound with olive oil and preserved it in a dark place away from heat or sun, she could use it as a love potion to smear on Heracles's garment if ever his affections for her waned (Soph. *Trach.* 555-7; Hyg. *Fab.* 34; Ov. *Met.* ix. 129-33; Sen. *Her. O.* 517-34).

Diodorus Siculus says that Nessus's seed that had spilled on the ground had to be added to the mix as well (iv. 36. 5), making the claims of some authors that Nessus did not succeed in raping Deianeira especially suspect. According to Diodorus, "Heracles shot the Centaur with an arrow, and Nessus [was] struck even while he was having intercourse with her." (iv. 36. 4).[4]

And so, when Heracles was offering thanksgiving sacrifice to his father Zeus for the massacre of Oechalia, where after slaughtering her father and brothers he carried Iole captive, Deianeira decided to make use of Nessus's "charm." Deianeira "the manslayer," the supposed daughter of Oeneus, who appears to be an Amazon in disguise, for she was really the daughter of Althaea by the god Dionysus, and she drove chariots and trained for war (Apollod. i. 8. 1; Hyg. *Fab.* 129).[5] In Diodorus, Deianeira, in fact, appears among the Amazons who were treacherously slain by Heracles during his ninth labor to bring back the girdle of Hippolytê (iv. 16. 3). She is among the most obscure characters in myth, which is partly due to the fact that her myth and the death of Heracles are, no doubt, accounts concerned with the Great Mysteries.[6] That she might have been an Amazon in disguise is enough to cast an entirely different light on the myth. Judith Mossman observes that in Sophocles's play, *Trachiniae* (*The Women of Trachis*), when asking about Iole's family, Deianeira frames her question asking first who her mother is "when the conventional order would place the father first" (496):

Who is her mother and who is her father that gave her life?
τίς ἡ τεκοῦσα, τίς δ᾽ ὁ φιτύσας πατήρ? (Soph. *Trach.* 311)

According to Mossman, Deianeira's endearment towards Iole is calculated to bring out her maternal tenderness, which Sophocles uses in order to create the needed contrast between Deianeira's terrifying image as "man-destroyer" and her feminine image as loving wife and mother. Though this contrast might serve well in tragedy, it does not have to be an empty image—if Deianeira asks first who Iole's mother is, this is because she follows Amazon custom which did not trace lineage through the father. If this is true, Zeus's prophecy that Heracles could only be killed by the hand of a dead enemy, someone whom he had previously slain, becomes doubly true, making the Amazon and the Centaur conspirators.

So, how can the slain Amazon and Heracles's wife be the same character? Logically, they must be two different characters of the same name, and this is the reasoning that most, if not all mythographers naturally follow. It will be remembered, however, that it was during the hero's visit to Hades to take Cerberus at the command of Eurystheus, his twelfth and final labor, that the marriage between Heracles and Deianeira was arranged. There, we are told, he met Deianeira's half-brother, Meleager, the son of Ares and Althaea (Apollod. i. 8. 2; Hyg. *Fab.* 171),[7] and on hearing the story of his death by his own mother for having mistakenly killed in battle his two maternal uncles, "for strong-spirited Ares does not discern a friend in battle," Heracles was moved to tears, and asked Meleager: "Is there, in the halls of battle-loving Oeneus, any daughter, unsubdued by love, whose appearance is like yours? I would gladly make her my splendid bride." To which Meleager responded: "I left behind at home Deianeira, with her neck like a fresh olive; golden Cypris, charmer of mortals, is still unknown to her." (Bacchyl. *Epinic.* v. 130-75).

Now, Artemis was worshipped as a guinea-hen (*meleagris*) in the island of Leros and, according to myth, all of Meleager's sisters except Deianeira and Gorge were transformed into guinea-hens by the gods when they would not stop lamenting their dead brother (Ov. *Met.* viii. 532-45; Hyg. *Fab.* 174; Athen. xiv. 655c; Aelian *N.A.* 4.42). This suggests that Meleager was either one of Deianeira's transformed sisters or, in all likelihood, Deianeira herself. What is certain, in any event, is that Meleager could not have been male.[8]

According to pseudo-Apollodorus, when Heracles descended into Hades the souls fled before him, save Meleager and the Gorgon

Medusa. "And Heracles drew his sword against the Gorgon, as if she were alive, but he learned from Hermes that she was an empty phantom." (ii. 5. 12). But the Centaurs and the Gorgon Medusa are closely related and both had the power to warn off against violations of the Mysteries (Baur 1912; Graves 2012), since their depictions on Melian stones as early as the geometric period were used as amulets. On some gems of the sixth century BC, in fact, the Medusa is represented as a Centaur or Centauress.[9] This is significant and brings up again a possible conspiracy between the Amazon and the Centaur. Deianeira's sister, Gorge (Γόργην), then, might herself be none other than the Gorgon (Γοργείην).

Bacchylides, on the other hand, says that Heracles drew his bow at Meleager not at the Gorgon, and was confronted by the dead warrior: "Son of Zeus, stay where you are! Calm your heart, and do not send a fierce arrow in vain from your hands against the spirits of the dead. You have nothing to fear." (*Epinic.* v. 79-83). Meleager's guileful words certainly strike a stark contrast with Zeus's prophecy that Heracles shall die by the hand of a dead enemy.

The mythographers deny that Deianeira was among Meleager's sisters that were transformed into guinea-hens, and especially that it was her that Heracles might have met in Hades, to account for her subsequent betrothal to the hero. Yet, as an account of the mysteries, the myth is concerned precisely with the capability to cross between the two worlds at will. When examined closely, Deianeira appears strikingly similar to Artemis herself. In any case, she knew her craft well. In Seneca's play her decision to send Heracles a tunic to which Nessus's mixture was applied is far from the act of an ignorant and credulous housewife: "I shall not go unavenged" (*non ibo inulta*),[10] she says, "Though you have borne the heavens and the whole world owes its peace to you, a worse pest than Hydra waits you – the wrath of an angered wife." (*Her. O.* 282-5).

The words *iratae dolor nuptae*, with which Seneca seems to take a shot at the weaker sex, may be understood in the opposite sense as well, i.e. if Deianeira the warrior was accusing Heracles. Her charge anticipates and surpasses Marx and Engels's analysis of hetaerism and adultery in monogamous patriarchal societies by two millennia. "Monogamy introduces two permanent social characters that were formerly unknown," Engels writes, "the standing lover of the wife and the cuckold. The men had gained the victory over the women, but the vanquished magnanimously provided the coronation. In addition to monogamy and hetaerism, adultery became an unavoidable social institution—denounced, severely punished, but irrepressible." (963-5). This narrow view of the conflict is given a wider breadth by Seneca in the words of his Deianeira: "*adhuc timebam monstra; iam nullum est malum, cessere pestes, in locum venit ferae invisa paelex*", generally rendered as, "Until today had I feared monsters, but now evil is no more. The pests have vanished and in the place of wild beasts comes the hated harlot." (288-90). A riddle. On its own the Latin *invisa* means "undetected, unseen," i.e. invisible. *Paelex*, on the other hand, is a concubine. Together they are rendered as "a hated rival," implying that the danger of concubinage lies in its concealment. Yet, as a concubine Iole was all too visible. It was not to Iole that Deianeira was referring but to herself:

> Evil is no more. Instead of the wild, the invisible foe.[11]

In their poetic ambiguity, these words seem to point in two directions at once; first, Heracles has cleared the world of its chthonic monsters. Second, it refers to the transformation that has occurred as a result of their disappearance: by subduing all that is wild and unrestrained and forcing it to go underground, he has made the world apparently safer but less bright. The world becomes ordinary and the repressed aggressive instinct more insidious in its effects. Evil becomes banal, as Arendt succinctly put it, murder made commonplace, bureaucratic and mechanical; murder not recognized as murder but as upholding the law. The new world order begins with the conversion of the hero into statesman and city official; his murders are institutionalized because he does not kill men but monsters. [12] Deianeira's act, on the other hand, belongs neither to an institutionalized deed nor to a regular and lawful engagement. Hers is perhaps the first example in the history of mankind of asymmetrical warfare.

This concern with the unseen, the unspeakable, or the unthinkable is voiced again a few lines below in Seneca's drama:

> O grief that no revenge can satisfy, seek him some dreadful, unthought-of, unspeakable punishment, (*quaere supplicia horrida, incogitata, infanda*); teach Juno herself the power of hate; for she knows not to rage enough (295-8).

The accusation suddenly turns upon the vanquished; they failed because they did not know how to exploit and aim their rage. They could not harness their personal anger and transform it into an all-pervading universal rage. Deianeira seeks a deed "unthought-of," which therefore cannot be uttered and consequently becomes impossible to judge. After the deed, she is quickly exonerated because she commits suicide.[13] Yet, in Seneca's play this is premeditated: "happy lies the one who crushes those he hates." (350). In short, the one who extends her life does so at the expense of rage. Deianeira's wrath prevails because it invites destruction even upon its bearer, raising the stakes to the breaking point: "Strike me like some unexampled scourge, like an evil far worse than stepmother's wrath. Launch a weapon like that launched once against the straying Phaethon; for I too, in Hercules alone have ruined nations." (851-5).

Even though in Seneca's *Hercules*, Deianeira seems to take a hostile stand with respect to Iole, in Sophocles's *Trachiniae*, she felt more pity than resentment for the beauty that became the cause of Oechalia's ruin (298-313; 329-32; 460-5). And so, applying some of the mixture prepared from Nessus's blood and semen to a shirt that Heracles was to put on during the priestly ceremonies in honor of his divine father, she placed it in a chest and sent it off with Lichas, whom she instructed that under no circumstances should it be exposed to light or heat before Heracles was about to wear it (Soph. *Trach.* 604-9; Hyg. *Fab.* 36).

There is no doubt, however, that Deianeira's revenge was a premeditated act, not of a jealous wife against her cheating husband, not even merely of an Amazon against the patriarchal order, but of the barbarian against the civilized world. Nevertheless, her belligerent acts have traditionally been interpreted as no more than the acts of a credulous housewife who believed the intentions of her rapist to be good. The new world order was better off believing that than concede to the fact that a much more diabolical foe might be lying in its midst. The knowledge of the latter would no doubt have undone the precarious balance that was even then struggling against more ancient religions and their mysteries. Even Sophocles's words describing the death of Heracles are generally criticized as some of the most horrific and abhorrent verses in tragedy, testifying to the shock and denial this grave treachery induced in the minds of the classic interpreters until not too long ago:

> When the blood-fed flame began to blaze from the holy offerings and from the resinous pine, a sweat broke out on his skin and the tunic clung to his sides close-glued at every joint, as if by a craftsman's hand; there came a convulsive, biting pain in his bones; and then the venom, like that of some deadly, cruel viper, began to devour him. (*Trach.* 765-71).[14]

Coursing through his limbs, Hydra's venom corroded the flesh. Attempting to rip off the shirt, which had become one with his flesh, he tore his flesh away with it, exposing the bones and tearing away his limbs (Ov. *Met.* ix. 166-71; Sen. *Her. O.* 828-31). Mad with pain, he came upon Lichas, who trembling with fear was crouching near the altar, and believing him to be the culprit, picked him up by the feet and hurled him into the Euboean waters (Soph. *Trach.* 779-82; Sen. *Her. O.* 808-22; Ov. *Met.* ix. 211-8; Apollod. ii. 2. 7). Then he ran to a stream nearby and plunged headlong in it but the venom burned even fiercer than before. Fleeing over the mountain tearing up trees as he went, he finally reached the foot of Oeta, where summoning his son Hyllus, he gave him instructions to build a pyre and burn him there (Soph. *Trach.* 1191-200; Sen. *Her. O.* 1481-7).

No one of those present, however, dared light the pyre but Philoctetes, to whom in gratitude the hero bestowed his bow and poisoned arrows, passing along the curse of the deadly bile. In the fire, the maternal and mortal part of his body was consumed, while whatever he derived from his father, was preserved, and after Zeus struck the pyre with a thunderbolt, ascended to Olympus (Apollod. ii. 7. 7; Hyg. *Fab.* 36; Ov. *Met.* ix. 239-75; Sen. *Her. O.* 1725-57, 1940-76).

4.3 The Rise and Fall of Consciousness: From Bicamerality to Narcissism

I am able to transform: the landmine of civilization—this is my name
  (a sign)

—Adonis, "This is My Name"

In Seneca's play Deianeira brings forth a number of accusations against the hero, many of which even though appearing to stem from personal concerns, are too general to seriously be considered mere recriminations between husband and wife. Among these hypocrisy stands out, particularly his feigning madness in order to do murder with impunity and rid himself of unwanted wife and children. "Thus does Alcides throw away his wives; such is his manner of divorce. Yet no one can make him guilty! He has made the world believe his stepmother answerable for his crimes." (431-4)

This indictment refers to the episode in Heracles's myth, in which blinded by Hera, the hero murders his own children, and according to Euripides, also his wife Megara (*Her.* 999). The charge of hypocrisy, however, cuts deeper than merely the suspicion Heracles might have "feigned" his madness and blamed it on the goddess. It refers to an epoch when the gods truly intervened in human affairs, a time in which man was directly moved by their will. The hypocrisy consists in the fact that now the hero is a defender of the new world order and of the higher powers of rationality and reason. Either the previous madness must have been feigned, Seneca seems to reason, or the present logic is weak and vulnerable. Even more importantly, in juxtaposing two mutually exclusive ways of viewing insanity, he points to the overall civilizing arc of Heracles's mythos, which more precisely may be understood as the struggle between an older mentality, what Julian Jaynes calls the bicameral mind, and the emergence of a new consciousness.

116

The above sources have been ordered with a view to subject matter only, with little regard to their chronology. Obviously, there are great differences between the tragedians of the fifth century BC and Seneca in the first century AD. For one thing, the Greek tragedians do not so openly question Heracles's madness as does Seneca. Insanity in the modern sense is not yet possible, though already with Plato things begin to change.[1] But above and beyond the chronological ordering of the authors, the myth itself is a vast collection of stories, all sewn together from different times and places.[2] However, a detailed sorting of the different sources used by the authors, as well as their own later moral embellishments is not necessary, and would be beyond the scope of this work. It is enough to point out the difference and compare briefly between the two eras, that of the older bicameral societies and the modern conscious civilization – Heracles's myth spanning the whole period of transition between the two. If *Odysseus* is "an odyssey toward subjective identity and its triumphant acknowledgment out of the hallucinatory enslavements of the past," as Jaynes asserts ([1976]2000, 277), Heracles's myth, with its superimposed layers, is the retrospective extension of this subjective identity beyond its own beginnings into the bicameral past, as well as the barbarian's own puncturing of the future. The fact that the myth is a mosaic made up of diverse stories, often all heaped together contradictorily, permitted later authors to retrofit and assert their own worldview into the past, as well as inject their apocalyptic vision into the future. The myth is, in short, a good measuring device of both the odyssey toward subjective identity and of the dissent and radical critique to it from more esoteric poetic cliques.

The Bicameral Mind

According to Julian Jaynes, "at one time human nature was split in two, an executive part called a god, and a follower part called a man. Neither part was conscious." (84). The relationship between

117

man and god was "by being its progenitor—similar to the referent of the ego-superego relationship of Freud or the self-generalized other relationship of Mead." In short, these gods took the place of consciousness, and were "what we now call hallucinations." (74). To put it simply, if somewhat incorrectly, before man could think his thoughts he heard his thoughts as commands given by the gods. Incorrectly, because these auditory hallucinations were not yet thoughts, or even his, but the voices of his own tribal chiefs or ancestors, commands spoken earlier now ringing inside his head like the wind inside an empty skull.

Differently from the thoughts of self-conscious modern man, however, the bicameral man did not recognize the voices as his own, and if they commanded him this way or that, he obeyed them instantly. These commands obviously were not something abstract. They were instructions received by someone in authority, which instead of being stored in memory, rang out as auditory hallucinations. Jaynes warns against supposing that they were like tape recordings, though they might have begun as such. In the face of some novel situation for example, the hallucinations might have improvised to provide an instruction that the chief had never uttered. (140). Their function, therefore, was more synthetic than analytic.

For right handed people, auditory hallucinations seem to originate in the right hemisphere of the brain, in what corresponds to Wernicke's area in the left hemisphere, the part concerned with the comprehension of language. In ancient times, this area of the brain "may have organized admonitory experience and coded it into 'voices' which were then 'heard' over the anterior commissure by the left or dominant hemisphere." (104). The reason that the language of men was involved with only one hemisphere, Jaynes argues, is in order to leave the other free for the language of the gods. (103-4). So, the bicameral man with his decision-making auditory hallucinations was very similar to schizophrenics today, in fact for Jaynes schizophrenia is merely a vestige of the bicameral mind.

Having evolved as "a side effect of language", these auditory hallucinations may have "operated to keep individuals persisting at the longer tasks of tribal life." (ibid.). Another evolutionary advantage might have been tirelessness. As Jaynes points out, this is observed even in schizophrenics today, who "are capable of tremendous feats of endurance" and "may move about day and night, or work endlessly without any sign of being tired."

> This suggests that much fatigue is a product of the subjective conscious mind, and that bicameral man, building the pyramids of Egypt, the ziggurats of Sumer, or the gigantic temples of Teotihuacan with only hand labor, could do so far more easily than could conscious self-reflective men. (426-7)

Since the bicameral man could hear his king's voice when the king was not physically present, it follows that he could continue to do so when the king was dead, at least for a time, until the hallucinated voice began to fade away and the command was taken over by his successor. Statues, effigies, idols and figurines of every shape and size have been used, Jaynes conjectures, to reinforce such fading hallucinations, which suggests that the auditory hallucinations might have had also a visual component to them. "Like the queen in a termite nest or a beehive, the idols of a bicameral world are carefully tended centers of social control, with auditory hallucinations instead of pheromones." (144). The origin of the gods, therefore, is in the dead king and his lingering voice. The continued presence of these voices which had to be obeyed, Jaynes asserts, "was the absolute prerequisite to the conscious stage of mind in which it is the self that is responsible and can debate with itself, can order and direct... In a sense we have become our own gods." (79).

However, the difference between the thoughts or affects of subjective conscious men and the auditory hallucinations of bicameral men cannot be fully grasped without appreciating the fact that the gods' voices originating in the right hemisphere of the brain, had absolute authority over the man part in the left. This, according to Jaynes, is a property of sound itself, which is the least controllable of all sense modalities (97). We would not be able to comprehend someone's speech if we did not suspend our own consciousness briefly, and meet them half-way, as it were. "Consider what it is to listen and understand someone speaking to us." Jaynes says.

> In a certain sense we have to become the other person; or rather, we let him become part of us for a brief second. We suspend our own identities, after which we come back to ourselves and accept or reject what he has said. But that brief second of dawdling identity is the nature of understanding language; and if that language is a command, the identification of understanding becomes the obedience. To hear is actually a kind of obedience. Indeed, both words come from the same root and therefore were probably the same word originally. This is true in Greek, Latin, Hebrew, French, German, Russian, as well as in English, where 'obey' comes from the Latin *obedire*, which is a composite of *ob + audire*, to hear facing someone. (ibid.)

There are, Jaynes explains, two ways to counter such obedience. One is by maintaining a comfortable spatial distance between oneself and the speaker, which, as every cultural anthropology student knows, is culturally conditioned. The second is to counter the effect of other people's authority over us by our opinions of them. "Our personal judgments of others are filters of influence." (98). But for the bicameral man neither of these methods availed, since he could not escape or back away from voices emanating within, nor could he judge as beneath him these voices he believed came from the gods. "The explanation of volition in subjective conscious men is still a profound problem that has not reached any satisfactory solution", Jaynes states. "But in bicameral men, this *was* volition. Another way to say it is that volition came as a voice that was in the nature of a neurological command, in which the command and the action were not separated, in which to hear was to obey." (98-9).

4.4 Exilic Consciousness: The Sea People

One day I will sit on the pavement…the pavement of the estranged.
I was no Narcissus; still I defend my image
in the mirrors. Haven't you been here once before, stranger?
Five hundred years have passed, but our breakup wasn't final,
and the messages between us never stopped…

—Mahmoud Darwish, "One Day I Will Sit on the Pavement"

One objection to Jaynes's theory is that in the face of these uncompromising and unpredictable bicameral voices demanding absolute obedience from their subjects, utter chaos ought to have prevailed, with everyone following their own private hallucinations. The only way for bicameral civilizations to exist would be that of a strict hierarchy, each individual hallucinating and obeying the voice of his immediate superior, up to the kings hallucinating gods (Jaynes, 79). But the world of the *Iliad* is very different from this. According to Jaynes, this is because later poet-singers (*aoidoi*) brought together under its theme other stories, but also because the chaotic world of the *Iliad* might be the time when the bicameral mind was breaking down and subjective consciousness beginning. For Jaynes, this occurred as a result of a number of cataclysmic events, such as, the Thera explosion in the mid-second millennium BC and the series of vast migrations that followed. These migrations became the great invasions of the 13th and 12th centuries BC marked by the Trojan War and the collapse of the Aegean civilization. This is the time of raging warriors like Achilles, who caused such staggering destruction as to deserve the epithet "slayer of warriors", or "sacker of cities" and "destroyer of men." This is also the time of the "Sea Peoples," a conglomeration of tribes that abandoned their lands to form a formidable pirate alliance in whose wake all cities fell, from Mycenae, Thebes, Tiryns, Knossos, and Cyprus to the

Hittite and Egyptian empires (Bierling 2002). In the words of Ramesses III at Medinet Habu:

> ...The foreign countries made a conspiracy in their islands. All at once the lands were removed and scattered in the fray. No land could stand before their arms, from Hatti, Kode, Carchemish, Arzawa, and Alashiya on. ... They were coming forward toward Egypt, while the flame was prepared before them. Their confederation was the Philistines, Tjeker, Shekelesh, Denye(n), and Weshesh, lands united. They laid their hands upon the lands as far as the circuit of the earth, their hearts confident and trusting: "Our plans will succeed!" [*ANET*, 262][1]

One of the tribes among them were the Philistines and another the Danaans (Denyen), who were also part of the expeditionary force at Troy. In the records of Ramesses II, the Dardanians (Da-ar-d(a)-an-ya) are also mentioned. In fact, as Neal Bierling argues, many of the hardened warriors who took part on both sides of the protracted Trojan War might have later joined the Sea Peoples who turned up in Egypt according to the Pharaohs, and in Palestine according to the Old Testament.

In the 1990 afterword addition to his book, Jaynes retracts the view that the breakdown of the bicameral mind was a consequence of some cataclysmic event, emphasizing instead that the overpopulation resulting from the success of theocratic agricultural societies, naturally brings with it the seeds of its own undoing (454). Group size is delimited by communication and hierarchy, and the strictly leveled organization required for the control of bicameral societies, breaks down under uncontrolled population growth.

Be that as it may, for bicameral societies, rapid population growth would have roughly the same effect as a catastrophic natural event *because* it would result in migrations. Jaynes himself asks what would happen to the city god's voice if the distance between bicameral men and its source increased, as must be the case for sailors and merchants who, furthermore, might be in daily contact and probably even speak the language of men ruled by a different pantheon of voices. "Is it possible that something like a protosubjective

consciousness occurred in these traders at the boundaries of different civilizations?" (211). One may follow the implications of this
question to a study by Susan Sherrat, who traces the apocalyptic
events of the 13ᵗʰ and 12ᵗʰ centuries directly to the Sea Peoples and
the destabilizing effects their aggressive decentralized trade had in
the region. For Sherrat the artisanal economy of the Sea Peoples
might have resulted from "the lack on [their] island² of centralized
or tight 'palatial' forms of economic and political control." (1998,
306). These tight "palatial" forms, as the ones found in Minos's
palace in Knossos, or Cadmus's palace in Thebes, are precisely those
needed for the existence and welfare of bicameral societies (Jaynes,
79-80), and if the Sea Peoples' decentralized culture was the consequence of their lack, this suggests that these terrible seafarers were
already post bicameral, though, it would seem, without the inhibitions of the later subjective mind. They were gods unleashed.

Apart from the evident military threat, however, they constituted also an economic and political threat to the Egyptian and the
Hittite theocratic states (Sherrat, 307). For Sherratt, too, the seeds
of this "insidious economic and political threat ... were included
in the long-term evolution of the structures with whose collapse it
is associated." (ibid.).

In the end, it would seem that no matter where we look for the
catalyst to these world-transforming events, whether some natural
cataclysmic occurrence that set in motion vast migratory waves, or
the success of theocratic agricultural societies resulting in overpopulation and migration, or yet again to the decentralized artisanal
trade of the Sea Peoples that Sherrat envisions as archetypes of
homo economicus, one characteristic is common to them all; an
exilic consciousness for which all borders have dissolved. Suddenly,
the world stands face to face with an enemy that is both strange and
familiar, in the materialization of whose features it recognizes both
an alien arriving for the first time and its own rejected offspring
returning. For, if the change from the bicameral mind to subjective
consciousness had risen within a sedentary culture, one would expect the change to be gradual, the bicameral voices slowly fading

away. Instead, the change is abrupt. Jaynes asserts that before fading out the voices multiply to a hullabaloo of commands and counter-commands that shatter all hierarchies and social institutions (cf. the story of Babel). The gods go rogue no longer upholding the laws of the universe, seeking to annihilate all that stands in their way. It is a war of all against all – *bellum omnium contra omnes* – as Hobbes feared again, and rightly so, a few thousand years later.

This same theme of great upheaval and destruction, runs also through the Norse prophecy of the end of days, which it is foretold will result in the twilight of the gods (*Ragnarøkkr*) as they battle an array of monstrous giant beasts to the end, a theme similar in many respects to the battle of the Olympian deities against the giants. And as the gods above, so the men below. In the end, the seas will rise and giant waves will swallow everything. Then, silence!

Half-dead, the post-apocalyptic man washes ashore and awakes to find himself abject, alone, and abandoned by his gods. Suddenly he turns his gaze upon himself only to see that there is no one there. The temple is empty. A terrifying void stares back at him. Narcissus, the archetype of subjective consciousness, is born. To fall in love with an empty image is easy—he already worshiped idols before. But the narcissistic consciousness is fetishistic because it averts its eyes in terror. To use Metzinger's terminology, Narcissus first fixed his eyes upon the "model of selfhood," realized the sheer depths of its emptiness, and horrified withdrew his gaze in self-hypnotic contemplation. Simply put, he followed the well-known advice that when in panic, take deep breaths and count to ten. There was a moment, then, during the transition from the bicameral mind to subjective consciousness, that the model of selfhood was not transparent. It may well be that it is still opaque, the ego operating like a maze of mirrors, creating the illusion of transparency. In other words, the model is unaware of itself, not because it is transparent and can see through itself (Metzinger 2003), but because the mirror maze directs its gaze elsewhere. Immediately after its emergence, then, the new consciousness is muzzled again through the birth of the subject and his ego. This stuttering new subjectivity emerging from the ruins of the bicameral mind begins its awkward walk wavering at every corner, stumbling with every step it takes, for man's new labyrinthine self awareness does not tell him what to do or where to go. Exhausted, his earlier ambition for great deeds and glory is gradually replaced by a desire for rest and comfort. He cannot find the strength within himself to affirm anything. This period is unsurprisingly marked by a frantic search for the lost gods. Yet, man searches for the gods while at the same time fearing in his heart that he might truly find them. Hence, he finds demons instead.

4.5 The Poets: Intellectual Exile

...Nothing hurts me.
Not the air, and not the water... There is no basil in your morning, no
iris in your evening that hurts me after this departure...

—Mahmoud Darwish, "In Exodus I Love You More"

Jaynes does not deny the possibility that certain individuals might have been conscious before the rest, though for him this is perhaps not significant enough:

> Did consciousness really come *de novo* into the world only at this time? Is it not possible that certain individuals at least might have been conscious in much earlier time? Possibly yes. As individuals differ in mentality today, so in past ages it might have been possible that one man alone, or more possibly a cult or clique, began to develop a metaphored space with analog selves. But such aberrant mentality in bicameral theocracy would, I think, be short-lived and scarcely what we mean by consciousness today. (221-2)

One must be cautious, however, not to judge the evolution of consciousness from one's own position of subjective understanding, according to which, its evolutionary pathway seems inevitable and is taken for granted. Jaynes, for example, does point to an interesting dimension – and possible alternative – with his suspicion that the god side of the bicameral man appears to have approached consciousness before the man side, "the right hemisphere before the left." (277). This might have been the case, as we saw, with the Sea Peoples, though the god-side may not necessarily have approached *subjective* consciousness, as Jaynes then asserts. Subjectivity, in fact, was a censuring or inhibition to a consciousness in which man and god (or instinct and reason; the synthetic and the analytic functions), seem to initially have merged.

But apart from the Sea Peoples, and more generally from the migrants and exiles traced through the geographical landscape, one may also look to another kind – the intellectual exile. For Bruno Snell, these individuals were the poets. Even though reaching quite different conclusions from Jaynes's theory of the bicameral mind, Snell's study of the rise of consciousness in Greek philosophy and literature provides some glaring instances of this. Both authors, however, agree on the crucial point that a decision must rise out of a *tension* between two (or more) conflicting impulses. For Jaynes, in fact, *stress* and *decision-making* are the same thing:

> It has now been clearly established that decision-making (and I would like to remove every trace of conscious connotation from the word 'decision') is precisely what stress is. If rats have to cross an electric grid each time they wish to get food and water, such rats develop ulcers. Just shocking the rats does not do this to them. There has to be the pause of conflict or the decisionmaking stress of whether to cross a grid or not to produce this effect. If two monkeys are placed in harness, in such a way that one of the monkeys can press a bar at least once every twenty seconds to avoid a periodic shock to both monkey's feet, within three or four weeks the decision-making monkey will have ulcers, while the other, equally shocked monkey will not. It is the pause of unknowingness that is important. For if the experiment is so arranged that an animal can make an effective response and receive immediate feedback on his success, executive ulcers, as they are often called, do not occur. (93-4)

For bicameral men, stress is the mechanism that triggers hallucinations to providing a decision. The stress threshold for releasing auditory hallucinations, then, must have been considerably lower in the bicameral era, "the only stress necessary was that which occurs when a change in behavior is necessary because of some novelty in a situation." (93). Conversely, the stress threshold must be much higher for the conscious man to start hearing voices instructing him what to do, requiring a decision by other means. According to Bruno Snell, this stress or inner conflict is intensified to harsher new realities by the conscious tragedians. "This is most clearly shown in Aeschylus's last tragedy, the *Oresteia*."

> Orestes is under an obligation to avenge his father; this means he must slay his mother. He performs this deed only after experiencing the cruel difficulty of his decision to the full. This is the discovery of the contrast between freedom and fate, between duty and doom, a discord which sunders

the world of men from that of the gods. Orestes stands between two divine commands, and in the last play of the trilogy the tragedy actually issues into a struggle between two hostile camps of gods, the Erinyes who desire to punish Orestes for the murder of his mother, and Apollo who eventually clears him of his guilt.

With two deities making irreconcilable claims on him, the human agent is forced to confine himself to his own resources. Values which previously were unambiguous are cast in doubt; man becomes irresolute and incapable of spontaneous action, and finds himself pressed to consider in his own terms the problem of right and wrong. (Snell, 123)

It will be noted that Orestes's inner conflict resulting from the irreconcilable demands made on him by the two deities, corresponds exactly to the multiplication of the gods' voices during the breakdown of the bicameral mind. All the tragedian had to do to point to the human (in)decision was to accentuate this, by interpolating two perfectly antithetical demands. Hence, the tragedians' tendency toward even images.

The same decision emerging out of an implacable conflict characterizes Euripides's tragedies. But in *Medea* he goes even further than Aeschylus in reaching that decision through a monologue. In fact, as Snell points out, "before Euripides the genuine monologue had not existed in tragedy." (126). And this is significant also in that it highlights man's existential solitude in the face of ever receding gods. Medea's decision to murder her children is conscious insofar as she reaches it herself, though she does recognize her anger as a mover: "I know what crimes I am about to commit, but my anger is stronger than my reason." On the other hand, Jason, the civilized Greek hero who unquestioningly follows his community's tradition, though rational – in fact, all-too-rational – is less conscious than she is.

This should not come as a surprise, however. The subjective conscious man today is no different in that subjectivity is a mode that can operate just as unconsciously as the bicameral mind's hallucinations. If man does not hallucinate today this does not necessarily mean that he thinks. Decision-making can easily be taken over by habit, and in any case, there is a proliferation of instructions/commands everywhere one turns today, that to find one's way from home to work and back, one only has to follow the signs. In many ways, thinking is disadvantageous and even outright discouraged in today's civilized world. As Martin P. Nilsson says, "primitive mentality is a fairly good description of the mental behavior of most people to-day except in their technical or consciously intellectual activities." (qtd. in Dodds 1951, 35-6).

It has generally been assumed that in Euripides's plays the gods are slowly becoming more abstract and equated with morality. But more than anything this explanation seems a forced solution to the irresolvable conundrum Euripides has left us with. Snell argues that in *Medea* he advances the instinctual and the irrational over Jason's rational, and because of it, dull, mentality; "From the very beginning Medea appears as an extraordinary, a strange and mysterious woman beside whom the reasonable and well-intentioned Jason must strike us as shabby and commonplace. This is how Euripides draws the hero of the Greek myth, and the barbarian witch." (Snell, 125).

Unlike the poets criticized by Socrates, Euripides knows exactly what he needs to say, and proceeds with an almost otherworldly precision. "In Aeschylus Apollo holds the field against the Erinyes, i.e. the purer faith triumphs over the hoary superstitions, and the somber plot is brightened by a meaningful end. In [*Hippolytus*], however, the two chief agents perish, and the two deities continue to face each other across an irremediable breach." (Snell, 127). Snell misses the point, though, when he points out Euripides's emphasis of the irrational. Rather, in Euripides one may catch a glimpse of something higher than the philosophic ass, in a flash of the *arational*, since he does not call for a return to an older mentality, which would have been irrational (nostalgic), nor does he provide some great destiny toward the future to be called a moralist (utopian). His use of morality is more a coaxing for the common man who otherwise would find only naked threat in his tragedies. Looking past Euripides's moral spins, Aristophanes distinctly perceived this threat, and, in diametrical opposition to modern critics that make Euripides a moralist, accused him of being immoral. But, as Snell states, "immorality is not the only count on which Aristophanes indicts Euripides. He also calls him a clever sophist, and accuses him of splitting hairs and other cunning manipulations."

> And yet it was Euripides who first placed the accent on the irrational forces in man. Medea and Phaedra are great women because they are passionate; it follows that Euripides cannot be a one-sided champion of reason and enlightenment. On the contrary, it might well be maintained that Euripides reduces reason and reflexion *ad absurdum*: in both plays reason plays a negative role, doubly negative indeed, for on the one hand it acts merely in a warning and deterring capacity, and secondly it does not succeed in that function, unlike the *daimonion* of Socrates which is also confined to a repressive role. Moreover the 'reasonable' figures in the two dramas, Jason and the nurse, are contemptible and immoral precisely because they are reasonable. Still it would be wrong to define Euripides in terms of a contrast between reason and irrationality. Aristophanes has some justice on his side when he places Euripides among the company of the Sophists and Socrates, for his moralizing is largely that of a philosopher and dissenter. His discontent, his skepticism shatters his faith in the gods and in the ancient meaning of life, and tinges his creative temper with nihilistic overtones. In his later plays the characters have a hollow ring, their action is devoid of any significance or higher mission. In the *Iphigenia in Aulis* the brothers Agamemnon and Menelaus easily unmask the idealistic motives which each alleges to the other; the principles which really control their actions are egotism, lust for power, and—cowardly fear of the other. With biting cruelty Euripides has shown us the true nature of these Homeric heroes who now find themselves isolated in a world stripped of the gods, a world that makes no sense. With no illusions left to support them, they totter and threaten to fall. This is the gain which has accrued to man from his newly-found independence: he has no firm ground to stand on, and is helplessly exposed to the hazards of life. (129-30)

Euripides, then, is not a naïve herald of universal reason, but at odds with both the older mentality and the new. He is not simply situated in the middle, at a transitioning period between these two modes of social control, but viciously attacks them both. His universal reason is eternal strife.[1]

In periods of social upheaval and identity crises, society anxiously seeks to forge another identity for itself. The transition from the bicameral mind to subjective consciousness, therefore, marks the prototypical mode of social control based on identity politics. Euripides's fierce nihilism can only be understood in this light. It is an onslaught against identity politics. It is not at all obvious that consciousness should have evolved only in the way it did, i.e. as subjective consciousness. Subjectivity, more than an evolution of consciousness, is its reins and muzzle. One may envision ways in which the breakdown of the bicameral mind branches off in different directions, and instead of foregoing the hitherto automatic command of the gods, it appropriates and transforms it. But first it must be brought to a full halt. Man must endure nothingness. In the implacable conflict of the gods, Euripides's gesture points toward the disappearance of the human into a yawning abyss of (in)decision, dipped into the waters of the Lethe, or primordial chaos. What emerges, is something altogether different, something far more dangerous than the gods with their unchanging nature, uncompromising demands, and dependence on the human for the execution of their commands. For if something must emerge at all, it is the kind that can act beyond the sanction of the divine or the logic of the human. The gods too, owe their existence to this universal conflict, not the other way around. All proper mythology starts with chaos. Graves (2012) summarizes a number of creation accounts bearing witness to this:[2]

1- The Pelasgian Creation Myth:

In the beginning, Eurynome, the Goddess of All Things, rose naked from Chaos, but found nothing substantial for her feet to rest upon, and therefore divided the sea from the sky, dancing lonely upon its waves. (xii).

2- The Olympian Creation Myth:

At the beginning of all things Mother Earth emerged from Chaos and bore her son Uranus as she slept. (1).

3- Two Philosophical Creation Myths

a) ...Darkness was first, and from Darkness sprang Chaos. From a union between Darkness and Chaos sprang Night, Day, Erebus, and the Air... (3).

b) the God of All Things—whoever he may have been, for some call him Nature—appearing suddenly in Chaos, separated earth from the heavens, the water from the earth, and the upper air from the lower. (4).

The first philosophical creation myth is based on Hesiod's *Theogony* (211-32) and taken up by Hyginus, Apollodorus, Lucian, and Pausanias. In its misconceptualization of original creation, "Darkness was first, and from Darkness sprang Chaos," it adds nothing of value to the more free-flowing Pelasgian and Olympian myths. Nevertheless, from this first blunder, an interesting sequence of unions between opposite elements follows, giving rise to a plethora of monstrous entities,[3] making it a very productive conceptual error.

The second philosophical creation myth is found in Ovid's *Metamorphoses* (i-ii). The subject of the separation of opposites found in the Pelasgian creation myth and expanded by Ovid is interesting in view of Hesiod's account where from their union spring monstrosities, for this abyssal union between relentlessly annihilating opposites is precisely the non-localizable birthplace of the barbarian. Unlike the political animal, who seeking an ordered universe,[4] inhabits only one element at a time, the barbarian rides them all, bringing with him chaos and destruction.[5] It was Daniel van der Velden who stated that conservatives and realists love the earth and liberals love the cloud, and the barbarian, as McFarlane succinctly put it, is neither a liberal nor a conservative, but the pinnacle of violent hybridity.

It would be futile to dwell at length over the fact that the present time is the age of nihilism. But differently from what is generally assumed, nihilism is not a revolt against the instinctual. This revolt has already occurred. Rather, nihilism is a counter-revolt against subjective consciousness and all that it entails. It, too, traces its roots to the breakdown of the bicameral mind and the emergence of the new subjective consciousness, and can be first perceived clearly in the work of the poets.

Nevertheless, it is not enough to say that the poets were seeking for another consciousness. They were seeking a new command as well. And what they discovered (or forged) was *suggestion*, a type of encrypted command that had not hitherto existed. Given the fact that the hallucinated voices of the gods were already inside one's head, they had no need of suggestion: their voice was an immediate and direct instruction in the nature of a neurological command.[6] But once they faded away, the space they previously occupied became susceptible to invasion from without. The ego was conjured up as the watchdog to guard this inner space from outside invasion. The coded command of suggestion, therefore, served to throw off the scent of this new Cerberus in that another's instruction could subtly be implanted on the audience's mind as if it were its own. It was the smuggled seed of a future command grown in the home soil of one's own head. From here on language became a proper virus, able to reprogram one's whole constitution. And as rhyme, rhythm, sound patterns, etc. functioned for poetry, logic became the primary modus operandi of certain other insidious and invasive methods of suggestion, since by demanding consistency, it helped clear away the new habitat inside another's mind from all that was at odds with the implanted suggestion. As Jaynes points out, "The very reason we need logic at all is because most reasoning is not conscious at all." (41).

It is as a result and in compliance with the rules of logic that philosophy grew out of tragic poetry. It is no coincidence that Euripides's assault on subjectivity and the ego reaches new heights with Socrates. In virtually all his interviews, for instance, Socrates deliberately compliments or scolds the ego of his respondent, an act that enables him to harness it like the reins to a beast and direct the attention of his interlocutor where he pleases. What Socrates achieves can only be understood in light of the well-known fact that the excitation of the ego always inhibits or momentarily suspends cold reason. The subject whose ego has been flattered or insulted loses in no small measure the capacity "to think straight." Socrates's masterful alternation between cajoling and deriding his respondent's asinine ego has the effect of making the subject conscious of it, which means precisely that the subject was not conscious of it to begin with, and that the ego is in fact a hindrance to consciousness.

However, while philosophy has time and again vied for authority with sophism, religion, science and other forms of knowledge, poetry preserves its function of an encrypted command to this day. In ancient times poetry was the language of gods, it was divine knowledge. "And after the breakdown of the bicameral mind, [it became] the sound and tenor of authorization", Jaynes says (364). Poetry commanded where prose could only beg, though as Socrates rightly observed, most poets did not consciously understand their own code.[7] Something else was still speaking through them. This prophetic and divine inspiration is consistently mistaken for mere catharsis in modern times, a way to express one's feelings, to "just get it out of one's chest" which, of course, would make poetry no better than verbal vomit. "Art is the mirror of the artist's soul," one hears ad nauseam today, a metaphor that only makes sense if one envisions the soul's contractions as no different than bowel movements.

Through art man sees the world as the gods do! Art is not some subjective endeavor unless one intentionally and narcissistically makes it so. Nor is it objective: art cannot explain itself any more than god can explain his own existence. And being not a dialectician's business it does not have to.

Tragedy, however, finding itself midway between poetry and philosophy, was more susceptible to becoming infected by its own viral logic—inculcated by the echo of a spell returning to its source. One can clearly observe this in Seneca's ambiguity in *Hercules on Oeta*, who now accuses the hero of hypocrisy, now recites the morals of the day in all their pomp, sermons which, one suspects were picked up wholesale from the very beginnings of tragedy. By Seneca's time they had acquired legitimacy as the very columns on which civilization was built; so much so that the author could inadvertently use them to divert attention from more dangerous assertions. Was Seneca pointing to the ongoing conflict between the barbarian and civilization? Or was he simply unconscious of the secret command he was uttering?

APOCALYPTIC TEACHERS

5.1 The Teachings of Chiron

Sky did not beget us, dust did not beget us
We are a foam evaporating from the rivers of words
Rust in the sky and its heavens, rust in life!
(a coded message)

—Adonis, "This Is My Name"

Toward the end of Seneca's play, Nessus and Deianeira slowly melt in the shadows as greater concerns pervade the myth. Heracles's murder is relegated to the second plane as the audience's attention is called to the hero's immortal ghost now rattling on crass, high-minded advice against unrestrained lamentations to his inconsolable mother Alcmene (1863-989). Influenced by earlier Hellenic platitudes against excessive mourning practices, this is Seneca's own moral adjustment to the myth and figure of the hero, who as a symbol and stalwart of civilization must, even in death, continue to spiel off all sorts of moral teachings.

Rarely does one stop to think that evidence of a conspiracy against him screams from every word of the story, that from the Amazons to the Centaurs, Deianeira is found in every camp against which Heracles fought, hardly the naïve housewife everyone makes her out to be, and much more proficient than him in the Great Mysteries, their wedding itself having been arranged in hell. That the focus now as then remains on her ignorance, only demonstrates that her threat is still valid, and that it is impossible for a civilization which cannot survive without its delusion of safety, to recognize what really stares it in the face.

Nessus's foresight, too, is recognized and quickly dismissed; it was prophesied that Heracles should die in order to become a god, so ultimately Nessus merely played his part in a vast celestial scheme set in motion by Zeus. Even though clearly intelligent, his role is no more than to bring death to the hero, a fateful pawn in the hands of an immutable destiny. Generally alone, working his tricks by the wayside or the river, Nessus is rarely seen in the company of other Centaurs. He stands an individual apart, not to be confused with others, not even his own savage race. It is significant that this was not always so, and that in the art of the archaic period, other Centaurs come to his aid against Heracles, a motif that was not preserved in literature. (Baur, 1912: nos. 32, 33, 36, 38, and possibly 108). In Attic representations of his encounter with the hero, with a few exceptions (nos. 66, 70), he is consistently depicted as cowardly and stumbling while attempting in vain to escape, head turned back in fear, hands stretched out in supplication. Is it not strange that the murderer of Heracles, the greatest hero of all, should be such a minor mythological figure? Yet, Heracles himself did not complain at learning that it was Nessus who killed him, for he considered him a worthy adversary (Sen. *Her. O.* 1464-87).

The myth clearly shows that even though the murderer of Heracles has to be set apart from savages including his own race, still it is impossible to imagine him as anything more than savagely cunning. In the end, he remains a canny beast, his duplicity and guile an innate characteristic of his kind that in him appears unnaturally exaggerated. In short, intelligent or not, there is nothing one can learn from savage Nessus. Merely an aberration to be used for astral agendas, he poses no difficulty to the civilized mind, no hidden mysteries, no enigmas to be solved.

Yet, a saying from early myth shows that this was not always so. Similarly to the Centaur, the Satyr too, was both savage and wise before becoming merely a jest appended to tragedy, a figure of ridicule meant to soothe the irritated souls of the audience. It was said in the olden days that young men who sought the secret of life were encouraged to go into the woods and ask the Satyr. And if one asked Silenus, Dionysus's tutor and companion, and if the Satyr deigned him with a response at all, he would get to hear an antinatal pessimist philosophy foreshadowing that of Schopenhauer, Zapffe or Ligotti today: "That not to be born is the best of all, and that to be dead is better than to live." Plutarch cites this passage from Aristotle's lost dialogue, *Eudemus*, in his "Letter of Condolence to Apollonius":

...they say that Silenus, after the hunt in which Midas of yore had captured him, when Midas questioned and inquired of him what is the best
thing for mankind and what is the most preferable of things, was at first
unwilling to tell, but maintained a stubborn silence. But when at last, by
employing every device, Midas induced him to say something to him, Silenus,
forced to speak, said: "Ephemeral offspring of a travailing genius and of
harsh fortune, why do you force me to speak what it were for you men
not to know? For life spent in ignorance of one's own woes is most free from
grief. But for men it is utterly impossible that they should obtain the best
thing of all, or even have any share in its nature (for the best thing for all
men and women is not to be born); however, the next best thing to this, and
the first of those to which man can attain, but nevertheless only the second
best, is, after being born, to die as quickly as possible."

(Plut. *Cons. Ap.* 27)

Of course, Plutarch's disappointing conclusion is, "It is evident, therefore, that he made this declaration with the conviction
that existence after death is better than that in life." What should
not go unnoticed in Silenus's reply is its abrupt severity, the tight-
ening grip of its wisdom besieging the mind from every side. Not
only is the best thing of all utterly impossible to obtain, but the
second best thing, too, is merely to look forward to your own demise, and possibly help it. This is not all. Silenus takes away from
Midas the one thing the king was in possession of, and the last best
thing possible to be attained by men, for having now received this
unwelcome knowledge is itself a violent blow. "Ignorance of one's
own woes" would have been bliss, a blessing now equally denied
him. There is no going back here, Silenus allows no escape, no safe
passage for retreat.

At any rate, the teachings imparted by Chiron must not have
been so different from those of Silenus. A cue to this can be found
in Heracles's own words tearfully expressed to Meleager,
Deianeira's brother in Hades, for they are almost word for word
taken from Silenus's reply to Midas: "For mortals it is best never
to be born, never to look on the light of the sun. But there is no
profit in lamenting this; one must speak of what can be accom-

plished." (Bacchyl. *Epinic.* v. 160). And what *can* be accomplished, according to Silenus, is, after having been born to die as quickly as possible.

The question whether Heracles borrowed these words from Chiron or Silenus is less significant than might at first appear, since Centaurs (horse-totem tribesmen) and Satyrs (goat-totem tribesmen) became differentiated only in later myth. (Graves 2012, 77, 178, 442, Padgett 2004, 4, 27). In this case, the most likely candidates to be the goat-totem Satyrs are the Lapiths, the Centaurs' hereditary enemies, who in early vase paintings are in fact, depicted as goat-men. Yet, even though blood-related, for both tribes are descendants of Ixion, in Greek myth the Lapiths stand for the forces of reason and order, battling against the wild and unruly Centaurs. This battle in which another civilizing hero, Theseus, partook as an ally of the Lapiths, and which resulted in the banishment of the Centaurs from Thessaly, was called the *Centauromachy* "the battle of the Centaurs," or, to distinguish it from the battle of Heracles on Mount Pholoe, the Thessalian Centauromachy.

On their road to civilization, however, the Lapiths distance themselves not only from their kin, the Centaurs, but also from their own totem animal, the goat. Hence, the legendary Lapiths and the mythological Satyrs stand opposite one another, the totem animal expelled from its people. But the totem represents the lifeblood of its people, their bare life. If this is perhaps the first myth in which the mystic connection between the exile and the totem animal can be clearly pointed out, it is certainly not the last. The same can be traced to the figure of *homo sacer* in Roman law, from whom the notion of the outlaw as a *wolf* or *wolf's head* is derived.[1] It is in this way that Agamben's notion of *bare life* must be understood. The exile is bare life precisely insofar as he is the totem of his people. "What defines the status of homo sacer," Agamben writes, "is ... both the particular character of the double exclusion into which he is taken and the violence to which he finds himself exposed. This violence—the unsanctionable killing that, in his case, anyone may commit—is classifiable neither as sacrifice nor as homicide, neither as the execution of a condemnation to death nor as sacrilege. Subtracting itself from the sanctioned forms of both human and divine law, this violence opens a sphere of human action that is neither the sphere of sacrum facere nor that of profane action." (1998, 931-5).

Severed from its people, their life conditions, customs and mores, their survival politics and sacred city walls, the former totem is the avatar of exilic consciousness par excellence. Again, what we see with the Satyrs or the Sileni are naked gods, stripped of their institutional power, belonging neither to the earth nor the sky. Unleashed from their human bonds,[2] they become vagrant gods of intoxication, laughter, rampage, and destruction. It is here that the exile meets the barbarian and is transformed into what is called the total enemy, both of the world of men and that of the gods.[3] For, these are stray gods; outcast, mercenary deities ready to sell their tricks and ruses along with the secrets of heaven and hell to the highest bidder. Chiron's esoteric teachings of the heroes, especially of music and medicine, and closely related to these, philosophy and the martial arts, only make sense if seen in this light. But the best evidence for his subversive teachings is provided by the secret diet he used for his pupils and their initiation into the mysteries. For he nourished them on the food of the gods, nectar and ambrosia, strictly prohibited to mortals as we know from the punishment of irreverent figures like Tantalus, and according to Graves, even the Centaurs' and the Lapiths' own ancestors, Ixion and his son, Pirithous.

5.2 Medicine and Music

Prophetic Chiron,
the son of Phylira,
laying hands
on the blond curls
of Achilles,
often declared Fate:
Scamander chokes
on the Trojan marauders.

—Bacchylides, frag. 27

The fragments that remain from *The Precepts of Chiron*, a work that according to Pausanias (ix. 31. 5), was probably composed by Hesiod, are too few to allow any insight on the matter. In the *Iliad* as well, there are only four references to Chiron in relation to his pupil, Achilles, though his other tutor, Phoenix, appears in it prominently and in person in the embassy sent to the hero's tent by Agamemnon. (ix. 168 ff. for Phoenix; see below for Chiron). This, "lamentable lack of detail" is somewhat strange, and raises more questions than it answers, according to C. J. Mackie (1997), considering that the allusions to the Centaur within the text imply that the audience is quite familiar with the Chiron/Achilles tradition (2). This, it is generally argued, is most likely due to the conscious exclusion of supernatural elements from the epic: "At a most basic level Phoenix is clearly a more appropriate figure for the poem because of his human form. One finds it difficult to imagine the embassy to Achilles being led by a centaur in a poem like the *Iliad*." (3). However, the suppression of the fantastic and the supernatural is only partial, as Rutherford points out: "the *Iliad* includes a cap of invisibility, a talking horse, a warrior who fights with a river god, and a body magically preserved against decay." (qtd. in ibid.). So even though Chiron is banished to the sidelines of the poem,

Mackie concludes, he is not totally excluded in order to account for Achilles's uniqueness and complexity, a role that Phoenix alone, being "a kind of generic old man figure" would not be able to fill (4).

The fact notwithstanding that the *Iliad* may not be the work of a single poet-singer named Homer, and that considerations concerned with the impression a scene might make on the audience are more appropriate to drama than to epic, still it is possible that certain elements having to do with the magic and the fantastic were gradually censured by the poets down the centuries, each in their own way. It is true, however, that the association with Chiron adds a distinct aura to Achilles's figure, accentuating his dark moods that seem to flow from a world incomprehensible to either men or gods. Yet, this dark aura does not limit itself to the "personality" of the hero, as Mackie then claims, but extends to the field of action. It precedes one's personal anger with the objects of frustration that might have caused it, brewing in calculative preparation, – traceable in this respect as far back as Chiron's training of Achilles's own father – standing the hero from engaging prematurely until all the plot lines will align, building its reserve of madness for a period stretched over long years during which anxiety, impatience, boredom, and the slow running of time, will work their magic and convert into calculated recklessness, so when the moment comes, it may unleash itself upon the world with an explosive fury that tears apart not men but societies.

Two of the four passages in which Chiron is mentioned describe Achilles's ashen spear, which no other Achaean can wield. (xvi. 141-4; xix. 388-91). Without the knowledge that it was a gift from Chiron, this devastating weapon would have been just another wooden spear with a bronze tip. The association with the cunning master, however, gives it a terrifying tinge, it appears almost as a biochemical weapon of mass destruction:

> And from its stand he drew his father's spear, heavy and huge and strong, that no other of the Achaeans could wield, but Achilles alone was skilled to wield it, the Pelian spear of ash that Chiron had given to his dear father from the peak of Pelion for the slaying of warriors. (Hom. *Il.* xix. 388-99)

Over a hundred lines in book 20 describe the great slaughter he wreaks with it (381 ff), reaching a climax in lines 490-4:

> As through the deep glens of a parched mountainside rages wondrous-blazing fire, and the deep forest burns, and the wind as it drives it on whirls the flame everywhere, so raged he everywhere with his spear, like some god (δαίμονι), ever pressing hard on those he slew; and the black earth ran with blood. (A. T. Murray's trans.)

In book 21, the corpses become so numerous they choke the Scamander river, who complains that his streams can no longer reach the sea (214-20). Other passages throughout the poem are too many to count, yet Homer never mentions that, like Heracles's arrows, the tip of Chiron's spear was poisoned. By itself this detail certainly would not broach on the supernatural, and the poets would have had no reason to exclude it. It is as if the poem is ever pointing to its power without giving away the source. The other two references to Chiron, however, describe his capacity as a teacher of medicine (iv. 217-19; xi. 828-32), which, in light of the poisoned ash-spear take on a special significance. Interestingly, these four references are evenly spread and indicate the opposite sides of the same coin: it is the same knowledge (of poison) that causes both the destruction and the healing. The story of Heracles's son, Telephus, who was wounded and healed by Achilles's spear makes this plain. That it might have been precisely this dark knowledge the authors were trying to suppress is suggested by the fact that Asclepius, another of Chiron's students is also brushed off quickly in the *Iliad*, as Mackie astutely points out:

> In Hesiod and Pindar Asclepius is a much more colorful figure whose healing powers extend to reviving the dead, thereby challenging the very nature of Zeus's role over mortals. There is none of this in the *Iliad* [where] Asclepius seems to be a rather ordinary Thessalian student of Chiron. [His] portrayal ... would appear to be a case of Homer's avoidance of magical healing in favour of a much more conservative and respectable form of medicine. If Homer does degrade Asclepius in the *Iliad* for his sins in reviving the dead there is of course every reason to degrade Chiron for much the same

146

reasons. Whether this same process takes place in the case of Achilles's healing powers we cannot say for certain, although there appears to be nothing
remarkable or magical about his medicine. One thing that is certain is that
the reference to Achilles as a healer, uttered by Eurypylus in the heat of battle, comes out of the blue, and sets him apart from the other princes. It
would seem to suggest rather strongly that healing was an important part of
the earliest accounts of the hero. (6)

The discrepancy between Hyginus's account in his *Fabulae*, in
which Achilles appears strangely ignorant of medicine, and Apollodorus's report of the same story in which he is medically proficient, lends support to this view. Wounded in battle by Achilles,
Telephus was in constant excruciating pain and upon consulting the
oracle of Apollo, was informed that "the only thing that could cure
him was the very same spear that had wounded him" (Hyg. 101).
Having received the knowledge that they could not capture Troy
without Telephus's guidance, the Achaeans entreated Achilles to
cure him, to which Achilles incredibly responded that he knew
nothing about medicine. At the suggestion of Ulysses, Telephus
was cured by shaving the rust off the spear, a procedure echoing the
myth of Melampous (Apollod. i. 9. 12; ∑ Hom. *Od.* 281). According to Apollodorus, however, Achilles did heal him (Apollod.
Epit. e. 3. 20), and, of course, in the *Iliad*, not only is he well versed
in the medicinal arts, but he has passed at least some of his
knowledge on to Patroclus as well. From this myth, we can deduce
that similarly, it was not from the Hydra but from Chiron that Heracles received the deadly bile in which he dipped his fateful arrows.
And this also answers the question of why it was that only Achilles
could wield the ashen spear – for only he knew the secret properties
of its venom. The devastating effect of the spear, therefore, does
not point to the infallibility of the hero as a marksman, as Mackie
argues, but to that of the poison, which made even the smallest
wound deadly.

The same suppression, it would seem, occurs in the *Iliad* in
regards to Chiron's training of Achilles in music, since if associated
with the Centaur, this too becomes a source of magic (see 5.3).

Centuries later, however, the references to Chiron resurface, though by this time they can be interpreted in line with a more natural view. According to pseudo-Plutarch, for example, we are told that "Heracles, Achilles, and many others had recourse to music, and their trainer, as tradition has it, was the paragon of wisdom, Chiron, instructor not only in music, but in medicine and justice as well." (*Mor.* 1146A). The author provides some insights into the function of this teaching. Taking his/her cue from the passage in the *Iliad*, in which Nestor, Odysseus, and Ajax arrive to Achilles's tent to find him "delighting in a lyre" as he sang heroic lays (ix. 186-9), pseudo-Plutarch argues that Homer tells us the proper way of employing music:

> Homer furthermore teaches us the suitable occasion for such employment, presenting it as a beneficial and pleasant exercise for one reduced to inaction. For though a warrior and a man of action, Achilles was taking no part in the fighting of the war, because he was wroth with Agamemnon. Homer believed, we gather, that it was fitting for the hero to whet his spirit on the noblest music, in order to be prepared for the sally into battle that was shortly to follow. That is obviously what he was doing when he rehearsed feats of long ago. Such was the music of olden times, and that is what it was used for.

> *Mor.* 1145F

Valerius Flaccus depicts a similar picture of the sage Centaur's teachings in his *Argonautica* in the words of Peleus, Achilles's father, to Chiron: "Let my little son marvel to hear thee speak of clarions and of wars; do thou teach him to wield his boyish weapons in the chase, and ere long to grasp my spear."[1] (i. 268-70). Most of the heroes on board the Argo, including Peleus himself, were, in fact, Chiron's older pupils, and it is interesting to witness the older generation departing as the younger takes its place.

Curiously though, these new more naturalistic or logical reinterpretations might not be too far from the truth. For what might have seemed as magic to the bicameral mind—that one could urge oneself on through music without need of the gods; that something or someone could issue commands to oneself and thus, induce the self to act of itself (*automatos*) — and man did not differ from inanimate objects in this regard in that he too was aroused and moved by forces beyond himself, — all this is only natural for the new subjective consciousness.

Of course, that something may be thought of as natural or logical from the standpoint of moderns is far from meaning that it has been explained. On the contrary, moderns may well know that music can play a motivational role, but what it is that makes it so, is a mystery, a few theories interpreting it as an expression of will notwithstanding. In this, the ancients had a better explanation; music is a prime mover because it comes directly from the gods. Chiron's magic, then, consisted in the appropriation of the gods' commands, and this may well be what the poets were trying to censure; not merely to seek more "natural" explanations, but ultimately to conceal the source of their own power.

5.3 Philosophy and Martial Arts

Brothers slay brothers;
Sisters' children
Shed each other's blood.
Hard is the world;
Sensual sin grows huge.
There are sword-ages;
Shields are cleft in twain;
Storm-ages, murder-ages;
Till the world falls dead,
And men no longer spare
Or pity one another

—The Decline of the Gods[†††]

Another source regarding Chiron's teachings is Dio Chrysostom's 58th Discourse, *Achilles*, which, even though the rhetorician's own embellishment,[1] or rather because of it, furnishes evidence that the barbarian's enmity against the savage/citizen-subject (s/c-s) civilizational lineage, was not lost to some authors, and centuries later had not in any way diminished.

In Chrysostom's moral tale, the nine-year-old pupil argues with his master about the use of the bow. To Achilles the bow is the weapon of cowards, since "it does not allow the foe to come near." "It does not allow the foe to get far away," is Chiron's reply. "The weapon belongs to men who flee," argues Achilles. "Nay; instead it is directed at men who flee," replies the Centaur. Afterwards, the argument grows abstract as the central issue becomes the difference between man and his tools, or in the specific case, fighter and weapon; if you overpower your enemy with a weapon like the bow, can you still say that it was you who overpowered the enemy and

---

[†††] In *Myths of the Norsemen: From the Eddas and Sagas*, ed. H. A. Guerber, Kindle Edition, (London: George G. Harrap, 1909), KL 391-2.

not the bow? Achilles answers in the negative, while similarly to Hegel, Chiron does not differentiate between the fighter and his weapon.

At any rate, if Achilles holds fast to his wrath, Chiron makes a case for sheer coldness.[2] Where Achilles bases his argument on the tacit assumption of the split between body and mind and the superiority of the former, Chiron, who does not subscribe to the body vs. mind wisdom – and being a Centaur, how could he?[3] – is bound by practical concerns to wear down not only Achilles's view of the superiority of the body over the mind, but also his arrogant presumption of his own superiority to others on account of his birth: His parents have spoiled him – his "briny mother," with pride of birth; and his mortal father with the tale of how the gods sang at his wedding. Chiron, however, denies that Achilles has any connection with either sea or sky. In a footnote to the text, the translator explains that this is only the unreasoning taunt of an angry man – an entirely superfluous comment, for in his philosophical tale, Chrysostom uses two well-known images to state that Achilles is earthbound—that he is incapable either of the abstraction associated with the sky, or the ever-restless movement and shapeshifting nature of the waters (recall here the wild transformations of Proteus, Nereus, and Thetis). Chiron continues:

> "…a warrior you will never be, though you will have that reputation with the unthinking, nor ever a leader of men, no matter where you may engage in warfare… Yet because of your audacity and fleetness of foot and physical strength men in flattery will call you most valiant of men. However, they will prefer to be ruled by other princes, while as for you, they will compel you by gifts and empty praises to do battle and risk your life for them until you finally meet your death. … But for all your arrogance, you will meet your death, not at the hands of some man of nobility, as you imagine; on the contrary, while you will find it easy to slay those who are like you, brave but stupid, you will be slain by a man of sagacity and military science, and, what is more, without ever having seen him."

In this outstanding prophecy, Chiron is squarely accusing Achilles of being a thoughtless savage. More subtle, however, is the master's erosion of the hero's belief in society and the flattering purpose society recites for his existence as its savior and defender. He ungrounds the future hero's belief in the truth and purpose spelled out for him. Chiron does not teach his student to strive for preservation; only to detach himself from the lofty ideals of those who would take shelter in them. Moreover, he teaches Achilles that his foe is not merely the noble savage (the brave but stupid—or the one who values the body over the mind) whom it is easy for him to slay, but also the civilized man of wile and deceit (the man of sagacity and military science—the one who values the mind over the body). The enemy, in short, is humanity itself from its savage beginnings to civilization, which is to say, the entire world.

This same mind vs. body or celestial vs. tellurian concern operant in Achilles's education, can be traced even more clearly in Heracles's mythos. A passage by Plutarch in *De E apud Delphos* (*The E at Delphi*) says that Heracles, before he had released Prometheus or had conversed with the sophists Chiron and Atlas, when he was young and unlearned, would do away with logical reasoning and attempt to solve any situation through the use of force.[4] However, "as he advanced in years, he also appears to have become most skilled in prophecy and in logic." (Plut. *Mor.* 387D).

It is, therefore, the wisdom of Chiron and Atlas that molds Heracles into the champion of civilization he is to become. But how can this wisdom be instilled into a mind that only knows brute force? For one must remember how Heracles murdered Linus, his music teacher, according to Robert Graves because he was offended by his effeminacy. Diodorus, on the other hand, says that the young student, "unable to appreciate what was taught him because of his sluggishness of soul" was punished with rods by Linus, became violently angry and killed him with a blow of the lyre (iii. 67. 2).[5]

Of course, these two accounts do not necessarily contradict each other, for a rude and artless mind generally considers a learned one weak and effeminate, though not always without reason. And this account raises the technical question of whether it would be at all possible for subjective conscious individuals to instruct bicameral men, especially if they lacked the necessary force and authority to accomplish the task. For in this particular episode, the bicameral hero appears side by side with the new consciousness and openly hostile to it.

That the episode of Linus's murder deals precisely with the period of transition between the bicameral mind and subjective consciousness, is attested to by Dionysius's report according to which Linus was the first to apply the letters brought by Cadmus from the Phoenician alphabet to the Greek language,[6] which is the reason perhaps, why Theocritus says that Linus taught Heracles to read and write (Diod. *Id.* 24. 105-7). The problem, however, is that the letters found in Cadmus's palace in Thebes (c. 1400 BC), same as the tablets found in Minos's palace in Knossos, are a syllabic script of the linear B type, precisely the kind that must have been used for the necessary records and instructions of bicameral societies (Jaynes, 80). The Phoenician alphabet, on the other hand, is a product of the conscious mind, and is made of 22 letters, all consonants. According to John Day, the evidence suggests that the Greeks took over the letters around 800 BC.[7] As they might have been brought to Greece by the followers of the post-bicameral cult of Dionysus, the story's confusion may be due to the fact that Cadmus was Dionysus's grandfather, and likely, the god's own bicameral aspect. In fact, the transformation of Cadmus and Harmonia into serpents, and their banishment to Illyricum by Dionysus, prophesying that after their exile they would return to Greece sacking many cities at the head of a vast barbarian host (Eur. *Ba.* 1330-7), possibly the Encheleis (Enkeledët) or Eel people of northern Epirus (Ruck 1986), might be a way to reconcile the god's older image with the new one by having it undergo the same exilic tribulations the post-bicameral god has passed through.

The time discrepancy may be due to the fact that, no doubt, these letters were at first not meant for widespread use, but reserved only for hieratic purposes. Orpheus, another of Linus's famous pupils[8] and contemporary of Heracles, also made use of them (Diod. iii. 67. 5). Founder of the mysteries bearing his name, he was the greatest poet and musician who ever lived, and according to Pliny the Elder, the first to spread the craft of magic from Thrace to the neighboring countries (*Nat.* xxx. 2. 7-8). His superstition grew from medicine, Pliny tells us, a craft in which he was also well versed. So then, from medicine to magic to music. Just as the Pied Piper of Hamelin who could lure away the rats and children with his magic pipe in the Middle Ages, so Orpheus could soothe even the savage heart of Hades with the sounds of his lyre. The same, of course, is said of Chiron. The following is Teuthras's song to Hannibal in the *Punica* of Silius Italicus:

> Long ago the nations of Greece—marvelous to tell—heard the shell of the tortoise sound, and the shell had power to draw stones and bring them of their own accord, to make walls for a city. The lyre on which Amphion played built walls round Thebes and bade the towers rise high at its music; and the stone climbed up of itself upon the ramparts that came to the call of the musician. Another lyre calmed the stormy sea with its music and arrested the seals; it drew after it Proteus in all his changes of shape, and carried Arion on the sea-beast's back. A third lyre, whose strains moulded the minds of heroes and the spirit of great Achilles in the cave of Mount Pelion—the lyre that Chiron loved, could quell the raging sea or the wrath of Hell itself, when he struck the strings. But the chords which Orpheus struck beside the Riphean Strymon, charming the gods above and the gods below the earth, earned a place in heaven and shine there among the bright stars. Even his mother, together with the whole train of her sister Muses, marveled at his playing. At his music neither Pangaeus nor Haemus, the mountain of Mars, nor remotest Thrace, could stand still. Wild beasts and forests, rivers and mountains, followed him. The bird forgot her loved nestlings, stopped her flight, and hung arrested in the motionless air. Moreover, when the Argo at Pagasae refused to launch out on the blue water which on land she had never known, the sea, summoned by the lyre, obeyed the music and came up to the stern of the sacred bark. The Thracian bard charmed with his quill the sunless land and the crackling flames of Acheron, and stopped the stone from rolling. Alas for the

cruelty of the Ciconian women and the madness of the Thracians! alas for Rhodope pronounced guilty by the gods! When the Hebrus bore his sev- ered head to the sea, both banks followed it; and then, when it was carried along by the rushing waves, suddenly the sea-beasts emerged from the water and bounded high at the low sound of that voice all over the sea. (xi. 440- 80)[9]

Already through music the poet could charm gods, animals, and even inanimate objects. It is true that he learned the art from the gods; it was Hermes who invented the lyre, Athena who in- vented the flute, but he surpassed them in skill. Orpheus's severed head, brought to Lesbos from Thrace, continued to prophecy for a long time, until Apollo, seeing that his oracles at Gryneium, Clarus, and Delphi had been abandoned, and Orpheus's head alone was giving oracles, appeared as he was prophesying and ordered it to fall silent (Philost. *Ap.* iv. 14).

These musicians, poets, and shamans, then, could still instruct the bicameral mind because unlike subjective conscious men, they spoke the tongue of the gods. In fact, they are the archetypal figures responsible for the multiplication of the bicameral voices which precipitated the demise of the old societies and their centers of social control. Heracles's fight with Apollo (see n. 4 above) perhaps indicates precisely this confusion of tongues that shatters the edi- fice of his long-standing certainties, corroding his faith and erasing his old ideas about the order of things and beings in the world. The most important part and perhaps the first stage of Chiron's teach- ing, then, consisted in severing the pupil's attachment to the earth and generally from all that kept him grounded, what Cioran calls the "timeless peasants' larval certainties" and "geologic reverie." (1968, 70). This is the Centaur's bile; a knowledge that erodes, the gaze turned inward. A venomous wisdom that Heracles spread far and wide in his travels.

It is out of this black bile that subjective consciousness also emerges, finding itself already at war with the older mentality with which it can no longer effectively communicate. To state it more concretely, it was not civilization that invented the barbarian, but an exilic or barbaric consciousness that forced civilization into being, casting the seeds of discord between the savage and his gods, twisting thus, the bicameral command (see schema IX). The discord instigated between the bicameral man and his gods, then, grew into the inner conflict of the civilized man, as well as the internecine war between him and his earlier self, the savage; a war of brother against brother who no longer understand each other.

In light of this we may traverse the whole spectrum of metastatic divisions in philosophical traditions, such as, vitalism/nihilism, and even materialism/idealism, or the dichotomous savage/citizen-subject progress of civilization in political theory, comprising its ancient mythological tellurian/heavenly antagonism, or its modern bipolar disorders, such as conservative/liberal, right/left, etc. through one simple element – the fact that it was from the barbarian that civilization received its first lesson.

In this sense, Heracles's murder of Antaeus, a son of the great Mother Earth, symbolizes this newly acquired corrosive knowledge and the technique religiously followed from here on against the savage: Noticing that Antaeus's strength was renewed every time he was thrust to the ground, Heracles lifted him up, cutting off the source of his power, and strangled him. The mention by Plutarch in the above quote of Atlas (*Mor.* 387D), the Titan on whose shoulders the sky rested, is not coincidental. Atlas is not merely holding the sky on his shoulder – he is separating it from the earth,[10] a feat that Heracles even relieved him of for a short time (Diod. iv. 27. 1-5).

Yet, before performing this deed, or even before being able to kill Antaeus, it was necessary for him to learn to control these elemental moods, and to summon them forth at will. Heracles's ultimate test, then, was to take hold of the old man of the sea, Nereus, in all his protean transformations until the god allowed him a glimpse into the depths of his abyssal knowledge (Apollod. ii. 11) – only then could Heracles gain mastery of the elements. Peleus, it will be remembered, was also required to master the transformations of Nereus's daughter, Thetis, in order to be worthy of wedding her, a task which Chiron set him on and even supervised in its accomplishment (see fig. 6).

Figure 6. Hydria. Vulci. Chiron raising his left hand encouragingly while watching Peleus and Thetis wrestle, as the goddess transforms into a lioness (Baur, 1912: no. 257).

In light of this, it is easy to see how Chiron could accuse Achilles of having no connection with either sea or sky. Yet, Peleus's marriage does not end well, for the enraged goddess abandoned him for interfering with her ritual of making Achilles immortal. Regretful, later Thetis promised immortality to Peleus, asking him to wait at the cave where he had first mastered her until she came to take him to her home into the depths of the ocean where they would live for ever, but never made good on her promise, and Peleus died on the island of Icos, old and forlorn.

This same theme of the impossibility to control these chaotic moods once and for all, is at work also in the education of Heracles, who, even though succeeded in seizing Nereus for a time, could not hold on to the knowledge thus acquired indefinitely. Or rather, it is precisely this attempt at absolute control that results in the crystallization of knowledge, of which Heracles can gather only the shards; fixed concepts, pure elemental categories that similar to Aristotle's elements, can no longer afford (or communicate with) each other. This is clearly represented in his split personality after death, when we find him both in Olympus as an immortal among the gods, and in Hades as a shadow of his mortal self.

This permanent schism of the earth from the sky as a symbol of the new world order, the rule of powerful but always more abstract sky gods, heralds also the professed victory of order over chaos, reason over instinct, and even of life over death as the Nether gods are distanced ever more from the everyday affairs of the world, and death is disavowed and kept out of sight until the appointed hour, veiled behind the lustrous façade of the social and the distracting priorities of the real. The abiding citizen is now ensconced in the delusion of safety encouraged and enforced by the austere Republic of reason. To the gods of the Underworld belong the night, the nightmare... the horror of the unreal stalking the new reality from behind its tall walls.

Heracles is at the forefront of this battle. He is among the heroes most exposed and thereby most afflicted by it. His now overly developed subjective consciousness is, in the words of Zapffe, "like a sword without hilt or plate" (qtd. in Ligotti 2010, 23), and if he is to use it, he must also turn one edge against himself. This is at its most transparent in the revolt of the giants, who not even the Olympian gods can defeat without his help. This is not surprising since they symbolize the hero's own nightmares, if one may assign property to them, since ultimately nightmares belong to everyone. But it was he who opened the door to the abode of the gods for them, darkening the heavens.

Hera prophesied, however, that not even Heracles would be able to fend them off until a certain herb of invulnerability was found. This herb, which grew in a secret place on earth, is never named by the mythographers, but Graves (2012) believed it to have been "*the ephialtion*, a specific against the nightmare," since *Ephialtes*, the name of the giants' leader, means literally "he who leaps upon," *incubus* in Latin. Another of the giants' names was *Mimas* "mimicry", which Graves argues "may refer to the delusive verisimilitude of dreams." A third was Hippolytus "stampede of horses" which "recalls the ancient attribution of terror-dreams to the Mareheaded goddess." (101) "These giants," Graves remarks, "are not flesh and blood, but earth-born spirits, as their serpent-tails prove, and can be thwarted only by the possession of a magical herb." (ibid.).

This deepens the dimension revealed by Silenus's grim philosophy. The separation of reason from instinct that is a prerequisite of civilization, proceeds on the path of a general paralysis; the suppression of certain destructive instincts which, with the aid of universal reason might have laid the world waste.[11] Perhaps an interesting analogy here would be the scientific notion of REM atonia, an almost complete paralysis of the body during sleep, which prevents the dreamer from acting out the dream so as not to hurt himself.[12] This dissociation of the brain from the body, so to speak, naturally occurring during sleep, is extended to the waking state in subjective consciousness. Hence, the erroneous idea that consciousness acts as an inhibitor to action. This is because consciousness, "parent of all horrors," as Ligotti christens it, "may have assisted our species' survival in the hard times of prehistory, but as it became ever more intense it evolved the potential to ruin everything if not securely muzzled." (41). It is precisely this surplus wisdom, then, that Greek "universal reason" cannot comprehend, which in a nutshell sums up both the naïveté and bad faith of civilization.

In addition, the mortal strife between the new reality and the unreal, brings up the fact that if acted out, if not dissociated from the nerves of the real, the spiritual or dream world would become the end of this narcoleptic civilization. This, then, may be another factor in the suppression of the fantastic in the *Iliad*. As Rosemary Jackson ([1981] 2009) puts it, "the fantastic is a spectral presence, suspended between being and nothingness. It takes the real and breaks it." (20). "[It] has constantly been dismissed by critics as being an embrace of madness, irrationality, or barbarism and it has been opposed to the humane and more civilized practices of 'realistic' literature. [This] implicit association of the fantastic with the barbaric and non-human has exiled it to the edges of literary culture." (172). The more uncompromising and threatening examples of the fantastic, are then relegated to the fringes of literature or reworked and reinterpreted in accordance with the sensibilities of a more domesticated audience (173-5). Hence, the Buddhist tenet "everything is illusion," is only acceptable if presented under the auspices of a so-called religion of peace. The same words uttered by the barbarian, would be un unbearable threat, a call to arms that would unleash all the heretofore paralyzed impulses and destructive energies which have accumulated under the weight of a comatose civilization for millennia.

Heracles's apotheosis itself is a sublimation celebrating the withering of his destructive instincts—his transformation from one with his feet on the ground to one with his head in the clouds. The schism of mind and body along the lines of sky and earth, stands as transparent as ever in his myth for, oddly, after his death we find two Heracles figures, one in Olympus, the other in Hades. It is revealing that in his bestowed immortality we find a completely senile Heracles whose existence after death would not have tempted even Plutarch:

> Heracles became the porter of heaven, and never tires of standing at the Olympian gates, towards nightfall, waiting for Artemis's return from the chase. He greets her merrily, and hauls the heaps of prey out of her chariot, frowning and wagging a finger in disapproval if he finds only harmless goats and hares. "Shoot wild boars," he says, "that trample down crops and gash orchard-trees; shoot man-killing bulls, and lions, and wolves! But what harm have goats and hares done us?" Then he flays the carcasses, and voraciously eats any titbits that take his fancy.
>
> Graves 2012, 528

Robert Graves apparently quotes this passage from memory from Callimachus's *Hymn to Artemis*. "The gods all laugh continuously at that one," Callimachus adds, "but especially his own mother-in-law." (145).

It is his mortal shadow that still preserves some of its old renown and "stalks about Tartarus, among the twittering dead; bow drawn, arrow fitted to the string. Across his shoulder is slung a golden baldric, terrifyingly wrought with lions, bears, wild boars, and scenes of battle and slaughter." (Graves, 2012, 528-9; from Hom. *Od.* xi. 605-12).

5.4 Chiron's Diet

*And [the serpent] said unto the woman, Yea, hath God said,
Ye shall not eat of every tree of the garden? And the woman
said unto the serpent, We may eat of the fruit of the trees
of the garden: But of the fruit of the tree which is in the
midst of the garden, God hath said, Ye shall not eat of it,
neither shall you touch it, lest you die. And the serpent said
unto the woman, Ye shall not surely die: For God doth know
that in the day ye eat thereof, then your eyes shall be opened,
and ye shall be as gods, knowing good and evil.*

Genesis 3:1-5

Many ancient sources mention Chiron's diet to his young pupil, Achilles. Statius says that he fed him on the flesh and marrow of lions (*Achill.* ii. 382 ff.). Pseudo-Apollodorus mentions the innards of lions and wild hogs, and the marrow of bears (iii. 13. 6). Philostratus the Elder has milk, marrow, and honey (*Imag.* ii. 2. 342K), while the author of *Etymologicum Magnum* mentions marrow of deer (*Euphor.* 81). Obviously, the commentators meant these victuals to explain Achilles's physical strength. During Thetis's visit on Mount Pelion, however, Chiron reveals them as Dionysus's gifts: "[he] begs her to taste victuals and Bacchus's gift, weaving various delights for her amazement." (Stat. *Achill.* i. 184-6).

Both the Satyrs and the Centaurs were worshippers of Dionysus, as it is well known, and Bacchus's gift has widely been assumed to be wine. The Wassons' studies on entheogenic mushrooms, however, have shown that what was at stake in the cult's mysteries was not merely the consumption of wine, but the food and drink of the immortals, *nectar* and *ambrosia*, which they reveal to be the highly hallucinogenic mushroom, *amanita muscaria*, also known as the *fly-agaric*.[1] Since it is extremely hot – Graves rightly describes it as liquid fire – those who consumed it used wine to wash it down.[2] The misanthropic shepherds of Southern Albania use it to this day, though they will not share its secrets with anyone. Its effects include temporal and spatial delusions, the gift of clairvoyance and prophetic insight, as well as extraordinary muscular strength often combined with a lust to kill and an overwhelming sexual desire. A few hours of this ecstasy are followed by complete inertia for one or more days. (Graves 2012, xvi; Graves 1960, 262). The well-known image of the Maenads roaming the countryside, in their frenzy tearing children and animals limb from limb, is enough to show how far the Dionysiac festivals could go. "At first his devotees drank beer laced with the toxic juice of yellow ivy," Graves explains, "hence, the sacred ivy-wreath, and only later took to wine. But they drank this, presumably, to wash down the fiery fragments of mushroom; because to tear even a kid in pieces, such fantastic muscular strength is needed as no beer or wine or maed can provide." (1960, 267).

To bring a more recent example of the use and effects of the fly-agaric, the trance-like fury of the Norse Berserkers who wrought untold havoc on the battlefield, and whose practice was outlawed by Royal proclamation in the Middle Ages, was most likely due to its consumption (262). The sagas consistently describe them as eating coals of fire, or biting down their shields, which may well be a way of saying that they used to gulp down mouthfuls of the fire-hot mushrooms. However, the food of the gods did not merely confer clairvoyance and muscular strength on the ones who consumed it, but literally transformed and bestowed immortality on them – the Norse word *Berserkgang*, in fact, aptly means "to change shape." And in his godly shape, the Berserker would cut down everyone in his path, no longer distinguishing friend from foe. This was also Meleager's fault when killing his uncles, or that of the god of war, Ares, whom Meleager calls father, and on whom he blames his blindness in Bacchylides's ode. During the fight with the Centaurs, Heracles, too, wounded his teacher and friend Chiron, though in an attempt to spare embarrassment to the hero, later commentators interpreted this as an accident, forgetting that Heracles's aim, like that of Achilles, was said to be infallible.

That the Centaurs' food was nectar and ambrosia, should be viewed not only as probable, but as indisputable within the framework of mythology, if any consistency might be ascribed to it, since Chiron was immortal. The fact that the Greeks placed such emphasis on the civilized habit of diluting wine with water, and that the battle between the Lapiths and the Centaurs ensued because the latter, being uncultured and, strangely enough, "unaccustomed to wine" (Apollod. *Epit.* i. 21), made themselves so drunk that they attempted to rape Pirithous's bride, suggests a euphemistic narrative. For, if the great mystery was merely wine, diluted or undiluted, these great myths would be nothing more than boring tales with moral endings. Can one really believe that the battles against the Centaurs were concerned with no more than an ancient prohibitionist story against wine by pagan puritans? "The ὠμοφαγία and the bestial incarnations", Dodds writes in his foreword to Euripides's *Bacchae*, "reveal Dionysus as something much more significant and much more dangerous than a wine-god."

> He is the principle of animal life, ταῦρος and ταυροφάγος, the hunted and the hunter—the unrestrained potency which man envies in the beasts and seeks to assimilate. His cult was originally an attempt on the part of human beings to achieve communion with this potency. The psychological effect was to liberate the instinctive life in man from the bondage imposed on it by reason and social custom: the worshipper became conscious of a strange new vitality, which he attributed to the god's presence within him.
>
> Dodds, Eur. *Ba.* 1987, xx.

All this notwithstanding, what concrete threat did the Dionysiac cult pose to civilization? For, considering the violent resistance offered to it in many locales and the lengths to which their rulers went in order to suppress it, it is doubtful this was merely a question of animalistic behavior or intoxication and disorderly conduct. The mysteries it promised to unlock must have entailed a much more essential challenge to the very foundations of civilization, though for reasons of political rhetoric, it is always more profitable to point out the primitive behavior of others, the advances and the elevated status of the present when compared with the savage past, and the dangers a reversion to the old ways might bring. But the fact is that civilization never left the old ways behind, and the fight against the state of savagery has itself always been more savage than what it was supposed to fight. One may, therefore, immediately rule out the widespread belief that what the communion with Dionysus achieved was a liberation solely on the level of the instinctual. If that were really the case, civilization would be no more in danger than if all the wild beasts had escaped from the zoo.

Nevertheless, Euripides's *Bacchae*, considered by many one of the greatest tragedies ever written, is tirelessly interpreted as a warning against the complete suppression of man's animalistic impulses by society, impulses which then might erupt in their full force and bring about the end of civilization. (Ruck 1986, 2540-1; Dodds 1987, xvi; Riedl 2012, 126). It tells of the ban placed on Dionysus's cult, first by Lycurgus, the king of Thrace, and then by Pentheus, the king of Thebes. Both "godfighters" (θεομάχος) were cruelly punished as a result and suffered a terrible fate; the first thrown to flesh-eating horses, the second torn limb from limb by his own mother and aunts.

Unlike most tragedies, however, the *Bacchae* is a play about an historical event; the introduction to Hellas of a new religion (Dodds 1987, xi). Dionysus says he came from Lydia (Eur. *Ba.* 464), though by the time we find him in Thebes the sect already has its strongholds in Thrace and Thessaly. That Theseus, the mythic Athenian king and reformer, sided with the Lapiths against the Centaurs, leaves little doubt that this battle was at bottom an early attempt of the Greeks to resist the encroachment of the Dionysiac cult upon their northern borders.[3] His slaying of the Minotaur in the underground labyrinths of king Minos's palace seems to tell of even earlier battles as far as Crete against the god.

By the time of Pentheus's murder, however, the cult had established itself on a firmer footing in the region and the question no longer was how to eradicate it, but how to live with it. Its worship was legalized and concessions were made (see, e.g. Hdt. v. 67), according to Graves, as a means of exercising some control over its orgiastic festivals which caused serious breaches of peace. (1960, 267-8). This acceptance, of course, did not come without a price and it must have severely curtailed some of the cult's former freedoms. A hundred years after coming under the legalized control of the *polis*, "Dionysus was civilized enough for enrollment among the twelve Olympians. After that, no more old-type outbreaks of Bacchic madness are recorded; nothing worse than cases of vinous abandon." (1960, 268).

But while the Dionysian festivals were brought under the law in the south, this was not so in the north.[4] Graves, in fact, argues that it was Dionysus himself who had covertly instigated the Centaurs' anti-social behavior. Pholus must have been his local agent, he concludes, for it was wine supplied by Dionysus that he was serving to Heracles on the occasion of the hero's fight with the Centaurs (1960, 276). However, considering the protracted battle and nightmarish chase that ensued, in all likelihood Pholus offered mushrooms to the hero, or wine spiced up with entheogens, as Ruck argues (see n. 2 above), the terrible fight being the result of his intoxication. The deliberateness of these actions may be seen in Euripides's depiction of the cult as a sort of world religion disseminated from land to land by missionaries as no Greek cult ever was (Dodds 1987, xx). Again, this cold-blooded premeditation is at odds with what is argued to be merely a release of the animalistic impulses in man.

Prohibitions

The most detailed and illuminating account of the dangers still posed by the cult of Dionysus to the authority of the state is found half a millennium later in Livy's report of the Bacchanalia purges by the Roman Senate in 186 BC. The sect was perceived as an alien and invasive religion by the Roman authorities, not on account of

Bacchus being a foreign god, for the ancients readily borrowed gods from other cultures, but on account of its apolitical dimension (Riedl 2012) which allowed the sect to grow without at the same time being assimilated into the Roman political life. The dreadful speed with which it had been able to recruit, spreading and metastasizing throughout the city, caused great consternation in Rome, for it was believed its ultimate aim was to infiltrate and finally overthrow the state. The response was therefore particularly brutal.

According to Riedl, this was "the largest systematic persecution of a religious group hitherto seen in Europe." (113). The great terror (*terror magnum*) that seized Rome in the face of this threat which had suddenly grown overnight like a tumor, is shown in the rashness and excessive violence the authorities used to suppress it. Of the 7000 people involved, many attempted to escape or committed suicide, the vast majority was executed, and the rest imprisoned (Livy, 39. 17. 5 – 39. 18. 6).

In Livy's report of consul Postumius's speech, the most serious charge brought against the Bacchants was impious conspiracy (*impia coniuratio*) with the ultimate aim to take complete control of the state. (39. 16. 3-4). This was supplemented with charges of murder and other violent crimes, debauchery, forgery, fraud, etc. The cult's secrecy and nocturnal gatherings were an additional cause for concern—in Rome any activity carried out with some measure of secrecy was regarded as suspicious.

The gravest danger posed by Dionysus's cult to the political dimension, however, remained its apolitical attitude. Riedl argues that "in the Bacchanalian affair, the cosmion of the Roman Republic defended itself against an enemy which was, as *religio externa*, an external aggressor and, as *intestina coniuratio*, a threat from within. Yet, whatever crime and violence might have originated from the Bacchic shrine, the real threat was a different one: The Bacchanalia questioned the meaning of the Roman cosmion." (122). Most importantly, however,

> A Bacchant cannot be a citizen. Should the city accept the Bacchanalia as *sacra publica* and as *religio civilis* it would mean the victory of Bacchus

and his destructive power. Postumius understood that the most significant differentiation is not the one between religion and politics, but between political and apolitical forms of religiosity. (124-5)

In this precise statement of the difference between the Bacchant and the citizen, Riedl unmistakably reveals the rift between the Roman microcosm and the Dionysus cult as that between the s/c-s civilizational lineage and the barbarian.

But in Rome, as in Greece, the Bacchic rites could not be entirely suppressed, or at least, not immediately. The state aimed to bring them under its control, which ultimately meant politicizing them. In the end, it should be understood, this politicization is a form of converting the Dionysian dimension into its own simulacrum. For Riedl, this forced matriculation into the political order meant that some room was left for the Dionysian dimension in order to prevent its chaotic propensity from breaking through in all its destructive force. In truth, however, to have restrained its unparalleled capacity for destruction, means to have turned the Dionysian dimension into Disney World, diluted many times over.

Nevertheless, in our own times this process of proliferating simulacra has picked up speed in the reverse direction and quite outside its original scope, as can be observed, for example, in the unexpected media savvy tactics of the Islamic extremists: these are not merely snuff films aimed at a repressed audience deriving its perverse pleasure in the privacy of their homes—these are snuff films aimed at drawing that alienated audience to act out its repressed fantasies in the world, a recruiting tool of great efficacy as the authorities are quickly learning; the citizen turned barbarian overnight. What defines these tactics still as simulacra, albeit violent to the extreme, is the fact that the viewer who is propelled to action, is acting in his sleep, as it were, going through the motions of the dream. The brain impulses that control muscle movement are expressed or released, but the individual continues to dream. The bad news for the simulacrum administrators is that the masterminds who have devised these tactics to turn the simulacrum thus against itself, are awake, and cannot be lulled back to sleep.

Considering that, as Hall has argued, the barbarian is generally believed to have been an invention of tragedy and playacting, it is interesting that so many commentators have expressed surprise at the fact that the terrorist as a barbaric figure should be found at the heart of the simulacrum he purports to be attacking. This short-sighted criticism tacitly assumes that the "desert of the real" must make its first appearance at the edges of the system and slowly close in (see schema N). This is an interesting problem because at the global scale, the system cannot possibly perceive what lies beyond its own horizons. The intolerable toxicity of the radical outside, therefore, seeps in from higher dimensions, turning the system inside out. In this sense, if the simulacrum was first and foremost conceived in order to contain and ultimately tame the barbarian by encapsulating the threat — provided that an original purpose may be ascribed to it at all — it only achieved the opposite; it paved the way for the threat to infiltrate and make its nest into the heart of the system. The simulacra is a repeated command that overloads and ultimately crashes the system. The commentators who are unable to comprehend this, whether implicitly or explicitly still subscribe to notions of purity in an age when there is nothing pure anymore. Even more, these absurd notions expect the barbarian, who was never pure to begin with, to bring purity to the system. In a world where there is no outside any longer, it is not the barbarian but the citizen who disappears.

5.5 Self Engineered Chimeras

If there were gods, how could I endure it to be no God!

—Friedrich Nietzsche, *Thus Spake Zarathustra*

Finally, a last prohibition that must be considered is the universal ban on sharing the food of the gods with mortals, the myth of Tantalus being its best known example. But Tantalus is not the only one. Ixion, one of the four great sinners of Greek myth, nearly always mentioned in the same breath with Tantalus, Sisyphus, and Tityus, might have well been punished for the same crime. Both were privileged to eat at the table of the gods, and both betrayed the law of hospitality (*xenia*) and the gods' trust.

Kazuhiko Yamamoto, in his comparison of the ethics of Homeric stateless society with the ancient code of the Albanian Kanun, brings up an old Japanese myth, according to which, twice a year God travelled incognito through the country (qtd. in Kadare 2011, 1862-8), revealing the roots of the Albanian code which equates the guest with God:

§ 602. The house of the Albanian belongs to God and guest.

If one refused a guest into his house, therefore, one might as well have refused God.[1] For this reason, the law of hospitality is sacred. Article no. 649 makes it clear that one may forgive the blood of a father or a brother, but never the blood of a guest killed while under one's protection. Consequently, Tantalus's and Ixion's crime is aimed directly at one of the most important institutions of stateless, or to bring Yamamoto's theory up to speed with what has been said so far, bicameral societies, without which there can be no order, and at Zeus as the guarantor of that institution. Similarly to the sons of Lycaon who cut up and cooked their brother Nyctimus for Zeus in Arcadia, Tantalus put his own son's flesh at the table of the gods, and Demeter, being too "distraught" over the loss of Persephone, even took a bite from the shoulder as the other gods cringed in horror. Graves reminds us that Demeter's "error" recalls the Maenads, in their revelries tearing apart infants and probably consuming their flesh. For the crime of cutting up his son Pelops, and for sharing the food of the gods with his mortal friends, Tantalus was hung waist deep on a marshy lake from the bow of a fruit-tree, condemned to perpetual thirst and hunger. For the third crime of perjury, for he falsely swore by Zeus's name, a black crag ready to slip and fall at any moment, threatening to crush his skull, hanged over his head. This third crime is interesting because verbal oaths would be impossible to break for bicameral men.

Ixion, too, broke the law of hospitality by killing his own kinsman, the first crime of its kind in Greek myth, for which he was refused purification (*catharsis*) by all his neighbors and driven mad by the Furies until Zeus took pity on him, inviting him at his own table on Mount Olympus — an act of kindness for which Ixion repaid him by attempting to rape his wife, Hera. These one-sided versions of the myth notwithstanding, the fact that in other accounts it is said that Zeus had previously raped Ixion's wife, Dia, and probably fathered Pirithous on her, a crime for which no higher tribunal existed for Ixion to turn to, reveals the sky god and guarantor of the law of hospitality as an unfair judge, who similarly to the God of the Jews, ruled by brute force, expecting thanks and obedience even when the fate of his subjects was only grief and sorrow.

Ixion, on the other hand, was dutifully punished for twice breaking the law of hospitality — the first time as a host, and the second time as a guest — and was eternally bound to a spinning fiery wheel. According to a lesser known account, however, both Ixion and his son, Pirithous, appear next to Tantalus sitting on a golden bench, starving before a royal feast they can never taste (Verg. *Aen.* 601-7). This second account which does not fit the crime, points to an act similar to that of Tantalus. Graves, in addition, points out an Etruscan bronze mirror from c. 450 BC, in which a fungus, probably the amanita muscaria, is depicted at the feet of a winged Ixion swirling on the fiery wheel.

This raises an interesting issue: A common explanation for these myths is that Ixion and Sisyphus are ancient deities probably related to a cult of the sun overthrown, or as was his custom, taken over by Zeus. Their sharing of the food of the gods with mortals, however, cannot easily be reconciled with this view. The question is, why did they only decide to share their knowledge at this time, and not before? Was this act merely an impotent and self-denying attempt to nibble at Zeus's throne by the deposed gods, now left without real means of resistance? The general argument in this case is that the transgressions of these dark (or rather, darkened) figures, and the punishments meted out to them, were not part of the "original myths" (as if such a thing existed), but priestly rationalizations added later as formal warnings against human hubris in front of the gods. But as the evidence is scant in this direction, this reasoning leaves the problem that the same argument may be formed against any part of the myths that does not fit neatly to whatever theory one happens to favor. In short, the objection is too general and can be applied to anything.

A solution to this conundrum is only possible when considering that in bicameral times, the food of the gods was nothing exotic, as man shared his own food with them. They were his own dead ancestors, and they ate what he ate, viz., they continued to eat what they had been eating while still alive, as shown by archaeological remains the world over. Nectar and Ambrosia do not come into prominence until the breakdown of the bicameral mind, similar to the Hebrew *Manna*, the bread from heaven which the LORD gave the Israelites to eat during the 40 years' exodus (Exod. 16:15).[2]

> It was like coriander-seed, white; and the taste of it was like wafers made with honey.
>
> Exod. 16:31

R. G. Wasson's findings confirm this, the consistent use of entheogens going back as far as the half of the second millennium BC, as evinced in the hymns of the Ŗg Veda. What this means is that like the Satyrs, these shamans consuming *Soma* were themselves post-bicameral deities freed from their human condition.

It is worth remembering in this context that at first Zeus did not care for human beings, but was determined to wipe them out. In accordance with this plan, he had initially taken fire away from them, reverting the human race to the status of beasts. Strangely enough, it is Prometheus (*forethought*), a chthonic deity, who first sets out to thwart his plan by bringing back fire to humanity. The fire, as Ruck (1986) reveals, holds herbalist connotations, and may well be a symbol for amanita muscaria.

If Ruck is right in his supposition that the main point of these myths is the negotiation and joining in matrimony of the house of the Olympians to that of the netherworld gods through the shared bridal figure of Persephone, reconciling thus "more primitive traditions to the new era of gods headed by a father in the heavens" (1816-23), a negotiation moreover, in which an ad hoc intermediary role is conjured up for humans as the matchmakers of this great festivity, making them indispensable and thus sparing Zeus the trouble of having to wipe them out, it would seem that ultimately it is both the sky and the chthonic gods who got the short end of the stick, for over time they are reduced to resembling always more the meagre stature of the intermediary beings in between. From an enlightened atheistic perspective one may well argue that this should, in fact, be the case, since the gods are man's own inventions, and as such they must resemble their creators. The problem, of course, is that the new gods are in no way worthier of respect than the old ones, not to speak of a dearth of gods entirely, which should make the atheists ashamed at the low opinion they hold of themselves and of everybody else.

Again, the question is, if this intermediary role for humanity was only made possible by the use of the entheogenic mushroom, which Zeus, who wants to protect his power, prohibits, but Prometheus who loves the human race, brings back to earth, then why did the use of entheogens continue to be prohibited? The fact that the food of the gods would confer not only the gift of sight on those who consumed it, but immortality as well, does not fit so neatly with Ruck's view. The knowledge that Prometheus shared, shook the vertical power structure of the universe, making heavenly gods and subjective humans pointless. It is only in this sense that these fallen deities can be reconciled with their so-called rebellious and sudden revolutionary nature. They are not deities of peace, or ancient humanists.

This view, finally, provides the answer to the question of the imminent threat which civilization perceived so distinctly in the cult of Dionysus. Through the consumption of the entheogen, man not only could directly communicate with the gods and have intimate access to their divine knowledge; he could be god, as also Yahweh's terror at Adam and Eve's consumption of the fruit of the tree of knowledge demonstrates. The tree of knowledge and the tree of life were one and the same (Gordon et al, 1986). More concretely, however, what made their consumption so dangerous was not merely the reawakening of an older bicameral mentality, but its coupling with the new consciousness and its subsequent dissociation with subjectivity, thus, the lifting of its inhibitory nature. The reawakened gods were therefore both old and new. More than the liberation of the instinctual life in man from the bondage of reason, the question was that of the liberation of his consciousness from the yoke of subjectivity. It is no wonder, then, that these cunning new teachers could multiply the bicameral voices at will, and it is precisely this that posed the gravest peril to the emerging civilization. They knew the recipe of the food of the gods and had broken away from their central command, issuing instead their own autonomous commands.

This transgression was not merely a matter of breaking the chain of command, however. It allowed these terrifying figures to break away from their own lineage and the intermediary place assigned to them in this great system of reciprocity, where each part has its destiny inscribed into its DNA. Just like cancer cells that have hijacked and unleashed the body's immortality by transcribing their own message back into its DNA, so too, these self-engineered chimeras could mutate at will, shape-shift, metastasize, and contaminate all that stood in their path.

Pessimism, Optimism, and the Dagger in Between

6.1 Pessimism and Nihilism

And I gave my heart to know wisdom, and to know madness and folly: I perceived that this also is vexation of spirit. For in much wisdom is much grief: and he that increaseth knowledge increaseth sorrow.

—Ecclesiastes 1:17-18.

Nihilism is ... not only the belief that everything deserves to perish, but one actually puts one's shoulder to the plough; one destroys.

—Friedrich Nietzsche, *The Will to Power*

The fact that Chiron's pupils were not only heroes who died young, but heroes who actively sought to die young, flies in the face of a good deal of psychological research in comparative mythology, the best known perhaps being Joseph Campbell's seminal work, *The Hero with a Thousand Faces*, according to whose Jungian approach, it is always trouble that finds the unwilling hero, not the other way around. Similarly, circular arguments derived from natural selection theory highlighting now the individual now the community, as the case may require, are a favorite shorthand in academic circles that can never fail to explain away the destructive impulses and recklessness of the hero's actions since, it is often said, what is not necessarily good for the individual may prove to be good for the community (and vice versa). Xenophon wrote that Achilles, nursed in Chiron's schooling, "bequeathed to posterity memorials so great and glorious that no man wearies of telling and hearing of him." (*Hunt.* I. 16). Yet, if one is even capable of counting a single good derived by the community from his deeds, the muse, unsurprisingly, never bothers with it. Inexorably drawn to his explosive rage, she sings only to the great devastation he brings both to the Greeks and the Trojans, threatening not only his enemies but the whole species.[1] That the knowledge of his own untimely death did

179

not discourage or paralyze him, but instead fueled even more his rapacious thirst for destruction, does not require any special insight to see. The deeper the rivers of blood, the higher the flames in his wake, the better spent his life is.

To modern ears it might sound surprising to hear that these so-called pessimistic or nihilistic views were not so isolated at that time of innocence. Herodotus, for example, relates a custom of the Thracian tribe of the Trausi, according to which, when a child is born, the kinsfolk sit round and lament how many sufferings the infant must endure now that it has entered the world, and go through a whole catalogue of sorrows; but when someone dies, they bury him with merriment and rejoicing, pointing out how happy he is now, and how many miseries he has at last escaped. (v. 4. 2).

Other examples abound, from the story of Solon, the Athenian statesman who, when visiting Croesus in Sardis, narrates more than one tale to support the view that only a dead man may be truly happy (Hdt. i. 29. I – 34. I) to Xerxes's dialogue with his uncle Artabanus during their camp at Abydos. Solon's argument, however, is sophistic and circular. Similarly to Silenus, he at first argues that it is better to die than to live (i. 31). Yet, it is not being dead that is important for Solon. In order to understand whether or not one was truly blessed, one needs to know how one lived in conjunction with how one died. Solon's solution, then, which Plutarch unquestioningly follows, is semiotics in action: he passes judgment because he is still alive and therefore, still able to speak – a judgment for which the dead do not care. For the one who is still alive and well and leading a comfortable existence, Solon reserves the adjective "fortunate," not "blessed," which can only be applied after one dies, because, so he reasons, one's good fortune may slip away and become misfortune. But this would be an argument precisely not to use the word "fortune." For if Solon merely meant fortunate now, but possibly unfortunate at another moment, then one needs to consider that the blessed/cursed compound is just as unstable. It is too facile to argue that death results in the stabilization of these terms, since for this self-proclaimed live Rhadamanthus, judgment is entered by the living not the dead, and the living may at any moment change their mind and send to hell those who were previously in their good graces, as Dante unflinchingly does in his *Comedy*. So, even though it appears as if Solon joins life and death at the precise moment of judgment, in point of fact he achieves exactly the opposite, a reasoning that was preserved with great care in later times.

While Solon's tales are filled with moral lessons preaching moderation, temperance, and humility, as was usually his habit, Xerxes's story might be of more interest. This was during Xerxes's march to Greece as the army had set camp at Abydos, the day after their stop at the citadel of Troy. After a review of the army and a rowing match won by the Phoenicians of Sidon, Xerxes, so Herodotus tells us, "was pleased with the race as with his army. But when he saw the whole Hellespont hidden by his ships, and all the shores and plains of Abydos thronged with men, Xerxes first declared himself happy, and the moment after burst into tears." His uncle Artabanus asked him the reason for this strange contradiction, to which Xerxes replied that it occurred to him as he surveyed the army how pitifully short human life is, and that of the multitude of men now standing in front of him, not one would be alive in a hundred years' time. (vii. 44. I - 46. 2). "Yet," answered Artabanus, "we suffer sadder things in life even than that. Short as it is, there is not a man who is happy enough not to wish — not once only but again and again — to be dead rather than alive. Troubles come, diseases afflict us, and this makes life, despite its brevity seem all too long. So heavy is its burden that death is a refuge which all men desire." (vii. 46. 3).

Xerxes's melancholia about the great slaughter that is life — which surpasses any human war, for, whether or not the battle at hand will have claimed them, in a hundred years' time not one of the multitude now present will remain — allows only two outcomes; either total paralysis in the face of terror, or raising the stakes to such heights as to equal the overkill of life itself. One may rashly object that this is the bet of losers, but in the end, no one comes out of life a winner. In light of this, a strange question insinuates itself; did the Greeks really win the war against all odds, or did Xerxes annihilate his own army, throwing it in droves at them?

Perhaps the answer to this question is not that difficult to divine, but first a distinction between nihilism and pessimism must be drawn. While fancy philosophical distinctions, obviously, already exist, the distinction needed here is rather something elemental, similar to that between action and reaction, or acceleration and inertia.

In his book *The Conspiracy Against the Human Race*, Thomas Ligotti asserts:

> Immune to the blandishments of religions, countries, families, and everything else that puts both average and above-average citizens in the limelight, pessimists are sideliners in both history and the media. Without belief in gods or ghosts, unmotivated by a comprehensive delusion, they could never plant a bomb, plan a revolution, or shed blood for a cause. (43)

It remains to be explained, therefore, how Hasan-i Sabbāh, the founder of the order of the Assassins, could say on his deathbed, "Nothing is true. Everything is permitted." In the above quote, Liggoti seems to agree with Žižek, who asserts that the opposite is true: If God is dead, i.e. if nothing is true, then nothing is permitted.[2] Hasan-i Sabbāh contradicts both of these authors' argument, not only in argument, but also in deed. On the other hand, one may read Liggoti to mean that pessimists could never plant a bomb, plan a revolution, or shed blood for a cause, but could very well perform these acts without one. Or else, some distinction between pessimism and nihilism must be maintained.

Perhaps a quick way to draw this distinction would be to take Nietzsche's own differentiation between passive and active nihilism, applying the former to pessimism as used in this context, and the latter to nihilism. A distinction even as simple and broad lined as this has two surprising implications: first, that those who with Žižek claim that if nothing is true nothing is permitted, are seen to be optimists only on condition that God exist. If God does not exist, then the optimist is revealed to be a pessimist at heart. This, in fact, is the problem of our times, if one may use the phrase loosely enough to comprise a few centuries or even millennia. The enlightened person is paralyzed; the idiot, to use Žižek's own designation for that larger category of humankind, is strong and able. "Good schollers are never good souldiers," as Burton says (Radden 2002, 137). Hence, if you want to build an army, do not recruit enlightened persons. They have too many doubts. But above all, do not tell them the truth, viz., that nothing is true and that you are throwing them in droves at the enemy to be annihilated because everything is permitted.

Ultimately, the optimists' inclination, which in their own jargon is called "choice" or "free will," only permits them to choose their butcher, however, because even if God existed, He too is throwing them in droves at the enemy to be annihilated because everything is permitted. The example of decision-making stress mechanisms makes this obvious, since the tragic man in Aeschylus's tragedies is no different than the ulcerous rat in Weiss's experiment. This brings us to the second implication: that if God existed, a few pessimists would still be pessimists and reject him, which would make them active nihilists. The rest would resume their daily lives alongside the conditional optimists, happily awaiting the day of reckoning. The difference between the pessimist and the nihilist, then, is that the pessimist needs some transcendental, universal force or foolproof reason to affirm the world for him, after which he would be happy to be an optimist. Of course, no reason is foolproof without a fool. On the other hand, the nihilist can reject an authorized world and affirm an unauthorized one.[3] At least in this sense many self-proclaimed pessimists may fit more closely the description of the nihilist. As Ligotti himself states:

> Every negation is adulterated or stealthily launched by an affirmative spirit. … Without a "yes" in our hearts, nothing would be done. And to be done with our existence en masse would be the most ambitious affirmation of all.

Here, then, we have the whole range of possibilities in the face of an orphaned creation: For Hasan-i Sabbāh nothing is true and everything is permitted. For Thomas Ligotti nothing is true but at least one more grand act is still possible. For Slavoj Žižek nothing at all is permitted without some decree from above. Needless to say, that, for the sake of civilization, the views held by the first two need to be suppressed. Happily, the need to suppress these views in self defense, furnishes also the decision-making stress providing the decree demanded by Žižek. Hence, the advantage of having a self to defend.

Besides the three possibilities or categories already enumerated, there is also a muddled fourth, mentioned by Ligotti; those who recognize the futility of life, but who continue as if this were not so. These are that category of people, who not only think truth exists but also know what it is, opting nevertheless for the lie, which would include most of humankind.

> Controverting the absolutist standards of pessimism and optimism ... are "heroic" pessimists, or rather heroic "pessimists." These are self-styled pessimists who take into consideration Sully's unfavorable pole but are not committed to its entailment that life is something that should not be. In his *Tragic Sense of Life in Men and Nations* (1913), the Spanish writer Miguel de Unamuno speaks of consciousness as a disease bred by a conflict between the rational and the irrational. The rational is identified with the conclusions of consciousness, primarily that we will all die. The irrational represents all that is vital in humanity, including a universal desire for immortality in either a physical or nonphysical state. The coexistence of the rational and the irrational turns the human experience into a wrangle of contradictions to which we can bow our heads in resignation or defy as heroes of futility. Unamuno's penchant was for the heroic course, with the implied precondition that one has the physical and psychological spunk for the fight. In line with Unamuno, Joshua Foa Dienstag, author of *Pessimism: Philosophy, Ethic, Spirit* (2006), is also a proselytizer for a healthy, heroic pessimism (quotes implied) that faces up to much of the dispiriting lowdown on life, all radically pessimistic visions being cropped out of the picture, and marches on toward a future believed to be personally and politically workable. Also siding with this never-say-die group is William R. Brashear, whose *The Desolation of Reality* (1995) concludes with a format for redemption, however partial and imperfect, by holding tight to what he calls "tragic humanism," which recognizes human life's "ostensible

insignificance, but also the necessity of proceeding as if this were not so ...
willfully nourishing and sustaining the underlying illusions of value and
order." (47-8)

In other words, if God is dead, we still have the economy, politics, and the latest news to worry about. But for civilization to
continue to willfully nourish and sustain the [once] underlying illusions of value and order, which like buried old wires are now exposed and corroded in places where the ground has begun to erode,
thought unconstrained and unhinged from economic and political
concerns has to be purged. "Sorrow of the world," in short, has to
be suppressed. And this is not a modern solution to an old problem, but the only solution tenaciously prescribed since the very beginnings of narcissistic conscious civilizations.

It is no coincidence, then, that both Aeschylus's *Persae* and Seneca's *Hercules Oetaeus* end by emphasizing the concern that unrestrained grief presents for the preservation of civilization.
"*Excessive* mourning practices were considered 'barbaric' and discouraged at Athens", Hall says (84). It was in the sixth century BC,
in fact, that Solon's legislative reforms had prohibited certain funeral and mourning rites. Plutarch regards them with admiration,

> for he (Solon) made the Athenians decorous and careful in their religious
> services, and milder in their rites of mourning, by attaching certain sacri-
> fices immediately to their funeral ceremonies, and by taking away harsh and
> barbaric practices in which their women had usually indulged up to that
> time. Most important of all, by sundry rites of propitiation and purifica-
> tion, and by sacred foundations, he hallowed and consecrated the city, and
> brought it to be observant of justice and more easily inclined to unanimity.

Sol. 12. 5

Demosthenes gives a detailed account of Solon's law limiting
the number of female mourners allowed at funerals. This law permitted only women relatives "within the degree of cousinship to
enter the chamber where the deceased lies, and it permits these same
women to follow to the tomb." (Oration 43. 62-3).

185

For those who may not be familiar with tradition, Solon's law seems to be aimed at paid women wailers whose presence in funerals was thus curtailed. We see, therefore, a direct concern with sorrow and mourning, not only in Attic drama, but also in political thought.[4] These bans might have provided a further impetus and inspiration for tragedy to pick them up, sublimating them beyond personal grief.

In contradistinction to Nietzsche's view that the new art had its roots in Dionysian dithyrambs, Ismail Kadare (2011) asserts that the origin of tragedy is to be found rather, in funeral rites:

> The Dionysian festivals, excessively sensational and raucous, were readily declared to be the mother of tragedy ... [By] reason of their superficial resemblance to theatre, they unjustly supplanted the two most important ceremonies in life, that of death, and that of the wedding.
> I think that precisely these two rites, that of death in the first place, and that of the wedding as its ancillary, were the parents of tragedy whose parenthood was unjustly denied. ... These two rites ... that both differ and resemble each other (as has been said, a funeral rite with the Albanians is nothing but a wedding turned on its head), for millennia have been the primary cultural institution of the Balkan people. Their similarity is not a coincidence: it is a consequence of the perception of life and death as the two dimensions of a single phenomenon, which are inherent in each other. (2001, 314-28)

The fact aside that it amounts to nothing to say that funerary rites and weddings are primary institutions in the Balkans, since they are so the world over, Kadare is quick to dismiss Nietzsche's insight, without considering that the Dionysian festivals were the commemoration of Dionysus's sorrows and his death at the hands of the Titans. In addition, the fact that tragedy came early on under the sponsorship of Dionysus, and that many poets were undoubtedly privy to its mysteries and often hinted at particular aspects of these, all bespeak to more than a mere intellectual acquaintance. The two views, however, do not have to be mutually exclusive.[5]

These political currents – the reluctant legalization of Dionysus's worship, and in diametrically opposite fashion, the ban imposed on certain more radical funeral rites – created an
environment that lent both depth and vigor to the new art, whereas
tragedy became a façade to ancient funeral rites, linked as they are
through Dionysus's death, burial, and rebirth. So it happens that
tragedy worships and renounces, sublimates and abhors, all at the
same time. Kadare's view, then, adds this deeper dimension to the
study of tragedy, which materializes and incarnates what is abstract
and incomprehensible not only for moderns, but must have already
been far removed even for those civilized Hellenes of the fifth century BC.

Strangely passed over in silence by the author, is the fact that
funeral rites became strictly controlled in Greece with Solon's legislation, and especially that paid wailers who did not belong to the
family of the deceased were outlawed, which must have provided a
more than suitable environment for the emergence of the art that
would sate man's need for affliction as a gift that must be shared.
To prohibit its expression means to recognize the threatening and
contagious nature of affliction, for the function of keening as an
ancient funeral rite, especially when performed by paid professionals, is to sharpen and transform grief and sorrow into such an acute
existential pain that no social foundation can withstand it; to in-
tensify it and heighten it to such a degree as to crack the universal
ceiling.

It matters little whether the dead is a loved one or a stranger;
to witness the keening of the women wailers is an experience that
transfigures space-time—the citizen cannot remain detached and
aloof as Plato would have wanted him. But while in the case of a
loved one the hearer may impute his grief to the experience of loss,
in the case of a stranger, grief will choke one just the same, and the
anguish will spread as far as the sounds will take it.

The sing-song will begin faintly, almost inaudible, at first rising
slowly, unlocalizable, as if from the depths of the earth. A low mur-
mur is transmitted through the crowd like a wave and then a deep

silence arrests the air, as spellbound everyone turns in one direction. To localize the source of this astonishingly beautiful and eerie sound and look directly at the keeners, kneeling like black birds by the side of the coffin, as if looking at the gorgons singing in a siren's voice, is petrifying. They do not look anyone in the eye, their gaze passes over you as if over smoke, though you cannot take your eyes off of them. Then, you will make out their words, which, until a minute ago, were incomprehensible. They are calling to the dead and speaking to him as if he were alive, beseeching him to rise to console and hold his mother in his arms once again, entreating him both with affection and with curses.

Appalled at the coarse language, for you did not know one could speak like that to the dead, the dead body's stiffness has now been transferred on to you—a frightful exchange occurs here, as in your mind you expect the corpse to really rise. You may tremble, turn away, leave, or endure the macabre scene, but one thing is certain; life cannot go on as it always has. Death is no longer a far and unfathomable event—you were able to take a glimpse of it in the stony eyes of the black mourners. The tall walls of the real have cracked and crumbled and with them all safety has vanished, but at the same time the air has been suffused with a strange vitality and is ready to combust. The world opens up and man stands in all his vulnerability face to face with the whole universe.

Kadare has keenly noted the danger that "artificially carved pain" presented to civilization and the state, not only with regard to paid wailers, but also to the art that followed in the wake of this ancient rite's prohibition. The act that releases into the world the chained truth of personal affliction, becomes a universal law of art:

> Despite the grand organization of dramatic competitions, the Greek state had never forgotten the threat posed to it by the theatre. Indeed, the more brilliant and sublime the dramas that were put on stage, the more watchful became the eye of the state. That watchful eye would never forget that behind these verses of sudden charm, behind the entrancing resound of the actors' voice, beneath the mesmerizing array of guises and masks, an old evil might always lie concealed. (980-3)

Kadare refers to two particular incidents from the cultural-political life of Athens. The first, narrated by Plutarch in his *Lives*, tells of the dispute between Solon and Thespis, the legendary tragedian. After a spectacle put on stage by Thespis, Plutarch tells us, the retired statesman accosted him and asked him if he was not ashamed to tell such lies in front of so many people, to which Thespis replied that there was no harm in talking and acting that way in a play. Whereupon Solon smote the ground with his staff and said, "Ay, if we honor and commend such play as this we shall find it some day in our business." (*Sol.* 29. 4).

The second reference is to Herodotus's account of the Athenian citizens' distress at the play called *The Capture of Miletus*. "When Phrynicus produced his play," he says, "the audience burst in tears. The author was fined a thousand drachmas for reminding them of their own evils, and they forbade anybody ever to put the play on stage again." (vi. 21. 2).

These two examples may suffice to show how powerful and controversial the new art was, but attempting to gain a glimpse of its nature based on a simple distinction between ancient or contemporary subjects, as some do, sounds somewhat trivial. Solon's legislation against keening appears somehow to have escaped them. That knowledge alone is enough to understand that the forces that would rip tragedy apart were already present at its birth. The tragic poets had a double role to play: they were to be the voice of reason, but the tools at their disposal were the darkest and most destructive of instincts. When reason finally won, it had turned into black bile deadlier than what it had attempted to counter in the first place.

This is not merely a metaphor. Although the ancient theory of the humors has been thoroughly discredited by modern science – insofar as modern science can discredit anything anymore in this moment of post-truth – in its inception at least, the Greeks were already pointing to the stress related psycho-somatic problems of decision-making. In fact, if in its similarity to the old fictions, the modern biochemical imbalance theorizing can address the problem at all, it can only do so with a heavy bias toward the body, demonstrating that fact without fiction is just as weak as fiction without fact. Even with what may appear to be great progress on the subject, this ideological rift has left the understanding of decision-making mechanisms at its most rudimentary level. Hence, for modern man volition remains a mystery in a two-fold sense: the first time overshadowed by subjectivity, and the second time by objectivity.

6.2 Acedia

The one whose gaze sets moths aflame
Will not look at me.
So blackened is my hanging corpse,
So deformed the tree.

—Pir Iqbal the Impaled

In book 30 of his *Problemata*, in "Problems connected with intelligence, thought, and wisdom," Aristotle asks:

> I. Why is it that all those men who have become extraordinary in philosophy, politics, poetry, or the arts are obviously melancholic, and some to such an extent that they are seized by the illnesses that come from black bile, as is said in connection with the stories about Heracles among heroes? Indeed, he seems to have been of this nature, and this is why the ancients named the illness of epilepsy "sacred disease" after him. And his insanity regarding his children and the eruption of sores that occurred before his disappearance on Mount Oeta prove this; for in many cases this occurs as a result of black bile. And these sores also afflicted Lysander the Spartan before he died. Further, there are the stories about Ajax and Bellerophon, of whom the former went completely insane, whereas the latter sought deserted places, which is why Homer wrote (of Bellerophon) in this way:
>
> > But when indeed he was hated by all the gods,
> > Verily over the Aleian plain he wandered alone,
> > Devouring his spirit, avoiding the path of men.
>
> And many other heroes have obviously suffered in the same way as these men. Now in later times, of the well-known people there are Empedocles, Plato, Socrates, and many others. Further, there are most of those connected to poetry. For in many such men diseases have come from this sort of mixture in the body, whereas in others their nature clearly inclines toward these conditions. (xxx. 953a10-30)

According to Hippocratic theory, black bile is one of four humors in the body, the other three being blood, phlegm, and yellow bile. In the healthy person the humors are perfectly, if precariously balanced. Illnesses result if one of them increases at the expense of the others. For Galen, the renowned third century physician, an overabundance of blood results in inflammation. An excess of phlegm brings about tubercles, pustules, catarrh, and nodules of lymph. Jaundice indicates a superfluous amount of yellow bile. For cancer, Galen reserved black bile, the deadliest of all the humors. As Mukherjee explains in his *The Emperor of All Maladies: A Biography of Cancer*, "Only one other disease, replete with metaphors, would be attributed to an excess of this oily viscous humor: depression."

> Indeed, *melancholia*, the medieval name for "depression," would draw its name from the Greek *melas* "black," and *khole* "bile." Depression and cancer, the psychic and physical diseases of black bile, were thus intrinsically intertwined. (48)

It is certainly no coincidence that melancholia, or *acedia*, the noontime demon (*dæmon meridianus*) of the desert monks of the fourth century, was both a carnal and a spiritual affliction. At this time, it had not yet been upgraded to the status of a sin; it was still a primitive temptation, a demon assailing the solitary monk by turning his own thoughts against him. And these demonic thoughts, it should not be hard to understand, could only spring into existence from that chasm between the soul and the body, or to pick up the previous line of thought, the divide between reason and instinct associated with the rise of subjective consciousness. For ultimately, vices (*vitia*) can work their evil only if the afflicted person is still stirred by the passions and desires earthly goods. "The flesh lusteth against the spirit," as Paul enlightens us (Gal. 5:17). Hence, for Evagrius of Pontus the highest reward of the ascetic life was the attainment of ἀπάθεια, freedom from disturbing passions (πάθη), obtained through the unswerving control of reason over one's senses, desires, feelings, and even of memory.

Nevertheless, cancer and depression were by no means the only two diseases imputed to an imbalance of black bile, nor even the only ones replete with metaphors, as Mukherjee argues after Susan Sontag. Perhaps not as "metaphorical" as depression, other diseases of a more mystical or divine nature were epilepsy and apoplexy, as exemplified in the (pseudo) Aristotelian quote above, or in Galen's and Avicenna's writings. To these two may also be added the ulcers in Brady's executive monkeys. In Albanian, it is worth mentioning, the sacred disease of epilepsy is also referred to as *smundë e tokës*, which in English is the same as "the falling sickness," but literally, "the earth sickness." While the meaning of "falling sickness" is certainly appropriate, the literal meaning might reveal a deeper history, as we shall see.

The concept of melancholia, then, has a long history which has undergone myriad transformations, while at the same time fiercely preserving its essential characteristics: From the ancient notion of the extraordinary man with his superfluous amount of black bile resulting in states of divine madness, epilepsy, the eruption of sores, ulcers, and cancer, to the grievous demon of acedia in Christian mysticism or the sin of sloth with the Church. From its status as a demon and a sin with the Church Fathers to a return to the extraordinary man with the Italian Renaissance and the brilliance of the melancholy man in art, philosophy, and politics, the creative energies balancing out his black moods, a view which eventually gave rise to the notion of the man of genius, or the mad artist, followed by the escapism of the sensitive nostalgic and the *mal du siècle* of European Romanticism. From the great man in whom genius and madness were intertwined, to circular insanity (*la folie circulaire*), manic depressive states, and bipolar disorders in psychiatric nomenclature.[1] "The tower of Babel," Burton says, "never yeelded such confusion of tongues, as this Chaos of melancholy doth variety of Symptomes." (Radden, 149-50). In fact, for Burton his research on the subject of melancholia and its plethora of symptoms became a lifelong obsession, which he compared to the task of "capturing a many-headed beast."

The cyclic, or rather coiling, palingenetic nature of melancholia, then, observed in its oscillation between bouts of melancholy

moods and mania, giving rise to the peculiar psychiatric terminology, mirrors the constant and sudden shifts of the concept's own
evolution, which in this is not dissimilar or even unrelated to
McFarlane's oscillation in juridico-political models between the
savage and the barbarian, or Hardt and Negri's immanent/trans-
cendent oppositional divide. In Sloterdijk's exegesis of Greek psychology and thymotic dynamics, these historical cycles can more
clearly be delineated in relation to the vice of pride, because of its
accentuation of the *thymotic* pole, which, he notes, in Europe had
to wait until the Renaissance to rise again (17-8). And of course,
it is during this period that, similarly to the ancient concept, melancholia, too, is judged again as a quality inseparable from the creative energies and the brilliance of extraordinary individuals and
their achievements. "The classic catalogue of cardinal sins,"
Sloterdijk points out, "still provides an image that balances between
erotic and thymotic vices."

> This is based on the assumption that one rightly can assign *avaritia*
> (avarice), *luxuria* (voluptuousness), and *gula* (intemperance) to the erotic
> pole, while *superbia* (arrogance, pride), *ira* (rage), and *invidia* (jealousy, en-
> viousness) belong to the thymotic pole. Only *acedia* (melancholia) does not
> fit into this categorization because it expresses a sadness without subject
> and object." (227 n. 15)

One of the chief characteristics of acedia, however, more than
any of the other sins, is its capacity to shape-shift, often in sudden
and unpredictable ways; it moves, coils, metastasizes and invades,
growing and expanding in the same way as a cancer does. According
to Cassian's psychological concatenation of vices, acedia is related
to wrath and belongs to the irascible part – "it springs from sadness, which in turn arises from wrath..." (Wenzel [1960]2015, 21,
see also 193). In other words, where rage has consumed itself, emptiness takes its place.

For Freud, melancholia was the mourning for the lost "object"
(the parent as incorporated other), which then could spread and
infect all life. Similarly for Kristeva, "depression is the hidden face

of Narcissus." (1989, 5). In the ascent of its unstoppable fumes, however, of which Narcissus falls short, acedia could swallow the whole world, and indeed all the other sins, being the result of a will far beyond that of its parents, in which sadness (reason) and rage (instinct) have merged. It is for this reason that to the desert monks, acedia (ακήδεια or ἀκηδία) was "the most grievous of all [the demons]" (Evagrius, *Praktikos* 28). It entailed a hatred for one's surroundings (*horror loci*) that like acidic vapors might spread to infect and corrode everything in this world and beyond. There were no boundaries that could obstruct its fumes. At its apogee, it could turn against God.

In this it appears to belong to the thymotic pole, since at least one meaning of the Gr. θύμος, same as Alb. *tym*, is smoke. In fact, in Albanian it still links to the old Homeric *thymos* in the expression, *m'u ba tym* "to become angry, to lose control" but literally, "to become, or turn into smoke." Another expression meaning more or less the same thing, only now the anger is turned upon oneself, is *me ngranë vedin me dhamb*, which means "to consume oneself with anger," or literally "to gnaw at oneself (with one's own teeth)", which recalls Homer's description of Bellerophon devouring his spirit.

The most original addition to the debate of whether acedia belonged to the thymotic or the erotic pole comes from Avicenna, who theorized that black bile is one of the heavy sediments of the blood. Combustion of these sediments allowed overheated vapors to diffuse throughout the body and reach the brain, resulting in melancholia. One of its symptoms was a craving for coitus. This, it must be noted, is in direct opposition with Freud's description of melancholia as a loss of libidinal desire, and places acedia at both sides of the erotic/thymotic pole. For Avicenna, it preserves and even intensifies the libido, equating acedia with the apocalyptic imagination, since libidinal desire exhibits itself entirely uninhibited only in these two states; in dreams, as Freud well knew, and at the edge of life and death.

It is no wonder, then, that acedia was one of the most egregious demon-thoughts waging war against the ascetic in the desert solitude, particularly during the oppressive hours of the noonday heat. Evagrius enumerates eight such demons, or basic categories of thought: "First is that of gluttony, then fornication, avarice, sadness, wrath, acedia, vainglory, and last of all, pride." (*Praktikos* 6). While most of these demons assailed the monk in the dark, turning his thoughts inside-out, acedia was the exception; it illumined the day with shafts of dark light, "a deadly disease striking at noon."[2] In this it clearly appears as the atavistic or Dionysian aspect of Apollo, "a black sun," to use Kristeva's imagery. Strikingly, while the spiritual affliction readily manifests itself, in its physical aspect, cancer, it moves stealthily beneath the skin like a crab scurrying about under the sand.

The seven capital vices, emerged after Pope Gregory's merging of acedia with dejection (*tristitia*), vainglory with pride, and the addition of envy (*invidia*).[3] At that time the formal list was thus endorsed as, vainglory, anger, envy, dejection, covetousness, gluttony, and fornication. It is only later (in the 12th century) that acedia returns once more, surprisingly ousting Gregory's more authoritative version with his preference for *tristitia*. Then, following in the footsteps of Cassian, it was finally reduced to the sin of sloth, and punishments appropriate to it were prescribed for the benefit of the masses that could not relate to its spiritual aspect (Wenzel, 22, 29 and Ch's. IV-V), giving the present list of mortal sins as, pride, wrath, envy, sloth, greed, gluttony, and lust.[4]

Apart from the above, the scholastics categorized the vices based on a number of other divisions, ranging from the threefold division of human nature into *spiritus*, *anima*, and *corpus*, where *anima* refers to the part of the soul that, in contradistinction to the spirit, has some connection to the body (43) – one may call it with Žižek "the indivisible remainder" – to the division between internal and external aims or goods (Wenzel, 44). Each of these categorizations grouped the vices together and thus forged a different concatenation. In the first case acedia was given relative freedom and allowed to move undisturbed between the realm of the *spiritus* and that of the *corpus* through the intermediacy of the *anima*. In every other case involving rigorously dichotomous categories, such as, inner and outer, it never failed to sidle across or underneath the lines drawn on the sand, moving them with it.

More disturbingly, this extraordinary capacity to blur the inner and outer boundaries or endogenous and exogenous spaces, is shown to be not merely a matter of theologizing, but unquestionably extending to the physical world with the evolving research on cancer. Not coincidentally, it was the discovery and subsequent research on the cancer-causing retrovirus, Rous sarcoma, that in 1970 delivered the fatal blow to the central dogma of molecular biology which postulated the unidirectional flow of genetic information: DNA → RNA → protein. Rous sarcoma, could become part of the genome of the cell by attaching itself to the cell's genes through reverse transcription (RNA → DNA), becoming thus "both an internal aberration and an endogenous infection" capable of writing history backwards, as Mukherjee puts it (352-54). Strikingly, these viruses (src, abl, etc.) had first weaponized themselves by smuggling the cancer-causing gene from human cancers, and thus mutating themselves into cancer causing viruses.

For Thomas Aquinas, on the other hand, the division of vices was based on their direct or indirect movement of the appetite (Wenzel, 45). In one of his descriptions, then, acedia becomes "the aversion of the appetite from its own good because of bodily hardships that accompany its attainment." (46, 49). But this in itself does not make it a special vice. For Aquinas, acedia is a special vice because it has no earthly object: its object is the *bonum divinum*— it is the "sorrow or aversion against God himself and the things that are directly related to Him. It is the opposite of the joy in the divine good that man should experience" (49), "the negation of *caritas*, the greatest Christian virtue." (55). For Aquinas, then, acedia does not refer to temporal sorrows, as Wenzel explains, "but only to the sorrow about the divine good," no doubt a forced argument to disqualify as instances of acedia Christ's and Paul's utterances (in Matt. 26:38 and II Cor. 6:10 respectively).[5] Nevertheless, just like its physical aspect, acedia begins locally, to then spread and obliterate everything else, including its own beginnings (reverse transcription). Aquinas does capture this movement in his description of "true acedia":

> *True acedia* is by definition a mortal sin, since it opposes the virtue of *caritas* and its special aspect of spiritual joy. But it must be considered that this sin is not always "perfect" or completed. Its beginning is an aversion of man's sensitive appetite against the divine good. This aversion per se is not a mortal sin; it becomes such only if reason gives its full consent." (50)

In its elevation to the rank of mortal sin in Aquinas' incisive words, acedia finally emerges as that very same threat that called for the ancient injunction against the Dionysus cult and its use of entheogenic mushrooms: the terrifying amalgamation of instinct and reason, of the analytic and synthetic functions in the post-bicameral mind, a consciousness as yet uninhibited by subjectivity. For if reason gives its full consent to instinct, the resulting consciousness may lay siege to the world.

Again, this is not some spectral analogy, for ultimately, even analogies exploit their own physical pathways. The food of the gods that could bestow immortality and wisdom came in the form of a mushroom. This was euphemistically referred to as *sciros* "parasol" in Greek, which also means "tumor, swelling" – a strange euphemism considering that on the one hand it conceals a mushroom, while on the other it displays a tumor. Just like the post-bicameral mind, the cancer cell has unleashed itself from the central control and enforced death sentence of the "normal" genome, hijacking its DNA and acquiring autonomous proliferation. It can issue its own commands in front of which, even the god-host which cancer is literally devouring trembles, impotent and helpless. In his description of the cancer cell, oncologist Siddhartha Mukherjee, writes,

> ...cancer stem cells have acquired the behavior of normal stem cells by activating the same genes and pathways that make normal stem cells immortal—except, unlike normal stem cells, they cannot be lulled back into

physiological sleep. Cancer, then, is quite literally trying to emulate a regenerating organ—or perhaps, more disturbingly, the regenerating organism. Its quest for immortality mirrors our own quest, a quest buried in our embryos and in the renewal of our organs. Someday, if a cancer succeeds, it will produce a far more perfect being than its host—imbued with both immortality and the drive to proliferate. (458)

Like cancer, then, the mushroom-tumor entheogenic compound carries an especially venomous knowledge with it: that to achieve immortality, one must pay with one's life, or more specifically, one's identity. Ultimately, this is inherently bound to the problem of what death is, since in nature there is no death, only transformation.

More disturbing however, is the fact that there is no long-term defense from this deadly wisdom or disease. Psychologically, or even socially and theologically speaking, our tactics today are no better than in antiquity. The only option, then as now, was to excise instinct from reason, a solution whose expediency Thomas Aquinas was well aware of.[6] It is in this way that one may read the words by Huguitius of Pisa in his dictionary: "*Acci grece, cura latine*" (qtd. in Wenzel, 219 n. 27), for it would seem the only novelty here was to apply the cures to the old ills in a new language. However, this recurrent excision, amputation, or division, which we have been tracing throughout these essays, is itself only an artificial emulation of metastasis, thus, in the end accelerating the effects of cancer, and the possibility of a system crash.[7]

"In scholastic thought," Wenzel explains, "*acedia* holds an interesting intermediate position between body and spirit." On the other hand, "in Thomas's more spiritualized conception it stems from the opposition between spirit and flesh." (60, see also 170). With the help of Aristotelian psychology, he was able to connect acedia with a main passion, to wit, Gregory's *tristitia*, and consequently to show that "the theological vice is very intimately linked to the deepest roots of man's affective and volitive life." (55). Of course, for Aquinas, then, this becomes a disorientation of will, a disorder of man's affective life, and thus the groundwork for the interpretation of acedia as a sickness instead of as a sin is already in place. From here on, a return to the theory of the humors is inevitable, and the problem is again laid at the feet of the physicians. This was a relief for the scholastics. As Wenzel points out, theologians were never comfortable with its dual aspect and often omitted to mention acedia altogether in their contemplation of the chief vices, "One finds many instances in which especially *acedia* is lacking—which may be another sign of the uneasiness experienced by theologians in having to place the vice into a flesh-vs.-spirit category." (248, n. 31).

In point of fact, though, the responsibilities seem to have been shared, however unfairly: while to the physicians were allotted the psychological burdens of melancholia, the church controlled its physical aspect in the form of sloth, which whatever dangers it posed, did not come anywhere near its dark side, cancer. On the authority of Galen's warning, who himself was following Hippocrates's advice, medicine was content to diagnose it and let it take its course, or at most, recourse to bleeding and purging when all other treatments had failed. As excisions were considered futile, the doctors limited themselves to the alleviation of symptoms with balms, ointments, salves, and all sorts of purgatives and laxatives. "In the seventeenth century, a paste of crab's eyes, at five shillings a pound, was popular—using fire to treat fire." Mukherjee says (48).

With few exceptions, medicine did not dare touch cancers until much later, tentatively at first in the second half of the eighteenth century, but picking up the pace with the invention of anesthesia and antisepsis in the nineteenth century, and quickly reaching an upper limit in the late nineteenth and early twentieth centuries with Halsted's horrendous radical mastectomies that sought to uproot cancer from its source. These were superseded by the even more nightmarish "ultra-radical" mastectomies of his disciples in the mid-twentieth century. "A macabre marathon," as Mukherjee calls it, of an army of surgeons armed with their scalpels excavating the patient's body until (supposedly) no cancer and very little of the patient was left on the operating table (64ff., 193ff.)

Following closely on the bloody trail of the cold knife was the hot knife solution, radiation, a paradoxical cancer contra cancer treatment that killed nearly all the pioneers who discovered it. Similar in its effects, chemotherapy – chemical warfare turned therapeutic, – literally enlisted even mustard gas in its battle against cancer. This, too, found its extreme application in marrow-transplant megadose chemotherapy, which is chemotherapy taken to its utmost limit, and which, if it did not kill the patient on the spot, it might even cure one type of cancer and bless the patient with a second, chemotherapy-resistant one, along with various other deadly diseases and infections. The multibillion dollar total war waged against cancer, or the "total hell" as the doctors themselves sometimes called it, no less a political and bureaucratic war than a medical one, with its own frauds and wartime profiteers in the private as well as the public sectors, has disaster after disaster inscribed in its annals, the massacre of thousands of bodies in "butcher shop" hospital basements and, as business grew, hundreds of thousands now dying in expensive, shiny, brand new clinics, all in the name of finding a cure for this evasive, chimeric, and shapeshifting disease, and ridding society of its ills. "It was trial and error on a giant human scale," Mukherjee describes it, "with the emphasis, it seemed at times, distinctly on error." (208). In oncology's persistent, and often deliberate denial of any dignity to the ill and the dying, patient and cancer were often reserved the same treatment.

As for the scholastics, their own futile taxonomical attempts at insulating and containing the desert demon, had two far reaching effects: I) they winded up acquiring the illness, and this resulted in the metastatic proliferation of a number of sects and denominations splitting from the body of the Holy Church, 2) that part which managed to flee the epidemic contagion, a flight which, of course, was interpreted as an assiduous fight, continued to feel its ominous and oppressive presence until, at last, the ill feeling was externalized when the golden idea was struck that this was no demon at all in fact, but merely an illness in need of medical attention. Needless to say, that this relegation of Church powers to the science of medicine, paving the way for the biopolitics of the nineteenth century, amounted to a total capitulation and surrender for theology, and is the main reason behind the slow secularization of the Church, for acedia was in more than one way its raison d'être.

If for the more urban monks under the care of Cassian, the spiritual aspect of acedia might have seemed negligible compared to the more tangible effects of idleness, for semi-hermits of the desert with no diversions like Evagrius, it was "the most oppressive of all demons." "He attacks the monk about the fourth hour and besieges his soul until the eighth hour." Evagrius relates.

> First he makes the sun appear sluggish and immobile, as if the day had fifty hours. Then he causes the monk continually to look at the windows and forces him to step out of his cell and to gaze at the sun to see how far it still is from the ninth hour, and to look around, here and there, whether any of his brethren is near. Moreover, the demon sends him hatred against the place, against life itself, and against the work of his hands, and makes him think he has lost the love among his brethren and that there is none to comfort him. If during those days anybody annoyed the monk, the demon would add this to increase the monk's hatred. He stirs the monk also to long for different places in which he can find easily what is necessary for his life and can carry on a much less toilsome and more expedient profession. It is not on account of locality, the demon suggests, that one pleases God. He can be worshipped everywhere. To these thoughts the demon adds the memory of the monk's family and of his former way of life. He presents the length of his lifetime, holding before the monk's eyes all the hardships of his ascetic life. Thus the demon employs all his wiles so that the monk may leave his cell and flee from the race-course.

> Evagrius, *Praktikos* 12 (Wenzel's trans., 5).

With acedia thus, the passage of time slows down almost to a standstill. The length of the monk's lifetime becomes a vastness stretching out to an eternity of boredom. The promise of heaven that might hold some appeal for the coarse peasant, becomes a curse and damnation for the ascetic who knows all too well the dreadful burden of eternity. Time and again Evagrius, and after him Cassian, point out that if the desire to leave the cell is satisfied, flight might become a habit, and this may cause the monk to abandon his profession altogether (Wenzel, 10, 19 et al.). The restive personality and exponential growth of acedia's *horror loci* (fear or disgust with the present location) may be seen, for instance, in the extension of the boredom with one's cell to encompass the whole world now conceived as a vast prison.

Nevertheless, the hauntingly beautiful words of Hugh of Saint Victor, as Edward Said is often fond of quoting, illustrate just how indispensable this perpetual flight — which then threatens to become a permanent exilic mentality — was for the mystic seeking union with God.

> It is, therefore, a great source of virtue for the practiced mind to learn, bit by bit, first to change about invisible and transitory things, so that afterwards it may be able to leave them behind altogether. The man who finds his homeland sweet is still a tender beginner; he to whom every soil is as his native one is already strong; but he is perfect to whom the entire world is as a foreign land. The tender soul has fixed his love on one spot in the world; the strong man has extended his love to all places; the perfect man has extinguished his.

> (*Didascalicon*, 101)

Unsurprisingly, while such a radical form of intellectual exile may be practiced to sever the ties with this world in order to strengthen the bind with the other, it has never been openly acknowledged that if acedia is seen as a capital vice preventing and even outright rejecting union with God, it is also what is required for the severing of one's ties with the earthly domain in the first place. Speaking of the discipline required for study, Hugh of St.

Victor names, among other things, a foreign soil. (*Didascalicon*, 94). This is proposed "since it gives a man practice. All the world is a foreign soil to those who philosophize" (101), or alternately, "All the world is a foreign soil to those whose native land should be heaven. ...so that man may see he has no stable dwelling here..." (216 n. 84). And if one learned the lesson well, one would know there is no stable dwelling anywhere. The true believer must carry the torch to heaven as well.

6.3 Oncological Creation: The Earth Sickness

TO STAND, in the shadow
of a scar in the air

—Paul Celan, "To Stand"

I am the Other Conqueror, and the Earth a
game, a
Mare entering the clouds /

—Adonis, "This Is My Name"

Omnis cellula e cellula, Virchow said. All cells come from cells. The corporeal and spiritual Janus faces of melancholia do not contradict this. In its corporeal form, cancer, black bile takes Virchow's dictum to its extreme breaking point. In its spiritual aspect, acedia, it follows its reasoning from this world to the next—from the earth conceived as a vast prison cell to the vault of heaven, cracking the walls of God's abode. Or rather, through wrath they crack, and through acedia they break, to recalibrate Victor of St. Hugo's words, who was speaking of the soul as a vessel.

Victor of St. Hugo's image is interesting in view of the fact that the opposite, the body as a vessel for the soul, is generally considered more appropriate. From a wider perspective comprising the heavens and the earth, however, his reversal does not appear inconsistent; the vault of heaven encapsulates the earth, the spiritual realm the physical. Even the word *sky* in fact denotes a vessel, for it is etymologically related to the Greek *kytos* (κύτος) "a hollow, receptacle, basket." In this sense, then, it also denotes a cell, for a cell is a vessel. In English, the word *cell,* i.e. both the biological cell and the cell as a small room, comes from the Latin *cella* "small room, store room, hut" (see, *cellar*). Κύτος is traced to a reconstructed

Proto-Indo-European root *(s)keu- while the root of the Latin *cella* comes from the P-I-E root *kel-*[(2)], Greek *kalia* "hut, nest." Redundantly, both mean the same thing, "to cover, conceal." (OED). The Lat. *cælum* or *cœlum* "sky," however, is of the same family as the Greek *koilos* (κοῖλος) "hollow, sunken," with a sense of being convex or swollen. As the sky was imagined as a vault or as an immovable firmament where the stars rested, these shapes must not strike one as strange. In addition, as the dictionary[1] explains, the convex shape on one side implies a concave shape on the other, which brings us full circle to the first Greek word, κύτος, related not only to English "sky," but also to the classical Sanskrit root *chad* "to cover," from which derives *chattra*, meaning "parasol" as well as "mushroom."[2]

These terms come together in all their variety almost with mathematical precision in Albanian:

Qiell, qell (Gheg *qīll*) is the sky, the firmament of heaven, just as *qiellzë, qellzë* (from *qiell* + diminutive suffix *zë*) is the palate, the roof of the mouth.

In the same way, *qelí* is a prison cell, just as *qelízë* (*qelí* + diminutive suffix *zë*) is a biological cell.

Meyer (2007) argued that *qiell* derives from Lat. *cælum*, though it would be more prudent to consider them related than to rash stratifying them in chronological layers.[3] In light of the above Greek and Latin etymologies, both deriving from P-I-E roots meaning "to close," *qiell* may be related to *çel* "to open; to hatch; to light a fire; to bloom," whose opposite is *mështel, mçel* "to close." It is also related to *çaj* "to split, to cleave." Jokl follows the root to an I-E *skel-*, almost an amalgamation of *(s)keu-* and *kel-*[(2)] (Çabej; *çel*).

Hence, *çel*, is not to be taken as a clear, cloudless sky,[4] but as the sky opening up, for example at dawn, or after the rain. Taking

206

into account all its meanings, in its most expressive form *çel* would mean the splitting of the skies by lightning. And as this phenomenon was credited with planting the divine mushroom through the sexual union between the lightning bolt and the fecund mother Earth (Wasson 1980, Wasson et al. 1986), in this singular event one may grasp the whole spectrum of the word and its meanings.

From this celestial mitosis[5] mushroom a proliferating number of metastatic tumors, God's authority hijacked and obliterated by a parallel oncological creation or oncogenesis. Ultimately though, the Earth itself is a tumor in God's throat, "the deep rising" (BW I:5); a protuberant excrescence in his larynx when God uttered...

The stages of this abnormal growth can be discerned in *The Book of Wars* Oncogenesis following each other in quick succession. At first it is almost an abstract entity, a scarring caused by God's own thunderous voice.[6] Initially, this may be equated with the empty, the void (*bosh*), coinciding with God's gape, i.e. with his uttering, whose words in I:3, "Let there be a wound (in Me) to tear the whole in four" (*Mû hap i vrrag me shkle tanën katërçika*) cannot be separated from the deed. In other words, before God uttered the words, he was in an aproprioceptive, prenoetic condition.[7]

The word *ban* "to make" p.p. *bërë* "made, created" which is etymologically the same as the Hebrew word בָּרָא (bara'), reveals this first act of speech as a strike; "First of all God burrowed a hole and made the void" (BW: II. *Mâ s parit Pernia kall varrën e bân boshtm*). The word remains unchanged in the established version of the Bible and is explained as follows by the NET Bible scholars:

> The English verb 'create' captures well the meaning of the Hebrew term in this context. The verb בָּרָא (bara') always describes the divine activity of fashioning something new, fresh, and perfect. The verb does not necessarily describe creation out of nothing; it often stresses forming anew, reforming, renewing. (3tn)

Nevertheless, a note to the KJ version explains: "(bara'): a primitive root; (absolutely) to create; (qualified) to cut down ... dispatch, do, make."[8] The Net Bible scholars are right in saying that the Hebrew verb does not imply creation out of nothing, for indeed the opposite is the case in the BW texts; the opening up of the void out of the solid. What seems to escape them is that there is no other "previous" creation to look for. It is out of this power vacuum that a tumorigenic earth grows. Hence, the notion of the deep swelling up obliterating God's boundaries.

In a note to the text of Genesis 1:1, the scholars conveniently draw the readers' attention away from this gap arguing that by "heaven and earth" the entire world is meant and not simply the two particular entities:

> (The heavens and the earth): Or "the entire universe"; or "the sky and the dry land." This phrase is often interpreted as a merism, referring to the entire ordered universe, including the heavens and the earth and everything in them. The "heavens and the earth" were completed in seven days and are characterized by fixed laws. "Heavens" refers specifically to the sky, created on the second day, while "earth" refers specifically to the dry land, created on the third day. Both are distinct from the sea/seas. (tn 4)

This explanation, however, was not enough, prompting the scholars to add the following note:

> The disjunctive clause (conjunction + subject + verb) at the beginning of v. 2 gives background information for the following narrative, explaining the state of things when "God said..." (v. 3). Verse 1 is a title to the chapter, v. 2 provides information about the state of things when God spoke, and v. 3 begins the narrative per se with the typical narrative construction (vav [ו] consecutive followed by the prefixed verbal form). (This literary structure is paralleled in the second portion of the book: Gen 2:4 provides the title or summary of what follows, 2:5-6 use disjunctive clause structures to give background information for the following narrative, and 2:7 begins the narrative with the vav consecutive attached to a prefixed verbal form.) Some translate 1:2 *"and the earth became,"* arguing that v. 1 describes the original creation of the earth, while v. 2 refers to a judgment that reduced it to a chaotic condition. Verses 3ff. then describe the re-creation of the earth. However, the disjunctive clause at the beginning of v. 2 cannot be translated as if it were relating the next event in a sequence. If v. 2 were sequential to v. 1, the author would have used the vav consecutive followed by a prefixed verbal form and the subject.[9] (5tn)

These mysterious "others" who translate verse 1:2 "and the earth became," and who the NET Bible scholars are content to leave in the dark, offer the key to understanding how oncogenesis was covered up one concept at a time in what seems to have been a centuries-long process. (For a comparison of the different versions, see Table I below).

The quest of the NET Bible scholars for a more elegant pattern when it comes to a clear separation between summary, information, and narrative proper, finds its answer in *The Book of Wars*. Moreover, this version unfolds their unsettling compromise to settle for unoriginal creation in an attempt to do away with the disturbing implications of an oncogenetic creation. In other words, in the absence of a real solution they try to save God's Original Creation by pushing its beginnings further into the primaeval darkness, as if the malign oncogenesis that supplants it were unable to reach deep enough in time to corrupt and obliterate its message.

From the perspective of the authorized version, what the most mysterious second version reveals is basically that something is working against God's Creation, or at the very least that the Creation was not perfectly made, and so, as soon as the heavens and the earth were created they began to degenerate, the earth becoming without shape, though, oddly, no change is detected in the sky. Comparing the structure of the three versions, then, clearly shows that the established version futilely struggles to conceal what *The Book of Wars* plainly admits, and which, the second version of the mysterious others attempts to reinstate, albeit, it only goes half way in this direction. The authorized version has to compromise Original Creation in order to keep itself standing, while the second version attempting to keep Original Creation in place, makes God erratic and superfluous. While the canonized scripture has to revert the Bible to a simple narrative, as if when God created the world he did no more than told a parable, the second version, while admitting its truth as fact has to place the doubt on God.[10]

1. NET VERSION	2. OTHER VERSION	3. EARTHMARE
SUMMARY: UNORIGINAL CREATION	SUMMARY: ORIGINAL CREATION	SUMMARY: ORIGINAL CREATION
1:1. In the beginning God created the heavens and the earth.	1:1. In the beginning God created the heavens and the earth.	First of all God [burrowed] a hole and made the void.
INFORMATION: THE STATE OF THINGS	JUDGMENT: REDUCING ORIGINAL CREATION TO CHAOS	INFORMATION: THE STATE OF THINGS
1:2 Now the earth was without shape and empty, and darkness was over the surface of the watery deep, but the Spirit of God was moving over the surface of the water.	1:2 Then the earth became without shape and empty, and darkness was over the surface of the watery deep, but the Spirit of God was moving over the surface of the water.	Formless was the trunk of the immeasurable whole.
NARRATIVE	RECREATION	NARRATIVE
1:3 God said, "Let there be light." And there was light!	1:3 God said, "Let there be light." And there was light!	1:3 Then [God] uttered, "Let there be a wound (in Me), to split the whole into four"; and there was a deep gaping wound [1:2] and the breath of God's desire hovered over dark waters gauging at itself [1:4] Thus He showed Himself to Himself [1:5] And He called this knowledge because He knew.##

⸻

Ditë stands both for knowledge and day in Albanian, and can be translated equally into "And this He called day because there was light."##

In the texts from *The Book of Wars*, the earth sprouts into existence on the first day, not the third, and like Ullikummi, the deaf, blind, stone giant in Hurrian myth (see 5.3, n. 10), quickly shoots for the sky (*qiell*), or the palate (*qiellzë*), i.e. the roof of God's mouth. The reason for the confusion between the versions springs partly from the fact that in the first day, the earth is only hinted to in the strange term *boshtm*. As yet this is only an obscure and almost abstract half-flesh half-word entity. Coined by the pastor who first translated the texts to capture the ancient composite concept "*bhuthshtm*" in all its subtleties, and its eventual breakdown into numerous words (or worlds), it is simplified as void (from *bosh*) in English but it also hints at an axis (*bosht*). This metaphysical (i.e. half physical) entity is precisely what turns out to be the bedrock of the earth (*botë*) in the following days of Creation.

Without getting into a full analysis of the following days, which will have to wait for another work, a few points must be mentioned. The first time the earth is referred to unmistakably, is the second day. It is called *Gjaja* "the Thing." The term *botë* "earth, globe, world,"[11] appears only in later days, when God attempts to counter the horror of "the Thing" by recourse to naming the unknown. This first mention is unmistakable because we already know *Gjaja* from Greek mythology: it is Mother Earth, Gaia (Γαῖα, Γῆ). Linguists suggest an obscure pre-Indo-European or at least pre-Greek origin for the word, perhaps of Pelasgian stock. The fact that it occurs in the second part of *Pelasgia* suggests that this is a composite word. Thus, the compound might be divided into its constituent parts *pelas* + *gē*. Hellanicus, the famous fifth century BC logographer from Lesbos, points out the mention of Pelasgic Argos as the "pastureland of horses" (Ἄργος ἐς ἱππόβοτο) in the *Iliad* (iii. 75, 258, vi. 144), suggesting a possible meaning of "horse" for *pelas*. In modern Albanian this is straightforward; *pela* specifically means "mare."[12] In English, Pelasgia thus denotes the Earth Mare, or Earthmare, considering that in this guise she indicates Demeter, the Mare-headed goddess who in the throb of her hoofbeat brings terror dreams to a heavily sedated mankind from beyond the confines of the real.

This is a breeding proliferating Mare. In relation to her son Pelasgos, the eponymous ancestor of the warlike Pelasgians (Πελασγοί), the stress falls on the sense of offspring, creature, foal; Alb. *pjellë* (n.) "sprung from one's womb," since in Arcadian myth, Pelasgos was the first man who grew from the earth like a tree. The tumor-like growth could hardly be more evident. Ancient sources consistently refer to him as the first man, or "the earthborn," and this, in fact, is literally the meaning of his name; *pellas* (i.e. *pjellë* "offspring") + *gē* "born of the earth."[13] Similarly, the sons of Earth, the Giants, derive their name from Gaia with a reduplication of the root, *gigas.*

Demeter's name, too, is a composite meaning Earth Mother, from *De* "earth" + *Mater* "mother." (OED). The shift from guttural [g] to alveolar [d], seemingly a satemized form of *Gē Mater*, is more likely to indicate a lost animacy gender, a possibility that seems to have escaped linguists somehow. A similar gender division into animate and inanimate can be observed in the ancient words for fire and water. As regards the element of earth, Gaia is the living Earth. In Albanian, it is related to *gja, gjë* "thing," with a sense of living thing (*gja e gjallë*), and perhaps even directly related to *gjallë* "alive, living; quick." On the other hand, *De* (Δῆ̃), related to Alb. *dhé* (def. *dheu*) "earth, dust," represents not only the inanimate gender, but literally means "dead."[14]

This same shift between guttural [g] and alveolar [d], is observed in numerous cases, not only within Albanian, but across different languages as well. The difference between Greek γη and Albanian *dhé*, therefore, may be a remnant of an obsolete animacy gender (Ge/De), especially since we find words clearly related to the animate γη in Albanian, and likewise, words related to the inanimate *dhé* in Greek. At the very least, this suggests a possible alternative to the antedated centum/satem theory of languages with its anachronistic east/west divide. The theory should have been discarded already in the early 1900's with the discovery of Hittite and Tocharian which did not fit its geographical distribution. Unfortunately, linguistic theories die hard. If Hittite and Tocharian are dead languages, Albanian is a living language which, being especially at odds with the arbitrary boundaries imposed on it, must adapt to the theory instead of the other way around.

Be that as it may, a detailed discussion of these theories will not be necessary here. It will suffice to mention a few examples of these terms cleft in twain that, following the dissociation between sky and earth, reason and instinct, life and death, etc. seem to mirror the earlier Albanian-Germanic divisions. The most interesting of these perhaps, are the words for *serpent*:

> **serpent** (n.) from Old French *serpent, sarpent* , from Latin *serpentem* (nominative *serpens*) "snake; creeping thing," from present participle of *serpere* "to creep," from PIE *serp- "to crawl, creep" (source also of Sanskrit *sarpati* "creeps," *sarpah* "serpent;" Greek *herpein* "to creep," *herpeton* "serpent;" Albanian *garper* "serpent"). OED

In Albanian, which is dismissively lumped together with the satem group of languages, but does not belong clearly to either, we find a centum (or only impartially satemized) term for serpent – *gjarpër* – while in Greek, which is a centum language we find a satemized word – *hérpo* ('ἕρπω). According to the theory, however, whenever such satemized words are encountered where they should not be, it is said that they are not really satemized but follow some other rule that, oddly, has nothing to do with the centum/satem isoglosses. These rules that function like a throw ring or flotation device to help keep afloat a theory which on its own would immediately sink, effectively block any attempt to disprove it. One wonders what urgent need there might be for a theory that clearly does not hold water, if such unexpected rescue missions are afforded to it, and most importantly, if that need has anything to do with linguistics.

In any event, since the meaning of *serpent* in all the languages mentioned is "to crawl, to creep," it is easy to see that this is a composite word, *gja* "earth" + (*r*)*për* (*nëpër*) "through." *Nëpërkë*, the

name for viper or adder in Albanian, reflects the same word formation, *nëpër* + *kë* (cf. w. Sumerian *ki* "earth"). Similarly to *adder*,
nëpërkë used to be a generic name for snake, as its etymology suggests, later applied to one particular genus. Viper, on the other
hand, comes from Latin *vipera*, contraction of **vivipera*, from *vivus*
"alive, living" + *parere* "bring forth, bear."

Although having long fallen out of use, the old gender distinctions are no longer easily recognizable, in Albanian it would seem
that the animate declension corresponds more closely to centum
words, while satemized words usually stand for inanimate objects
as in *gja/send* "living thing/object"; *gjallë/dek* "alive/dead" etc.
In certain cases they have even blended, forming undead composites
with a reduplication of the root, as in *gjësend* "something." [15]

The so-called satemization pathway of consonant articulation
from the throat to the lips — i.e. from gutturals to velars to palatals
to alveolars, and so on — follows the growth of the earth from a
scarring of the larynx when God spoke, to a hardened keloid lump
in the throat (*gjëndër* "gland; lump," literally *gjë* + *ndër* "thing going through") to a disturbing fist-like tumor growing into the
mouth, erupting through the palate, metastasizing, and finally
breaking out and spilling into the world. These metastasized cancers, then, are Earth's offspring, exhibiting their own personality
and behavior, as oncologists like to say, having accumulated a different set of genetic mutations.

In the context of earthborn Pelasgos, the Biblical myth of the
creation of man out of the earth, and of woman out of man's rib, [16]
cannot be passed over in silence. Adam's name which, in the generic
sense in Hebrew means "human," is related to *adamah* "earth, clay."
Fashioned out of clay, however, he was still inanimate until God
breathed the breath of life into him, instructing him to go out and
subdue the earth in his name. Taken out of the pathological pro-
trusion itself, Adam is a clinically grown specimen, perhaps singled
out for exhibiting a particularly antagonistic behavior even against
his own kin, thus "using fire to treat fire." This trait was carefully
selected for, and passed on to the next generations. There is a reason

Adam and Eve came last in God's list of new and perfect things. These are clearly the first steps in fashioning a long-lasting cure for the Earth sickness, a cure which, as is usually the case with cancer, turned out to be worse than the disease, since in only three generations, from Adam to Cain to Enoch, the godfighter, this aggressive strand is unleashed and totally out of control.

If the creation of Adam leaves any doubt, that of Eve is clearly surgical. Though the English translations use the word "rib," the Hebrew tells of God taking as much as a side (*one quarter:* צֵלָע – tsela`) from Adam's anesthetized body, inferring a monstrous growth in just a short time, out of which he fashions Eve, a transgendered clone of Adam, in an attempt to isolate and extract the very essence of the disease.

One might consider also earlier creations which were so offensive they had to be removed from God's presence, like Lilith, the night spirit that gave birth to demonic offspring at such an accelerated rate as to entirely obliterate his creation. Collectively, these forbidding creatures were called "the plagues of mankind." The emended records of canonized scripture subsequently excise all but one mention of her. This occurs in the same breath with the Satyrs[17] in Isaiah's apocalyptic visions of the Lord wreaking vengeance upon Edom (Isaiah 34:13-15). In the King James version, her name (לִילִית liyliyth) is translated as "screeching owl," but the Septuagint uses "onokentauros."

Eight types of beasts are enumerated in Isaiah, from which it may well be that Evagrius Ponticos later adapted his own desert demons. If this is true, one can easily guess what demonic position was reserved for the Satyr. As for Lilith, fornication would seem the most appropriate association, but as is usual with acedia, a clear line between it and the other sins cannot be drawn. Wenzel does not mention this possible source for Evagrius's eight demons in his work on acedia. "Of the various sin schemes that have been suggested as models for the Evagrian list, I have found nothing which in nature and importance would equal ἀκηδία." he says (17). A more appropriate source than the Satyr, however, can hardly be found.

The Biblical myth, has been interpreted as an appropriation of Mother Earth's creative power in favor of the Heavenly Father, who attempts to dispense entirely with Earth as creatrix, at the cost that everything autochthonous has always something alien in it. But if Adam is a tweaked version of the earth-grown Pelasgos or Lilith, Eve is twice removed. The keen medical student will immediately discern the sequence of these clonings described in the Holy Scripture as medical records of attempts to grow and study the earth disease under controlled laboratory conditions.

In more than one way, God's total war against the "earth sickness," or the "Thing disease," resembles the total war on cancer of the twentieth century. Isaiah's visions, to mention but one of countless apocalyptic invocations, are striking because his descriptions of the desolation of the land could easily be applied to a body gone through extensive radiation:

> And the streams thereof shall be turned into pitch, and the dust thereof into brimstone, and the land thereof shall become burning pitch. It shall not be quenched night nor day; the smoke thereof shall go up for ever: for generation to generation it shall lie waste; none shall pass through it ever and ever. (Isaiah 34:9-12)

These scorch trials by a medically proficient God, represent an escalating concern with a deranged abnormal growth that has flung open the floodgates of creation. It can neither be clearly separated from God's own consummate Creation, nor permanently assimilated for it accelerates its logic to the breaking point.

The philosopher might become more acutely aware of the problem this constitutes for ontology in the application of the ontological argument to cancer, for cancer grows precisely over and above the greatest thing that exists. If that thing continues to obsessively grow, in the mind or in reality, so does cancer. Medical ontology cannot provide a solution to God's disease by opting for an arrested view in time of the Whole called Being. With cancer there is no such thing as Being, only Becoming. The complete eradication of cancer, therefore, if at all imaginable, means absolute control over mutations, thus over chance happenings, and this means to put an end to all life. To counter death, in other words, one needs to eradicate life. For cancer, the gatekeeper, only lets us on to the secret of immortality if, by crossing that threshold, we agree to become something other, something monstrous and deadly to our own existence.

APPENDICES

Appendix A: Tracing the Scriptures

The first verse of the New King James (NKJ) and the New English Translation (NET) Bible versions reads: "In the beginning God created the heavens and the earth.§§§ The translator's note (1 tn) of the NET Bible explains:

> *Beginning.* The translation assumes that the form translated 'beginning' is in the absolute state rather than the construct ("in the beginning of," or "when God created"). In other words, the clause in verse 1 is a main clause, v. 2 has three clauses that are descriptive and supply background information, and v. 3 begins the narrative sequence proper. The referent of the word "beginning" has to be defined from the context since there is no beginning or ending with God.

A study note (1 sn) then adds:

> *In the beginning.* The verse refers to the beginning of the world as we know it; it affirms that it is entirely the product of the creation of God. But there are two ways that this verse can be interpreted: (1) it may be taken to refer to the original act of creation with the rest of the events on the days of creation completing it. This would mean that the disjunctive clauses of v. 2 break the sequence of the creative work of the first day. (2) It may be taken as a summary statement of what the chapter will record, that is, vv. 3-31 are about God's creating the world as we know it. If the first view is adopted, then we have a reference here to original creation; if the second view is taken, then Genesis itself does not account for the original creation of matter. To follow this view does not deny that the Bible teaches that God created everything out of nothing (cf. John 1:3) – it simply says that Genesis is not making that affirmation. This second view presupposes the existence of pre-existent matter, when God said, "Let there be light." The first view includes the description of the primordial state as part of the events of day one. The following narrative strongly

---

§§§ The King James version has *heaven* instead of *heavens.*

favors the second view, for the "heavens/sky" did not exist prior to the second day of creation (see v. 8) and "earth/dry land" did not exist, at least as we know it, prior to the third day of creation (see v. 10).[****]

Translations that follow the King James and New King James versions are:

1. New American Standard Bible (NASB)
2. American Standard Version (ASV)
3. Amplified Bible (AMP)
4. Darby Translation (DARBY)
5. Douay-Rheims 1899 American Edition (DRA)
6. English Standard Version Anglicized (ESVUK)
7. God's Word Translation (GW)
8. Good News Translation (GNT)
9. Holman Christian Standard Bible (HCSB)
10. New Century Version (NCV)
11. New English Translation (NET)
12. New International Reader's Version (NIRV)
13. New International Version (NIV)
14. New International Version 1984 (NIV1984)
15. New International Version – UK (NIVUK)
16. New Life Version (NLV)
17. New Living Translation (NLT)
18. Today's New International Version (TNIV)
19. Wycliffe Bible (WYC)

The New English Translation while retaining the KJ wording, twists the interpretation in agreement with the Torah.

Versions that follow the Torah translation are the Common

[****] See the NET Bible at: http://bible.org/netbible/. Compare this with the explanatory note in the King James Version: "Beginning. Hebrew: re'shiyth[…] the first, in place, time, order or rank (specifically, a firstfruit):— beginning, chief(-est), first(-fruits, part, time), principal thing." For notes on the King James Version, see: http://www.touchbible.org/index.php

English Bible (CEB), and Young's Literal Translation (YLT).

The Amplified Bible, which is based to a good extent on the American Standard Version (1901), and is therefore a revision of it, in an attempt to "amplify" the text in order to make accessible all the meanings of the original texts, translates, "In the beginning God (prepared, formed, fashioned, and) created the heavens and the earth." This is in direct opposition to the Torah translation, suggesting instead original creation in even more unequivocal terms than the KJ Version. The GNT also renders the first sentence as, "In the beginning God created the universe," making the explanation of the NET version (sn 1) useless. The NLV with its translation, "In the beginning God made from nothing the heavens and the earth," delivers another blow to the interpretation of the NET Bible scholars, who claim that Genesis does not affirm that God created the world from nothing. The same with WYC translating as, "In the beginning God made of nought heaven and earth." There is also a standard and established version, which in the choice of the first two words, is closer to the newly found texts than any of the above-mentioned versions: The Message (MSG), which reads, "First this: God created the Heavens and Earth."

The great number of contradictory translations in existence — and the list provided above is by no means exhaustive — must raise some questions, not to mention the problem of "authoritative scripture," i.e. what criteria were used to decide which scriptures qualified for inclusion into the biblical canon and which did not. The problem one faces in the choice of canonized scripture, however, extends and is even magnified in translation, as can be seen from the many copies all claiming to be the correct version and vying for authority. Just as the interpretations of the scriptures arrogate to themselves plenipotentiary powers that eventually oust the authorial or central agency entirely, so translations as twice removed interpretations, lose sight of their beginnings. Consequently, the NET Bible offers 60,932 translator's notes in a futile attempt to authoritatively lay bare once and for all the meaning of each word, in the process inevitably proliferating a vast number of twisted interpretations and heretic alterations through the now punctured and swollen text. It is our hope to live up to their inspiring example and amplify these heresies.

Ultimately, all translations are alterations, hence betrayals. The Italian expression, *tradurre è tradire*,[††††] illustrates the point perfectly. Gershom Scholem ([1969]1974) provides two examples from rabbinical experience which render even an attempted faithful translation inadmissible. The first is from the second century AD and comes from Rabbi Meir, one of the most important teachers of the Mishnah, who relates, "When I was studying with Rabbi Akiba, I used to put vitriol in the ink and he said nothing. But when I went to Rabbi Ishmael, he asked me: My son, what is your occupation? I answered: I am a scribe [of the Torah]. And he said to me: My son, be careful in your work, for it is the work of God; if you omit a single letter, or write a letter too many, you will destroy the whole world..." (39).[†††††]

The second comes from Nahmanides (1194 – 1270?) who

[††††] Literally, "to translate is to betray." It. *tradúrre* "to translate" contraction of the Lat. *tradúcere*, p.p. *tradúctus* "to make pass" from *trans* "through, other, beyond, outside" + *dúcere* (*condurre*) "to conduct." It. *tradire* "to betray," however, plays a pun on the etymology of the word which derives from the Lat. *trádere* "to give, to consign, to place in someone's hand," from *trans* "through, other, beyond, outside" + *dére* (*dare*) "to give, to consign," whence the second part of the word is taken to mean *díre* "to say," hence, making the meaning "betrayal" correspond to "altered sayings" or "between sayings." (DEO: **tradúrre; tradire**).

[†††††] In this context, it is interesting to bring up the words of William Carlos Williams in book III of his poem "Paterson," who writes, "It is dangerous to leave written that which is badly written. A chance word, upon paper, may destroy the world. Watch carefully and erase, while the power is still yours, I say to myself, for all that is put down, once it escapes, may rot its way into a thousand minds, the corn become a black smut, and all libraries, of necessity, be burned to the ground as a consequence." (New Directions Books, 1992), 129. It is often said of literature that everything that could be said has already been said. Hence, it is not outlandish or unreasonable to demand that all libraries be burned to the ground.

writes that "the entire Torah consists of the names of God," therefore "the Masoretic tradition concerning the writing of the Bible and especially the scrolls of the Torah must be observed with the utmost care. Every single letter counts, and a scroll of the Torah must be rejected for use in the synagogue if there is so much as a single letter too few or too many." (38-9). But even in Nahmanides' time things were no different. The *torah kedumah* (the primordial Torah), has been distorted innumerable times during the course of centuries. It is well known, for instance, that by 500 BC Hebrew became a dead language, and that by the time the Jews were allowed by King Cyrus to return to Palestine, the only men who knew Hebrew were Esdras and Daniel. From this time onwards, the original scriptures underwent a series of revisions and manipulations, from Esdras' revision of the Pentateuch which, after being introduced into the synagogues had to be interpreted by means of the Targums (interpretations), to the Essenes' deliberately misleading Greek translation in which they disguised the secret doctrine of their faith by the use of similes and symbolical imagery. (Gonzalez-Wippler 1977).

Appendix B: Semantic Shifts

The path for the semantic transformation of the Albanian expression *mâ s parit* (Tosk and Stand. Alb. *më së pari*) to something more consistent with "in the beginning" can be shown in the derivation of the word **mû** "exactly, precisely, till, until" from **më** "more," which with a darkening of *ë* gave *u*, whence the expression *më në fund*, literally "more towards the end; closer to the end" gave *mu në fund* "right at the end," (Çabej; **mu, mû**). and thus itself acquired a meaning more consistent with "at the (very) end, the farthest; finally." In the expression *më së fundi*, however, the meaning is more consistent with "beyond the end, over the edge," where as in *më së pari* "before anything, before first" a split can be discerned.§§§§ So, even though we find *mu në fund* to have derived from *më në fund*, the semantics of the newer form has retroactively influenced the older.

In addition, the particle *se, s* in non-interrogative sentences is a negation "not" — making a meaning consistent with "in the beginning" impossible. If *më* means "more," then, *më s parit* means "more than first." If, on the other hand, *më*, *mû* means a position, a locus from which something takes place "exactly, precisely, right at," then, *më s parit* means "where there is no one (no first)."

The formative power of the negation *se, s* can be seen, for example, in such formations as **smundë** "sick, ill, impossible" from *s* "not" + *mund* "able, possible, conquer, vanquish"; **as** "nor, neither, naught," from the particle *a* "or, before, ere" + *s* "not"; and **asgjë**

---

§§§§ Literally *më së* (*se, sesa*) *fundi* "more than the end." *Më në fund*, literally, "more towards the end; closer to the end" can mutate to *mu në fund* "right at the end" — the first expression describes a movement towards some destination without reaching it, the second indicates the destination itself, — but there can be no *mu së fundi* from *më së fundi*, just as there can be no *mu së pari* from *më së pari*. The correct expression in this case would be *mu në fillim* "right at the beginning."

"nothing, none" from *as* "nor, neither, naught" + *gjë* "thing, something."

The meaning of the ancient interrogative pronoun *se* (*me se* "with what" *për se* "what, for what" etc.) which in Albanian with a proclitic deafening of *e* to *ë*, gives *së*, further wrinkled into *s*, transitioned from *se çë* "what" to *asgjë* "nothing" similarly to new Greek, where τίποτε "nothing" derives from τί ποτε "what then." Later, Çabej notes, from *asgjë* "nothing" was arrived at *nuk* "not" where we find another analogy with New Greek where δεν "not" derives from ancient Greek οὐδεν "nothing." (Çabej; **s**).

Appendix C: Sound and Meaning

In his six lectures "On Sound and Meaning" first delivered in 1942 at L'École Libre des hautes études (the Free School of Advanced Studies) in New York, Roman Jakobson reevaluates two of the principles of Saussurian linguistics: 1) the linear character of the signifier, and 2) the arbitrariness of the sign:

> Saussure taught that in the word its 'signified' is not connected by any internal relation to the sequence of phonemes which serve as its 'signifier': It could equally well be represented by any other: this is proved by differences between languages, and by the very existence of different languages: the signified 'ox' has as its signifier b-ö-f (*bœuf*) on one side of the border and o-k-s (*Ochs*) on the other'. Now this theory is in blatant contradiction with the most valuable and the most fertile ideas of Saussurian linguistics. This theory would have us believe that different languages use a variety of signifiers to correspond to one common and unvarying signified, but it was Saussure himself who, in his *Course*, correctly defended the view that the meanings of words themselves vary from one language to another. The scope of the word *bœuf* and that of the word *Ochs* do not coincide; Saussure himself cites 'the difference in value' between the French *mouton* and the English *sheep*. (110-1)

Analyzing Saussure's theory that treated the phoneme as the smallest unit of language which carried no meaning in itself, but was constituted solely of relations, Jakobson argues that this ultimately leads to two paradoxes:

I. That the opposition between phonemes does not conform to the logical rules of opposition that are required for meaning to arise, such as large/small, far/near, black/white, etc. "Opposites," Jakobson says, "are so intimately interconnected that the appearance of one of them inevitably elicits the other." (77). In other words, the term *large* always evokes *small* without which it would have no meaning in itself. However, one can think of a phoneme *o* without at the same time evoking *a*. "There is no necessary connection between these two ideas." (ibid).

2. The second contradiction is that if the relations between phonemes were the primary values, and the phonemes themselves were only secondary and derived, the number of primary values would be larger than the number of derived values.

Jakobson takes as an example the vocalic system of the Turkish language which is composed of eight phonemes:

$$
\begin{array}{cccc}
o & a & ö & e \\
u & y & ü & i \\
\end{array}
$$

Following the mathematical formula for combinations, these eight phonemes produce twenty-eight distinctions. Contrary to Saussure, however, for Jakobson the phoneme is further decomposable into *distinctive features* which, as he says, "removes both contradictions with one stroke." (80). Continuing with the Turkish vocalic system Jakobson demonstrates how the "alleged" twenty-eight vocalic oppositions of Turkish can be reduced to three basic oppositions:

1- Openness and closure, in which the vowels o, a, ö, e are opposed to the vowels u, y, ü, i as open phonemes to closed phonemes.

2- Back and front, in which the vowels o, u, a, y are opposed to the vowels ö, ü, e, i as back phonemes to front phonemes.

3- Roundness and unroundness, in which the vowels o, u, ö, ü are opposed to the vowels a, y, e, i as rounded phonemes to unrounded phonemes. (ibid.)

It is important to recognize that these oppositions, which are limited in any given language, do not have to be the same across different languages. The phoneme *i*, for example, whose phonological content in Turkish is *closed, front, unrounded*, in American English and Russian may only be decomposed into two of these distinctive features; *closed, front* in English, and *closed, unrounded* in Russian.

Similarly, the French consonantal system is made of nasal consonants (ṇ, n, m) as opposed to orals, which in turn are divided between occlusives (k/g; t/d; p/b) and constrictives (š/ž; s/z; f/v). These can be divided further into centrifugals and centripetals, and these latter into dentals and labials. "Furthermore, Jakobson adds, "all the oral consonants of this system exemplify a binary opposition: presence and absence of voice. To the voiced *g* is opposed the unvoiced *k*, to *ž* is opposed *š*, to *d* is opposed *t*, and so on." (91).

The phonemes *d* and *t*, for example, which have much the same distinctive features in Albanian, are oral, occlusive, centripetal, dental. They only differ in that *d* is voiced while *t* is unvoiced. Thus, always keeping in mind that it is not the phoneme that carries some absolute and indestructible meaning, but only insofar as it can acquire these oppositive values to other phonemes, one may proceed to ascertain their function in particular signifiers.

Two somewhat controversial studies into sound symbolism offer some examples into what may be the most conspicuous cases of the signifieds of the phoneme. Margaret Magnus in her book *Gods of the Word* and Franco Rendich in his *Comparative Etymological Dictionary*, provide descriptions of the semantic values of the /v/, /r/, /n/, /t/, and /d/ phonemes that neatly fit our needs for all five of them.

According to Magnus: "Like the other voiced fricatives /v/ is infused with smooth, vibratory energy. [v] drives a process forward." (1051-7). Rendich's view is not too different: "The consonant *v* expressed the notions of 'detachment', 'distinction', 'propagation', "diffusion" or "removal". In Sanskrit, the consonant v also expressed the idea of 'vital energy' vayas, and was the force that had the power to break the two, div… In Latin, it will go on to maintain its semantic value as in the term vis and will grant man 'power': vir, making of him the male procreator: virilis." (23231-42).

Rendich also relates the Indo-European vṛ, **var** "to surround, to cover; to close; to obstruct; to hide; to protect; to envelop; to guard" to the opposite notion of "opening" as in Latin *apertus*:

> The ancient presence of the v is recalled both by the French ou-vri-r and by the Spanish abrir, given that the b is a late labial variant of the v. In the Latin verbs ape(v)rio and ope(v)rio, the dropping of the initial v of the Indo-European root vṛ "to cover" owes to the fact that, due to its dysphonia, the Romans did not utter and, therefore, never transcribed the phoneme vṛ in their language. Thus, it is evident that such verbs derive from apavṛ "to open", "to uncover" and apivṛ "to close" or "to cover", in which apa and api are verb suffixes [sic] with the meaning, respectively, of "away" and "above" (that which covers). (25234-8)

As for the sonorant /r/, Rendich distinguishes two allophones, one of which is a vowel, ṛ [ri], and the other a consonant, r [ra].

> ṛ [ri] to move toward, to reach, to go upward.
> r [ra] to move toward, to arrive, to reach.
> Indo-European uses the vowels i and ṛ to indicate, respectively, the acts of "continuous motion" and "motion toward" (1473-518)

For Magnus, "/r/ is active directed force." In her work, she conducts a test placing phonemes in different positions in the word (first position, second position... end position), and coupling them with different phonemes. In the case of /r/ in second position for example, depending on what phoneme precedes it, it falls under one of three designated categories: *rupture*, *fracture*, and *breaking*. "Rupture" she says, "is also one of the major phonesthemes which becomes apparent when you apply Test I to /r/ in initial position."[°°°°°] (1163, 489-566)

    [°°°°°] See also Margaret Magnus's "Outrageous /r/" at: http://www.trismegistos.com/MagicalLetterPage/.

As for the nasal ṇ [na], according to Rendich, it has a very specific meaning in Indo-European and Sanskrit: water. (96-117). However, /n/ appears to play a major role in negation as both Rendich and Magnus note, though for Rendich this initially becomes an obstacle in his analysis. (88-127).

The phonemes or stop consonants /d/ and /t/ are occlusives, and in the case of *vënd vënt* signify just that, stopping. However, according to Magnus and Rendich there is an important difference between the two that enables us to shed some light on the difference between the verb *vënë* and the verb/noun *vënt* as well as its later development into the noun *vënd* as chronologically envisioned by Çabej.

For Magnus, "/t/ expresses directedness toward an endpoint, generally along a linear track, but without indication as to whether the goal is actually reached." (1030-2). The phonestheme /d/, on the other hand, "occurs more frequently at the end of a word than at the beginning. /d/ is overwhelmingly downward." ⸶⸶⸶⸶ (997-1002). The same is observed in relation to the phonestheme /t/ by Rendich: "t [ta] motion between two points" (1455-88), though, not so for /d/ which he, similarly to Jakobson, associates with light.

The difference between *vënt* and *vënd*, then, seems to be found in their respective relation to motion and rest: *vënë* is a transitive verb—it only speaks of the object inserted or placed somewhere; *vënt* is ditransitive, it indicates both the object that is inserted and the one it is inserted into, therefore its location. Compare with *ta (ja) vura, vuna*, in which *ta* becomes suffixed to *vura/ vuna* resulting in *vërt/ vënt* (more on *vërt* on 3.2). It is out of this ditransitive verb that the noun *vënd* arises which, of course, designates only the location, the passive object which is pierced or transfixed.

⸶⸶⸶⸶ Note, however, that Magnus does not claim her conclusions to hold true between languages, and that her observations are limited to English, though, at least in this specific case they seem to hold perfectly in Albanian.

Appendix D: Semiotic Dams

Lacan's formula, the unconscious is structured like a language, depends not only on Saussure's first principle on the arbitrariness of the sign, but also on his second principle which asserts the linear character of the signifier: "The linguistic signal, being auditory in nature, has a temporal aspect, and hence certain temporal characteristics: (a) *it occupies a certain temporal* space, and (b) *this space is measured in just one dimension:* it is a line." (1666-8). This is because, according to Saussure, two phonemes or words cannot be uttered simultaneously: "Words as used in discourse, strung together one after another, enter into relations based on the linear character of languages. Linearity precludes the possibility of uttering two words simultaneously." (2647-8). This is the axis of succession. "Along this axis one may consider only one thing at a time... Combinations based on sequentiality may be called *syntagmas*." (1847-9). But "outside the context of discourse, words having something in common are associated together in memory. In this way they form groups, the members of which may be related in various ways. For instance, the word enseignement ('teaching') will automatically evoke a host of other words: enseigner ('to teach'), renseigner ('to inform'), etc. [...] This kind of connexion between words is of quite a different order. It is not based on a linear sequence. It is a connexion in the brain... We shall call them *associative relations*." (2653-9). In contradistinction from syntagmas which are ordered on the axis of succession, associative relations are arranged along the axis of simultaneity. "This axis concerns relations between things which coexist, relations from which the passage of time is entirely excluded." (1846-7).

"Syntagmatic relations," Saussure tells us, "hold in *praesentia*. They hold between two or more terms co-present in a sequence. Associative relations, on the contrary, hold in *absentia*. They hold between terms constituting a mnemonic group." (2659-61).

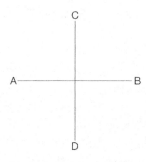

As Jakobson points out, however, though it may not be possible to emit two phonemes simultaneously, "it is perfectly possible to emit several *distinctive features* at the same time. Not only is this possible, it is what is normally done, since *phonemes are complex entities*." (99). Moreover, what we see in the topological constructions of *vënd*, shows, that a rotation of the axes of syntagmatic and associative relations, may, in fact, be possible, as touched upon in the alternation between linguistic suppression, psychological repression, and social oppression. What this implies is that psychological repression, although related to the subject of linguistic suppression, is not exactly the same. For, even though it may coexist with it, it may also, and has even more reason to exist, where linguistic suppression has not occurred. Hence, in a possible social rotation of the axes, whereas a buried meaning may be exhumed, this meaning will immediately be vested with its psychological opposite, such as for example, when an assertive or dominating female is said to be the one who wears the trousers. The unconscious, therefore, depends on all three pressures and not merely on language, and corresponds more to the rings of the Borromean knots, the Real, the Symbolic, and the Imaginary. Undo one, they all come undone.

What Lacan's formula cryptically states, then, is that the unconscious is not only what remains repressed but also potential in language—the current or the flow that rotates the turbines putting in motion the engine of the system. It is here that one can discern how "the re-turn of the repressed" is interpreted in accordance with the needs of the system, actualizing its potential through its rotation or kinesis. This outline clarifies Freud's technical question of how the ego represses the id if it draws all its force from it in the first place; in a way, the ego is merely the reinterpretation of the flow, the variety of different channels and sluices, valves and turncocks, gears and cogwheels carefully fitted together to control and economize the flow of the unconscious. It is the Minotaur's maze. Lacanian psychoanalysis, therefore, with its notion of *le sinthome* (Σ) functioning as a suture to the Borromean knots, or "tying together a knot which constantly threatens to come undone" (Evans 2006, 192), reveals itself as the maintenance department of a system that without this constant suturing would have collapsed long ago, letting the Minotaur loose to wreak havoc in the world.

This potentiality of language, is nowhere better depicted than in the semiotic bar which, Lacan tells us, is a barrier that resists signification (2006, 415), and is made into the very grounding that by separating the orders of signified and signifier, is converted into the axis on which the wheel of the system rotates,#### the prosthetic leg attached to the mundified stump, or the puttee that covers the wound to conceal the fact of the impossibility to ever putting a distance between the body and its lesion, the healthy part and the localized rot. The higher the successive succisions in order to remove the sphacelated tissue, the deeper and greater the advancement of the rot crawling ever closer as a violent *absent presence* (the phantom limb, the snatched away, the missing, what should have been there but is not), itself pointing to a *present absence* to which one has to continually sacrifice extremities and appendages (civilization's apotemnophilic jouissance), the unconscious chain of signifiers S1-S2-S3-S4... in reverse, $\lim_{S \to \infty} f(S) = 0$, where $f(S) = \dfrac{n}{S}$ where *n* is any nonzero number.

"To pinpoint the emergence of the discipline of linguistics, I will say that, as in the case of every science in the modern sense, it consists in the constitutive moment of an algorithm that grounds it. This algorithm is the following: $\frac{S}{s}$." (Lacan 2006, 414).

However, this bar which resists signification at the heart of the sign, throws the psychoanalytic or social equation off balance – while Lacan's schemas, generally, are balanced and equal zero, the sign separated by the bar can never be brought to a permanent balance, since signified and signifier can never exactly correspond.

This is because the Saussurean algorithm $\frac{S}{s}$, signifies on both sides of the bar not merely from top to bottom, as Lacan claims. While in any specific instance it may refer to any positive signified, on the whole, it signifies *present absence*; $f(S) \rightarrow 0$, wherein the bar as that which through violence makes communication possible, and through language prevents it from ever fully taking place, becomes a tectonic transformative site of relentless corrosion and messy annihilation. Consequently, the Lacanian subject that fleetingly appears above the bar when the signifier crosses it to become a signified, is always a mute and mutilated subject, "the victim burnt at the stake, signaling through the flames (Artaud 1958, 7) for in its abyssal depths the sign is always already absolute wound.

This gratuitous affliction, however, is immediately offered an excuse under the framework of psychoanalysis. The person who dreams of her father's funeral, we are told, and is filled with grief, is censoring from herself the fact that she wished for her father's death, and the grief really ought to have been pleasure were it not for defense mechanisms that will not allow such feelings to be consciously expressed, since then they would cause more anxiety than pleasure. The secret to this circular reasoning (I feel pain in order to conceal from myself the fact that I really feel pleasure, so that I will not feel pain), Freud is hard-pressed to admit, rests solely upon the seemingly infallible calculation on the part of the dreamer as to which of these anxieties is greater, and opting for the lesser. Flee the pleasure which creates displeasure, as Solon, the famous Athenian stateman said. Affliction is thus twice censored by psychoanalytic theory: the first time, when it must be avoided and denied at all costs, and the second time, when an excuse is needed for it, i.e. when gratuitous affliction is prohibited. To feel grief without some explanation, that is more unbearable than any calamity that could strike from above. The first universal axiom of every civilization is: there can be no suffering without a positive cause. The *acedic* who suffers without a cause is therefore, quite simply, not only insane, but incalculably dangerous and unaffordable. Psychoanalytic theory is therefore in close agreement with the Church Fathers, who defined the mortal sin of *acedia* as a sorrow or fear without a cause. Nor will the psychoanalyst admit that such a thing is even possible at all. In fact, neither will the insane, who will always devise some excuse for their affliction. Psychoanalysis is there to help them make it stick. "War against the plague," as Antonin Artaud says.

Political and juridical theories, too, and their evolutionary path toward political order, social peace, aesthetic harmony, theological oneness, etc. etc., despite their ceaseless articulations of the revolutions that shall bring about the new world order, must always steer clear of the dark energy fields and the shadows that lie beyond the supposedly holistic knots of the Real, the Symbolic, and the Imaginary.

Notes

1.1 THE DISEASE OF THE VOID

1. *Tanakh: A New Translation of the Holy Scriptures According to the Traditional Hebrew Text: Torah; Nevi'im; Kethuvim* (The Jewish Publication Society 1985), xxvi.

2. The two major dialects of Albanian are Gheg, roughly north of the Shkumbin river, and Tosk, south of it. The Standard Albanian is mainly based on the Tosk dialect while the present texts use the Gheg.

3. In fact, this is exactly what we find in the Albanian translation of the established version of the Bible; "Në fillim Perëndia krijoi qiejt dhe tokën." *Bibla: Dhjata e Vjetër dhe Dhjata e Re, Diodati i Ri,* Translation of 1991-94" based on the Textus Receptus.

4. New data on the fine-structure constant indicate that the laws may indeed change. See for example: John Webb, "Are the Laws of Nature Changing with Time?" Physics World, 2003, 33. However, the plane of science as a whole is still inclined toward the point of the origin (and consequently to that of the end), because calcified belief in eternal immutable laws is consistent with belief in a primal or first cause. Smolin (1997) expounds on this issue as regards scientific atomism when compared to its ancient counterpart, philosophical atomism: "According to the Greek philosophers, the elementary particles are eternal, never created or destroyed... Modern elementary particle physics does allow the elementary particles to be created and destroyed. But their properties are determined by laws, which endow each particle, when created, with certain properties, completely independent of whatever else may exist in the universe. These laws are presumed to be absolute and to hold for all time. Thus, the idea of the absolute plays an essential role for us, as it did for the Greeks. It has just been abstracted, from eternal atoms to eternal laws. That the laws of physics might be created or modified seems to us as nonsensical as it would have seemed to Democritus to build a machine that creates elementary particles. The idea that there is an absolute law of nature, which fixes once and for all the properties of the elementary particles, has been so successful it is difficult to imagine a scientific approach to understanding nature that does not begin there." (31-2).

5. Father N. "The Forgotten Science: The Disease of the Void," Notebook IX-C., ("Shkenca e Harrume: Smundë e Hiqit," Fletore IX-C).

6. Reza Negarestani in his "Globe of Revolution," lays the groundwork for a terri-topic model of trauma, building on the work of Sandor Ferenczi and his notion of Ururtrauma. An important notion, and perhaps the most important one, is that trauma is always plural, nested, never singular. At least three versions of this paper exist, one of them entitled "On the Revolutionary Earth: A Dialectic in Territopic Materialism". A free copy may be obtained at the Urbanomic blog: http://blog.urbanomic.com.

7. This is Nietzsche's argument in note 1066 of *The Will to Power*, "If the world could in any way become rigid, dry, dead, nothing, or if it could reach a state of equilib-rium, or if it had any kind of goal that involved duration, immutability, the once-and-for-all (in short, speaking metaphysically: if becoming could resolve itself into being or into nothingness), then this state must have been reached." ([1968]2011, 542-3). For an exposition of this view in physics, see, Errors in the Steady State and Quasi-SS Models by Edward L. Wright at: http://www.astro.ucla.edu/~wright/stdystat.htm. Cf. Anaxi-mander's notion of perpetual beginning (*apeiron*).

1.2. GUT THEORIES: THE BIG CREEP

1. This is what Bhaskaracharya says in *Lilavati*, the first part of his *Siddhantasirom-ani*, as an explanation for his conclusion that when a finite number is divided by zero, the result is infinity, which obviously would make every number equal: "any (non-zero) num-ber divided by zero is *khahara*, i.e. infinite." ([2001] 2015, 47). This is because "there is no change in infinite (*khahara*) figure if some thing is added to or subtracted from the same. It is like: there is no change in infinite Visnu (Almighty) due to dissolution or creation of abounding living beings." (48-9).

Same with Aleister Crowley who in *The Book of the Law*, says, "Every number is infinite; there is no difference." (1:4); http://www.spiritual.com.au/articles/crow-ley/the-book-of-the-law-aleister-crowley.html. Accessed on 10/03/2011.

2. From the context of the sentence, the word is more consistent with *çel* "to open" (or to spring, to bud; to light a fire). However, Demiraj in relation to the Indo-

European root *kehl only mentions kall; 'to stick (on, into) put (up)'; 'thrust'; 'insti-gate'. Other Albanian forms: kalloj, 'to kindle'. See Albanische Etymologien (Unter-suchungen zum albanischen Erbwortschatz), Bardhyl Demiraj, Leiden Studies in Indo-European 7; Amsterdam - Atlanta (1997) at:

http://www.win.tue.nl/~aeb/natlang/ie/alb.html. Same in Çabej, kall, këllás "fut; fut në dhe; shtyj një njeri për keq; ndez" (insert; put into the ground; instigate; kindle, fire up, ignite). SE V; **kall**.

3. Considering that kall(oj) also means "to kindle" and datë "date" derives from the PIE root *do, "to give, to offer," it may also indicate a Promethean gift or a sacrifice. This gift is the horrific gift of time: kall datën "to fill with fear," but literally, "to insert the date," i.e. to mark with an expiration date.

4. "Beginnings of Language: Etymology of the words in the Bible," (Zanafilla e Guhës: Etimillogii e Fjalvet t'Biblës) Marrash Journal (2005).

2.1. TERRA FIRMA

1. Eqrem Çabej does not see a common root between these words. Gustav Meyer who first brings varr, vorr "grave" close to vërë, vrimë, birë "hole, aperture, bore," later retracts this view and believes the word to derive from an Indo-European root *wer- "to wind, welter, mew, cover, shield." The base is thought to be an *or-n. The first view is found in FE; **birë**. The second in Albanesische Studien V, quoted by Çabej in SE VII; **varr vorr**. Çabej finds the root closer to Gr. ὀρύσσω, ὀρύττω, ὀρύχω "dig, burrow" ὄρυγμα "hole (in the ground), concave". Vladimir Orel in his Albanian Etymological Dictionary, goes back to the base *or-n and considers it a borrowing from a reconstructed Late Roman *orna, Latin urna "cinerary, urn".

2. These comprise different dialectal variations of the word. Çabej expects the older form to appear with the suffix -nt, but concedes that the proposed related toponyms with suffix -nd in the Balkan Peninsula of antiquity, remain convincing (e.g. Vendum of the Iapodes in Illyria, present day Croatia, and Οὐένδενίς [Ovéndenís] in Dardania), while preferring Pokorny's Celt comparisons in England (e.g. Venta Icenorum in Norfolk, Venta Belgarum in Hampshire, and Venta Silerum today Caer Went) attesting to the

Illyrian elements in Celtic languages (*SE* VII; **vend vënd**).

3. Cf. *AED* that traces *vë* ~ *vê* to some nonexistent Proto-Albanian verb **awena*, and its original meaning is "to put down", "to put inside", just as in Lat *pōnere* "to put". Lat *pōnere*, however, represents a variation of *(me) vënë* where *v* and *p* may vary according to Grimm's law of bilabials, small wonder the meaning is the same.

4. *Vulë* (n.), *vulos* (v.) "seal, to seal" from N. Gr. βοῦλλα, βουλλώνω (*FE*; **vulë**). As Tectumor (2014) writes, "[*Vulë*] is one of those lucky borrowings [which] had it not entered Albanian from the Greek, would have had to be invented to fill the lexical gap." (33). *Vulë* may well be borrowed from N. Gr. βοῦλλα, yet, it is also in line with Eng *weal, welt* alteration of *wale* "usually large bump or red area that appears on the skin because of injury or illness" that it is used in Albanian as in the expression *vula-vula* "black and blue."

2.2. WATER CHANNELS

1. *SE* VII; **vajzë**. This euphemistic naming is not an isolated practice, nor is it characteristic of Albanian only, nor in fact, a courtesy extended only to the female. See for example Alb. *feçkë* "small girl, daughter; vulva, cunnus, pudendum muliebre" that also takes its name from the female genitals; or late Lat. *fissa* "cunnus" basically from "fissure; crevice; chap" that in the southern dialects of Italy (e.g. Naples, Abruzzo) gives *fesse* "the female genital organ"; or Alb. *loçkë* "small boy" diminutive of *loqe* "testicles." (*SE* IV; **feçkë** and *SE* V; **loçkë**). In the same way that Alb. *vënë* "placed" is related to *vërë* "hole" and *varrë* "wound, fissure, crevice" from which *vajzë* "girl; maid; virgin" is derived, so too, late Lat. *fissa* "fissure, crevice, chap" is related to It. *fissare* "to fix" from Lat. *fixus* p.p. of *figere*, from which in turn derives *ficcare* "to poke, to transfix," according to DEO from an intensive form *figicàre, fixicàre*. See DEO; **figgere; fissare; ficcare**.

2. Europa's etymological understanding has always been along the lines of "broad-faced" from *eurys* "wide" from the PIE root **were-*(I) "wide, broad" + *ops* "face," literally "eye." Following the present analysis, however, it is more likely that the reconstructed PIE root **were-* is related to *varrë* "wound; split, tearing" also "broad stripe" by way of *vërë* "hole; opening," which is to say, "a widening hole; a tearing." The second

part of the name, then, is either derived from *ops* "eye" as OED explains, meaning the "eye or opening of the wound" or directly from PIE **upo*, Eng *open*, Alb *hap* (see *open* [adj.] at OED) in which case the meaning "opening wound" remains the same.

3. *Enantio-amelic*, in the sense of *limbless mirror-images*, so that if the left limb is lacking in one of the images, this is reflected in the mirror image as lacking the right limb. In the equation form $\frac{\text{vënd}}{\text{vërë}} \cong \frac{\text{world}}{\text{wound}}$ it is clear that we are looking at a body that is lacking a left arm and a right leg mirrored in the corresponding image as missing the right arm and left leg. But this is not all. The above equation form indicates not merely a butchery of body parts, but also the unsettling possibility of confusedly assembling the parts back together into monstrous forms.

4. Technically, it is an axiom. But Saussure expresses it as a self-evident truth that cannot be contradicted: "No one disputes the fact that linguistic signs are arbitrary" (1607-25). No one, that is, but Saussure, who it is no secret, explored the possibilities of phonic poetics, or sound meaning in poetry, later to be picked up and developed by Roman Jakobson in his own study on sound structure and the distinction between poetic and nonpoetic sequences. For a lucid account of Saussure's disreputable research into "anagrams" and Jakobson's subsequent revision, see Heller-Roazen (2013), chapters 9 and 10, 109-51.

5. Freud's notion of "penis envy" is one of the most prominent implications of this forced amputee position. This example makes clear that Noam Chomsky's (1970) differentiation in Saussurean fashion of a semantic component as *deep structure* from a phonological component as *surface structure*, cannot obtain. Although Chomsky speaks of larger grammatical units, what the present analysis illustrates is that the decomposition of language (as observed in the *virga/virgo* nucleus breakdown, i.e. the succision of the semantic component resulting in two opposite terms out of the same root [the oppositional couplet *virga/virgo*], followed by the dearticulation of the phonestheme, i.e. the further dislocation between phonology and semantics *vënd/vërë – world/wound*), which results in ever more specialized terminology, also brings about the abrogation of inner and outer boundaries, and hence of any permanent structures based on deep/surface meanings. In other words, the more specialized a term, the more its inner meaning is bled out.

2.3. THE STAIRCASE OF HEAVEN

1. *Vise* and *vêse* is the old form (the latter from the North Highlands, e.g. Malsia e Madhe and it is used that way in the Code of Lek Dukagjini), a view supported also by the fact that there is no singular **vis*. See *SE* VII; **vise**, and *Hyrje në Indoeuropianistikë* (2008, 150-1).

2. See: http://www.dianaalhadid.com/work/sculptures. Another equally compelling work by al-Hadid is entitled "Phantom Limb" and can be found at the same site.

3. http://5dal.com/2015/01/28/broken-staircase-2/

4. http://www.esv.org/

5. The explanation of "water" in Hosea of the Touch Bible's KJV is worth mentioning: "מַיִם – **mayim** dual of a primitive noun (but used in a singular sense); water; figuratively, juice; by euphemism, urine, semen:—piss, wasting, water(-ing, (-course, -flood, -spring)). 1. water, waters: a. water; b. water of the feet, urine; c. of danger, violence, transitory things."

2.4. CAPSULA MUNDI

1. http://www.capsulamundi.it/progetto_eng.html

2. http://5dal.com/2015/03/08/burial-pods/

3. In the latter, the intensive *rr* denoting the fact that *varrë* is a tearing of *vërë*.

4. **Wen** (n.) O.E. *wenn* "a wen, tumor, wart" from Proto-Germanic **wanja-* 'a swelling' (cf. Alb. *ënj* "swelling") from PIE **wen-*(2) 'to beat, wound'" (OED). The corresponding meaning in Albanian to the reconstructed PIE **wen-(2)* "to beat, wound" is still discernible in the adjective *vendçe, vëndçe,* or *vençe, vënçe* with Turkish suffix -*çe* "according to the customs of the place" as used in the so far cryptic expression *e rrahur vënçe* "a vigorous beating" where *vënd* still preserves its primary meaning of vigorous, virile. In short, the wound and its swelling, are brought together in such images as *wen* and *womb*. This coupling can be envisioned more accurately as strike → wound; insertion (insemination) → womb; but since *vë, vê, vû* (adj. *vënçe*) mean both strike and insertion, the images *wound* and *womb* collide. Other images in which this enantiosis occurs are *mound* and *tomb*.

3.1. TERRA NULLIUS/TABULA RASA

1. Two examples from the use of virginity symbols deserve mention: 1) The custom of the Africans of Mauritania to display the newlyweds' bed sheets outside of their home the day after the marriage is consummated to show the blood spot, proof of the maid's virginity (intact hymen), simultaneously demonstrating the man's virility while dispelling any doubts as to her honor which, in a more legal sense, is meant as proof that the male child born of the union is the legitimate heir of the father's estate. 2) In Deuteronomy 22:15-17 the tokens of a maid's virginity are to remain with her parents who in case of disputes between her and her husband will provide them as proof at the city's gates. Interestingly, in her *Greek Virginity*, Giulia Sissa shows that in Ancient Greece even though we find the hymeneal wedding song (*hymenaios*), the existence of the hymen does not seem to have played a role and virginity was conceptualized more in the sense of an opening like the mouth and lips which could be closed again, viz., it seems to have been renewable to some extent.

2. A note by Captain W.J.L. Wharton explains, "Nevertheless the natives do get out to the islands which lie farther from the shore than these reefs, as Cook himself afterwards found."

3. "The real issues, (the High Court) declared, were these: did the community of Murray Island have a system of land ownership which predated white conquest, and if so, was that system still valid?" See: http://www.nfsa.gov.au/digitallearning/mabo/info/doctrineOfTn.htm.

4. The full separate opinion of vice-president Ammoun can be found at the International Court of Justice webpage: http://www.icj-cij.org

3.2. THE CIVILIZATIONAL RNA STRAND

1. Michelet (1861, 247). The Albanian Bektashi poet Naim Frashëri, goes even further in saying, "Man [the human] has an ability in himself, he has been created to be king of the universe!" (1895, 122).

2. In this it is no different than the notion of "floating territory" or "swimming land," according to which vessels are said to fall under the jurisdiction of a single state, and which for maritime humans, as Schmitt remarks, "are entirely false references sprung

from the imaginations of land rats." (2015, 79) Schmitt distinguishes between autoch-
thonal or land-born peoples and autothalassic, i.e. "peoples purely defined by the sea,
who have never been land-dwellers." (8). "The jurists," Heller-Roazen expounds, "may
conceive of such a thing as 'mobile land' only because they have already presupposed a
purely abstract and formal being: a principle of 'territoriality' that may, when necessary,
be detached from any geographical segment of the surface of the earth." (2009, 127).
This fundamental rule to the law, is itself what establishes the fiction of the law (*fictio
legis*); "that device by which, for the purposes of reaching a judgment in court, 'the false'
may be accepted as 'the truth' (*falistas pro veritas accepta*)." (Baldus qtd. in ibid.).

3. It may be worth recalling that matrilineal societies generally prefer the opposite
fiction, in which it is the ultimogeniture who has the legal advantage.

4. Multiple and perhaps infinite etymons are possible simultaneously, in fact, etymons are never found isolated. The more etymons are brought to the fore the more the
truth is bled out. As a result, words tend to explode with an unbound meaning (cf. God's
Aleph on Mt. Sinai) after which meaning is lost altogether. Depth is replaced by width,
the vertical with the horizontal (cf. the 90° rotation of Sumerian cuneiform characters).
These spatial shifts and reconfigurations free all sorts of monstrous or menstrual abominations that thrived and fomented in the dark folds of the symbolic.

5. There are a number of passages where the Captain sometimes enthusiastically,
sometimes coolly mentions their nakedness. One particularly interesting quote deserves
mention for the peculiar thought expressed in it: "We could very clearly see with our
Glasses that the Woman was as naked as ever she was born; even those parts which I
always before now thought Nature would have taught a woman to Conceal were uncov-
ered." (6375-8).

6. Cf. the above quotation by Moynihan J. on the prestige related to gardening
prowess among the aborigines.

7. Literally, "the stone is heavy in its own place," meaning that man carries weight
in his own land.

3.3. THE BARBARIAN'S PROMISE

1. In analyzing Montesquieu's somewhat ambiguous position, McFarlane explains,

"Montesquieu is not normally viewed as a barbarist. As Singer points out, while Montesquieu cannot side with the Romanists, he equally 'cannot really be considered a German-
ist'. The reason for Montesquieu's neither/nor position is that he defends both
aristocratic freedoms, but also the elevation of the monarch over the aristocracy. However,
… it seems more correct to call him a barbarist than anything else – he is certainly not a
liberal nor a republican and aren't barbarians the pinnacle of violent hybridity?" (7).

2. One may observe, for instance, the paradoxical proceedings of the International
Court of Justice and the High Court of Australia, which, while openly condemning the
modern concept as defined by Pasquale Fiore, "which regards as terrae nullius territories
inhabited by populations … whose political organization is not conceived according to
Western norms," still demand to know if the natives or aboriginals had a system of ownership in place prior to white conquest. Such system of ownership, it goes without saying,
must display all the recognizable signs deemed appropriate by the Western norms it does
not have to follow. It is clearly not enough that one live there, i.e. inhabit the place. The
somewhat sinuous path, "less precise but more communal" in the vernacular of Karen
Knop, that Judge Ammoun used in his rejection of the terra nullius doctrine as practiced
by European powers since the time of the Roman Empire, testifies to this. Judge Ammoun
sought to find European precedents (or at least parallels), to Bayona-Ba-Meya's conceptualization, i.e. he "did not simply adopt Bayona-Ba-Meya's argument that *terra nullius*
must take its meaning for Africa from Africa." (Knop 2002, 127-8). And they were found
in the similarity between the notion of the human being and nature in African thought to
the Greek philosophy of Zeno of Sidon and his Stoic school, as well as in the reminiscence
of Bayona-Ba-Meya's views to African Bantu spirituality which, according to Father
Placide Tempel's *Philosophie bontue*, is analogous to Catholicism. "By presenting Bayona-Ba-Meya's account of the African spiritual tie to the land, Greek Stoicism, African
Bantu beliefs and Catholicism as fundamentally similar, Judge Ammoun predisposed us
to believe that a notion of *terra nullius* common to them might be found. The definition
he then proposed was that of Emmerich de Vattel, who restricted the notion of *terra
nullius* to land empty of inhabitants. Traceable earlier to Francisco de Vitoria, this definition belonged to the Western international legal tradition." (ibid.).

Similarly to the statement by Judge Ammoun of Vattel's definition of terra nullius,

Knop's statement that "this definition" could be traced earlier to Francisco de Vitoria is equally misleading. Writing of the Spanish conquest of Central and South America, for example, after some truly inspiring theo-juridical acrobatics to justify war waged by the Christians, de Vitoria concludes that the conquest was right (*bellum iustum*) on the grounds that Native Americans had unlawfully attempted to exclude the Spanish traders from their lands, and this was, of course, contrary to natural law. (Vitoria 1991, 231).

3. "Toka i takon atij që e punon" in the rhyme of the Albanian Labor Party, or according to a more recent statement by Bisheswar Prasad Koirala, the first elected Prime Minister of Nepal, "air, water, Sunshine, and Land belong to those who consume them. It is the tillers alone that must own the land." (Baral 2000, 100).

4. For Pythagoras's remainder (leimma) see Heller-Roazen (2011, 36).

5. For a historical discussion of the total enemy, see Thorup (2015).

6. The full note reads, "Overall view of the future European: the most intelligent slave animals, very industrious, fundamentally very modest, inquisitive to excess, multifarious, pampered, weak of will—a cosmopolitan chaos of affects and intelligence. How could a stronger species raise itself out of him? ... To fight upward out of that chaos to this form—requires a compulsion: one must be faced with the choice of perishing or prevailing. A dominating race can grow up only out of terrible and violent beginnings." After which follows the question and answer quoted in Hardt and Negri.

7. An Afterglow of the Mediatic: The Black Stack. With Benjamin H. Bratton & Metahaven. Transmediale/Festival. Auditorium Fri. 31 Jan, 2014.

8. (*immensa societate humani generis*). The translation is Heller-Roazen's. For Daniel's own question of the inclusion or exclusion of the pirate from the circles of obligation, and especially the "commandment to leave the domain of duty" to whoever comes into contact with the pirate, see *Enemy of All*, (2009, 20-1).

9. Marx's superb tactic has not escaped Foucault, who in his Lectures of '75-76, points out that in a letter written in 1882 Marx told Engels, "You know very well where we found our idea of class struggle; we found it in the work of the French historians who talked about the race struggle." (2003, 79). Which, of course, explains also where the Nazis found theirs.

4.1. FIVE PRINCIPLES

1. As Pythagoras and the ancients sought harmony in the properties of sound and arithmetic, Marx sought it in the field of politics; an ordered world that admits no in-commensurabilities. As Žižek remarks: "There is more than a historical accident in the fact that, in matters of culture, Leninists admired great classical art" (2006, 4). For a discussion of Pythagoras's incommensurabilities see, Heller-Roazen (2011). "The Pythagoreans," he writes, "were no strangers to the uncountable. Although they barred numberless relations from the domain of their arithmetic, they also named them in no uncertain terms. They called them unspeakable (ἄρρητοι), irrational (ἄλογοι), and "incommensurable" (ἀσύμμετροι). From such appellations, one might infer close acquaintanceship." (40). Apart from the obvious differences in principles 1 and 3, the distinction between the one who revolts against class misplacement and economic unfairness and the barbarian, becomes particularly clear in their relation to principle 2. While the barbarian is neither a contemporary nor an anachronistic figure, the world revolutionary on his road to sovereignty, is both.

2. Whether or not the myth of Heracles was put together into a more or less coherent whole before or after the Homeric epic is beyond the point. The events it narrates supposedly took place before, and in any case, by the time of the Homeric Trojan War, Heracles had already sacked Troy once before during the reign of Laomedon, Priam's father, and in that case it is Laomedon who goes back on his word. That the figure of the hero underwent extensive revisions, especially in the Classical period, but also in the Archaic and to a lesser extent in the Geometric period, is beyond doubt, and many of his battles became re-inscribed multiple times to fit the narratives of each particular era. It is precisely these reinterpretations that we are concerned with here, which in retrospect reach further into the past than the time of the Trojan War. In other words, once established, the historical beginnings of treachery and deception are pushed further into myth.

3. See the Indo-European Lexicon: Pokorny's Master PIE Etyma at the Linguistics Research Center at The University of Texas at Austin:

http://www.utexas.edu/cola/centers/lrc/ielex/PokornyMaster-R.html#P0171

4. See, for example, Heracles's own catalogue of triumphs in Seneca, *Hercules in Oeta*, 14-29.

5. This is so not only as regards a particular type of consciousness, as we shall see below, but also in the context of juridical theories. "The great adversary of this type," Foucault says, "is nature ... natural man, or the savage. 'Savage' is to be understood in two senses. The savage—noble or otherwise—is the natural man whom the jurists or theorists of right dreamed up, the natural man who existed before society existed, who existed in order to constitute society, and who was the element around which the social body could be constituted. [...] The other aspect of the savage, [is] that other natural man or ideal element dreamed up by economists: a man without a past or a history, who is motivated only by self interest and who exchanges the product of his labor for another product ... both the savage who emerges from the forests to enter into a contract and to found society, and the savage *Homo economicus* whose life is devoted to exchange and barter." (2003, 194).

4.2. THE APOTHEOSIS OF HERACLES

1. For a representation in archaic art of the young Heracles brought to Chiron by Hermes, similarly to the way Achilles is brought to him by his father, Peleus, see Baur (1912): no. 243. For Achilles, see nos. 242, 244-8, 250-4.

2. Chiron's depictions in art often allow us to differentiate him from the other Centaurs—he is generally draped, and carrying game such as a doe, a hare, and a fox, at other times a deer, sometimes accompanied by his dog, more rarely in the presence of his wife, Chariclo, and often but not always represented with human forelegs and horse's hindquarters. Over time some of these distinguishing features become a set iconographic formula. For example, in later times the full human body with the horse's body joined at the small of his back are only reserved for the venerable master, while the other Centaurs are more often depicted with all four horse's legs, pointing to their more animalistic nature. Pholus's iconography also takes over the branch holding game from him. These images reinforce those literary versions or interpretations of the myth according to which Chiron is unrelated to the other Centaurs, which in turn feed back into the visual arts. The other two civilized beasts, Pholus and Nessus, also appear draped in the geometric and archaic periods (Pholus more often so than Nessus).

3. An opportunity the hero does not make good use of, for according to Callimachus

he remains a glutton. (*Hymn* 3.160). Although it takes time for Heracles to lose his appetite, his apotheosis clearly constitutes a turn in the way the immortals are conceived. Their victory over the giants, titans, and all chthonic monsters is also the beginning of their fading away into the realm of the abstract.

4. For two non-traditional depictions in the archaic period of Nessus and Deianeira, in both of which she seems to be willingly riding away with the Centaur, see Baur (1912), nos. 78, 79. "She shows no resistance whatsoever," Baur points out. He attempts to explain away the odd scene arguing that she must have "become reconciled to her fate, because of her utter helplessness," which is strange considering that Heracles must have been close at their heels, even though the fragment depicting the hero in the red figure kylix is lost along with parts of Nessus's tail and hind legs. Had there been no inscriptions of their names on the kylix, Baur says, it would have been easy to identify them as simply Centaur and nymph.

5. The nom de guerre "manslayer" or "destroyer of men," from *de-* "to reverse, undo" + *anēr* "man, husband," might also be taken to mean "destroyer of mankind."

6. The fact that the ointment Deianeira applies to Heracles's tunic is not merely the toxic blood of the Hydra, but as Diodorus points out, a mixture of blood and semen, reveals that it was precisely a rite concerned with death and regeneration. This recalls Athene's all-heal medicine, the mistletoe (*ixias*), a name which Graves points out is closely connected to Ixion. "In Eastern Europe the mistletoe is a parasite of the oak, and 'Aesculapius,' the Latin form of Asclepius—apparently meaning 'that which hangs from the esculent oak,' i.e. the mistletoe ... was regarded as the oak-tree's genitals, and when the Druids ritually lopped it with a golden sickle, they were performing a symbolic emasculation. The viscous juice of its berries passed for oak-sperm, a liquid of great regenerative virtue" (2012, 145). The secret society of the Russian Skoptsy (скопцы), which has always mystified the authorities with the horrid mutilation of its members, continuing to exert a good deal of influence over a wide area even as far as the Balkans, draws its power directly from the Great Mysteries. Their leader is considered to be a god, who makes his appearance every time under a new form, using a different human body.

7. Dionysus and Ares were the most important deities of the Amazons.

8. The meleagrides are difficult to sex, Athenaeus quotes from Aristotle's student,

Clytus of Miletus, the females resembling closely the males (655e). Nevertheless, the sex of the meleagrides does not concern us. Only the fact that to be worshipped as Artemis, especially in their human manifestation, the meleagrides cannot be male. The explanation that Meleager's sister were transformed into guinea-hens (*meleagrides*) because they would not stop crying for their dead brother is merely an example of reverse etymology that derives the name of the bird from the name of the individual, when in fact, the opposite should be true.

9. A relief-pithos found in Boeotia depicting Perseus killing Medusa represented as a Centauress, of the second quarter of the seventh century BC, is now displayed at the Musée du Louvre, Paris. See also, Baur (1912), nos. 12, 240, and 274. For terracotta statuettes of Centaurs as Medusa types, see no. 207. The fact that in the early geometrical period, the Centaurs were used to decorate the head of the dead – in Italy they are occasionally connected with the lower world as guardians of the tombs, a tradition preserved by Dante in his *Divine Comedy* where the Centaurs are found in the Seventh Circle of Hell patrolling Phlegethon, the river of boiling blood and fire – and that, like Charon, they lead the spirits to the lower world, means that they had sepulchral significance. "In course of time," Baur holds, "they were considered guardians of the gates of Hades." (no. 5; See also nos. 282, 317). The same seems to hold true for Cyprus (nos. 205-6) as for Etruria and mainland Greece. See for example the Lefkandi Centaur named for the site of its discovery in Euboia, and dated to the end of the tenth century BC. This terracotta statuette might have been considered very valuable since its head was found in one tomb and the body in another and may well be the first representation of Chiron in Greek art, if the deliberate chip or gash on its left foreleg may be taken to represent the wound inflicted by Heracles's poisoned arrow (Padgett 2004, 7-9, fig. 3).

10. Repeating almost to a dot Nessus's vow: "I shall not die unavenged" (Ov. *Met.* ix. 131-2).

11. See for example, Brown (1995) who connects the Latin *paelex* to the Hebrew stem *piylāḡš-* and the Greek παλλακή, the latter also connected to πάλλαξ "young man," and Πάλλας as a title of Athena. According to Saul Levin from whom Brown cites, the Indo-European root is of Pelasgo-Philistine origin, the name Πελασγοί itself being a

form of the same word. "That will only work," Brown states, "if both 'Pelasgians' and 'Philistines' were a derogatory name, given by outsiders to the people, 'those of other stock, improperly married,' and then taken up by the people themselves in defiance as their own name for themselves." (65). If Deianeira was referring to herself as Pelasgian rather than to Iole as a concubine, the all but extinct Pelasgian tribes are speaking through her. In myth, this would indicate the older, more savage and bloodthirsty chthonic deities, i.e. titans, giants, and other earthborn monsters.

12. It is only in this sense that Adorno's oft misunderstood insight that "to write poetry after Auschwitz is barbaric" (34) can be grasped. Highly abstract, as it might seem, the statement has to be taken literally.

13. Seneca seems to suggest the notion of *mens rea* (criminal intent) here.

14. Sir Richard Jebb's translation (2004).

4.3. THE RISE AND FALL OF CONSCIOUSNESS

1. See, for example, Jaynes's own comparison of the early Plato in *Phaedrus* where insanity is a divine gift and the source of the chiefest blessings granted to men (244A), and the elderly Plato in *Laws* in which the family of those afflicted by insanity should keep them at home under penalty of a fine (934). (Jaynes [1976]2000, 405-7).

2. Herodotus believed the myth comprised the deeds of at least eight heroes named Heracles. Diodorus Siculus, however, only wrote of three. Cicero counted six, and Varro forty-four. The fact that Heracles's myth does not exist as a complete and consistent narrative, though there is a great visual component in it, allows for a greater range of possible interpretations. As the mythical components become more tightly knit or woven together, however, one can trace a certain evolution in the way the hero was perceived. At times though, he seems to regress, as when Heracles, the son of Alcmene is compared with his earlier namesake, Heracles the Dactyl, the founder of the Olympic games. See for example, Diod. v. 64. 3; Strab. viii. 3. 30; Paus. v. 7. 4.

4.4. THE SEA PEOPLE: EXILIC CONSCIOUSNESS

1. Qtd. in Bierling (2002, 40). A specific mention to the Sea Peoples in the bible may be found in *Numbers* 24: 23-4.

Sea-peoples shall gather from the north;

and ships, from the district of Kittim.

I look, and they shall afflict Eber;

but they too shall perish forever!

Kittim is Cyprus, while "the eponym Eber is here employed as a poetic term for the Hebrews." *The International Standard Bible Encyclopedia* (*ISBE* 3: 45) explains that the reading follows in part W. F. Albright, "who has shown that a more exact form of the original text can be obtained through a knowledge of ancient orthography."

2. Sherrat takes Cyprus to be the island from which the Sea Peoples staged both their trade and invasions.

4.5. THE POETS: INTELLECTUAL EXILE

1. While this has not gone unnoticed, it has rarely if ever been given its due credit. See for example, Carl A. P. Ruck (1986) who, while stating that in the context of similar tragedies, Euripides's *Bacchae* is unique in not expressly enacting a reconciliation and reintegration between primitivism and culture (2540-1), still obstinately clings to the idea that this is, in fact, what the tragedy ultimately aims at. Does this mean that Euripides was incapable of expressing his idea fully? Or did he expressly choose an underhanded expression? And why do that, if the idea was so fashionable, as Ruck claims?

2. For a full overview see *Early Greek Philosophy*, Vol. I-IX, ed. and trans. André Laks, Glen W. Most (Loeb Classical Library).

3. "From a union between Air and Mother Earth sprang Terror, Craft, Anger, Strife, Lies, Oaths, Vengeance, Intemperance, Altercation, Treaty, Oblivion, Fear, Pride, Battle; also, Oceanus, Metis, and the other Titans, Tartarus, and the Three Erinnyes, or Furies." (Graves, 2012, 3-4; See also Apollod. i. 1. 1).

4. This ordered universe can be religious and originary (e.g. Ovid's Kosmos) or political and constructed (e.g. Voegel's cosmion).

5. The destructiveness of the barbarian, however, is not an ideological exercise, unlike, e.g. Bakunin's vision (the most extreme of the creation/destruction dichotomy) who argues that one ought to first utterly destroy in order to later create, warning against even

thinking of creation before everything has been destroyed. These are all political musing camouflaged as anarchist thoughts, or alternately, negative nihilism badly disguised as political vision, for in the end they fiercely cling to the same old puritanistic ideas they purport to counter. In point of truth it is impossible to destroy anything without at the same time also creating. In Bakunin's extreme thought, politics meets religion in the deluded hope that a blank slate might in the end be achievable, and a chance at a new beginning after the deluge. Just as there exist utopias of creation there exist also utopias of destruction.

6. The rhyme used in these early instructions is not yet suggestive but merely a memorization device. In complex situations where a conscious decision is necessary, however, such simple rhymes turn into powerful suggestions. Lawyers still use them in order to influence the jury's decision with phrases such as "if it doesn't fit, you must acquit," etc. coined by O. J. Simpson's attorney Johnnie Cochran in his own tailored version, "if the glove doesn't fit, you must acquit." (Cochran and Fisher 2003, 108). Cochran provides other examples used in previous cases, such as, "If you pollute, we'll file suit." etc. This simple suggestion that the jury members will have no problem retaining in their memory (even perhaps longer than the more pertinent facts of the case) questions whether their decision was fully conscious.

7. It is not a coincidence that it should be precisely Socrates to understand this; for, as a hybrid specimen, his consciousness is both bicameral and subjective. It is interesting, for example, that many commentators associate, if not equate, his *daimonion* with reason, which is highly unusual, not only in light of the theory of bicamerality, but also from what is known of schizophrenia. One's first impulse should have been to associate it with instinct or the unconscious. Yet, in its repressive function, Socrates's *daimonion* defies this categorization as well. It may be tempting to place his consciousness at an intermediate point between bicamerality and subjective consciousness but this appears somewhat at odds with the fact that, in matters of logic, he seems to be well ahead of his contemporaries. Perhaps this is what Jaynes had in mind when he said, "It is as if the god-side of the bicameral man was approaching consciousness before the man-side, the right hemisphere before the left," but in this case, one should be prepared to admit the reality of the possibility that consciousness might have regressed again after its first baby steps.

5.1. THE TEACHINGS OF CHIRON

1. The first extant mention of *homo sacer* in Roman law is found in the law of the Twelve Tables c. 450 BC, which according to Livy were written after consulting the Solonian Constitution. This was a period of social and political turmoil for Rome, of the end of its existence as a kingdom and the beginnings of the republic, and of great political struggle between the plebeians and the patricians. See for example, C. F. Kolbert's introduction to the *Digest* (1979, 12). The tables were written in response to this social unrest, and as such seismic transformations touching all levels of society are always accompanied by an identity crises, it is not far-fetched to assume that the relation of the Romans to their old totem might also have shifted during this period. That the symbol of the wolf as a dark figure is older than its expression in law, and as with many things, the Romans merely repeated what with the Greeks had occurred much earlier, does not contradict this analysis. Cf. Lycaon's myth and the cult of Zeus Lycaon, which suggests that Lycaon was merely the atavistic aspect of Zeus, an earlier totem forced underground.

2. Pausanias (i. 19. 9) uses tellingly similar words in his description of a representation of Chiron after death as having been "freed from his humanity," though scholarly attempts at emending his text to a more "sensible" reading have not been lacking.

3. As Cicero says, where the gods care nothing for human welfare, there can be no piety, reverence, or religion. (*N.D.* I. 3; I. 115-6; I. 123).

5.2. MEDICINE AND MUSIC

1. The same in Statius, *Achilleid* (I. 185-94), though here it is Achilles who sings the songs taught him by Chiron for the pleasure of his anxious mother, Thetis.

5.3. PHISLOSOPHY AND MARTIAL ARTS

1. An already modern embellishment, in fact, that, to use a phrase by Sloterdijk, presents Achilles "as a delegate of extravagant parental ambitions." (2010, 11).

2. See Sloterdijk who says that the apocalyptic entrepreneur will discourage local rage projects that might endanger his masterplan. "This commits him to an extreme ascetics that will also affect his followers. ...the first precondition for collecting rage as part of a political project of global significance is cold-bloodedness. On the one hand,

this cold-bloodedness constantly needs to stir hatred and outrage. On the other hand, it is also necessary for securing restraint." (2010, 65-6). The project does not need to be political, however, though it is a given that the political will consider and treat anything that does not submit to it as merely its own opposition which, in this case will be denied apolitical status. In words that may be understood more clearly by the contemporary person, the political will attempt to turn everything into petty debate, a sickness that has for a long time affected philosophy as well with technical terms such as "dialectics," and all its derivations from the materialist to the ideological world, acquiring the status of both fine technical knowledge and virtue.

3. The Centaurs symbolized man's dual nature, according to the mythographers' own wisdom, the instinctual as well as the logical aspects of his being joined in one.

4. Plutarch refers to Heracles carrying Apollo's tripod at Delphi in anger when the Pythia refused to atone him for the murder of Iphitos, and even fighting the god for it.

5. According to yet another account by Apollodorus, he committed the crime out of a sense of justice, later citing in his own defense a law of Rhadamanthys, one of the three judges of the dead, that said "whoever defends himself against a wrongful aggressor shall go free." (ii. 4. 9).

6. Diodorus (or Dionysius) seems to use the terms Greek and Pelasgian language interchangeably: "the letters, as a group, are called Phoenician because they were brought to the Greeks from the Phoenicians, but as single letters the Pelasgians were the first to make use of the transferred characters and so they were called Pelasgic." (iii. 67. 1-2).

7. Qtd. by Oldfather in Diodorus Siculus, Library of History, Vol. II. (Books 2.35-4.58), Cambridge, MA: Harvard University Press, 1935, 307. n. 1. This was not long after the first Centaur figures started appearing in mainland Greece. Baur (1912, 6) argues that the first appearance of Centaur figures in mainland Greece is attested after the Mycaenean period, as early as the eighth century BC, if not before. However, the protogeometric Lefkandi Centaur, a possible depiction of Chiron, dated to the end of the tenth century BC, moves Baur's boundary of their first appearance by at least two centuries (Padgett 2003, 7).

8. Or brother, according to pseudo-Apollodorus (ii. 4. 9).

9. Cf. Ovid's, *Ars Amatoria*, i. 9-16.

10. This is openly stated in the older Hittite and Hurrian myths from which the Greek myths of Uranus and Cronus, and later, the revolt of the giants, have borrowed a great deal. (Guterbock 1951). Seeking to overthrow his own son the Weather-God Tešub, who now ruled over heaven and earth, Kumarbi conceived Ullikummi on a massive rock and hid him in the Nether world on the shoulder of Upelluri, "an Atlas-like giant who carries Heaven and Earth," and as Guterbock conjectures, perhaps the Sea, too (138). There, Ullikummi, a deaf and blind stone giant, goes unnoticed but growing like a tumor with terrifying speed in the sea until he reaches the sky where he is spotted by the Sun-God who hurries to warn Tešub. After an unsuccessful battle against Ullikummi, in which Tešub is defeated, Ea orders the older gods of the Nether world (like Upelluri and Enlil) "to provide the ancient tool with which Heaven and Earth had once been cut apart, and with this tool he cuts Ullikummi off 'under his feet'; that is, by separating him from the body of Upelluri on which he has grown, he magically breaks his power." (139).

11. See also, Weissman (1993), who in the context of bicameral voices enforcing a code of conduct, says, "The patriarchy of the *Iliad* includes both glorified male aggression and the rules that contain it, the rules that keep these warriors from becoming uncontrolled killers who would extinguish the species." (1). In the breakdown of the bicameral mind, then, and its coupling with the new consciousness, this aggression reaches new vertiginous heights, whose taming, it would seem, was the function of subjectivity and the resultant politics of identity.

12. REM Atonia is not dissimilar to the ancient notion of sleep as the "looser of limbs." See, Snell (Snell [1953]1982, 53-7) for a discussion of its ancient usage.

5.4. CHIRON'S DIET

1. See Wasson (1980), and Wasson; Ruck; et al. (1986) While Ruck argues that Demeter's draught made of mint-water mixed with pounded barley may have acquired its intoxicating property from ergot, Graves (1960) believes the ingredients to be an instance of a food ogham, "which is what the Irish bards called the device of spelling out a secret word by using the initial letters of other ordinary words," though this does not necessarily counter Ruck's opinion. It just means that the words for the ingredients were not ordi-

nary. The ingredients of the draught (*kukeón* "mixture") in the Homeric Hymn to Demeter (208-9) are given in Greek as Minthaion, Udor, Kukomenon, and Alphitos, the initial letters spelling **MUKA**, which is an earlier form of the word *mukes* "mushroom." The same can be shown for Ambrosia whose ingredients were a thick porridge of honey, water, fruit, olive-oil, cheese, and pearl-barley, giving no details as to what kind of fruit. In Greek, the ingredients are: Meli, Udor, Karpos, Elaios, Turos, and Alphita, the initials spelling **MUKETA**, which is the accusative of *mukes* "mushroom." And again for Nectar, whose ingredients are only said to be honey, water, and fruit: Meli, Udor, Karpos giving **MUK** (Graves 1960, 264-5). At times ambrosia is given as the drink and nectar as the food, suggesting that the terms might have been used interchangeably at the time of their conception, since they both referred to the same thing. Dionysus's feasts, of course, were called the *Ambrosia*, and took place during the mushroom season.

2. This is Robert Graves's supposition. Carl A. P. Ruck (1986) believes that intoxicant spices, including perhaps amanita muscaria or a substitute may have been mixed with wine, leading to the need to dilute wine with water (2221-40).

3. As Baur (1912) points out, in the art of the archaic period it seems as if the Lapiths planned the war for a considerable time after the wedding, since the battle is represented as taking place outdoors. It is not until the next or fifth century that the battle takes place indoors, in the banquet hall of Pirithous (no. 115). In addition, Diodorus tells of earlier battles between the Centaurs and the Lapiths, which had occurred as a result of the former making a claim to a share of Pirithous's kingdom, on the ground of their kinship. (iv. 70. 2-3). But see also Baur's example of the Etruscan amphora in no. 173A titled, "Heracles pursuing two centaurs, who have wounded a Lapith." This is the only known archaic example of Heracles participating in the Thessalian Centauromachy. "Etruscan vase-painters of the sixth century," Baur writes, "do not follow the traditions known to us through Attic art, they allow themselves privileges that would fill a dull conventional Attic vase-painter's heart with misgivings."

4. In archaic art, this is generally supported by the differing attitudes in the Centaurs' depictions between Attic and Ionic, (and even more conspicuously in Etruscan) art, whereas in the former they are in the vast majority of cases represented as running for cover, in the latter they charge vigorously, not only against the Lapiths but against Heracles as well.

5.5. SELF-ENGINEERED CHIMERAS

1. Such legends still exist all over the world, with a minor secularized element: God is replaced with a king who surveys his kingdom for any widespread injustices.

2. If Manna was *psilocybe* – the flesh of the gods or the divine mushroom (*teonánacatl*) of the Aztecs – a hallucinogen whose effects, similar to amanita muscaria, are temporal and spatial delusions, this would explain the unbelievably long time it took the Israelites to make their way from Egypt to the promised land (Graves 1960)

6.1. PESSIMISM AND NIHILISM

1. Cf. Weissman (1993, 1). See also Sloterdijk (2010, 9-10).

2. Though, it should not be difficult to grasp the fact that as man needs God to give meaning to his life, God needs chaos.

3. This is not to say that nihilism is a theory of pure transgression. Rejection in this sense must be read as an ability, not as an obligation or requirement. It is true that one does not need to desecrate anything for there was never anything sacred, to paraphrase Mohaghegh (2010), but one must also keep in mind that the sacred has always been enforced by community and tradition, never by the god of thunder.

4. Although they are not the only affects to be ostracized, they certainly make the top of the list. Plato, for example, expelled from his austere Republic of reason all emotion and transgressive energies. Rosemary Jackson counts "eroticism, violence, madness, laughter, nightmares, dreams, blasphemy, lamentation, uncertainty, female energy, and excess." (2009: 177).

5. See also Ruck (1986) who holds a similar intermediate position.

6.2. ACEDIA

1. For a collection of works through the centuries under the theme of melancholia, see Radden (2002).

2. Bamberger explains that the name is derived from the Hebrew text of Ps. 90:6 (Praktikos, 26). Unless otherwise indicated, this essay follows Wenzel's own translations instead of Bamberger's watered down version, which renders, for example, Evagrius's πορνεία "fornication, prostitution" as "impurity." The same applies to Thomas Aquinas's works.

3. For the history and development of the concept of acedia, see, Wenzel ([1960] 2015). For the process of transformation in arriving to Pope Gregory's list, see particularly pp. 23-4.

4. Cassian's practical shift of emphasis from acedia as a sorrow or weariness of heart (*tædium cordis*) to idleness, and the cure emphasizing manual labor he provides for it, resembles the communists' cure of handing out shovels to thinkers in order to cleanse them of the ills begotten from philosophically detached and abstract thinking. This was done in line with their own all-understanding perspective of dialectic materialism, which is supposed to have its feet on the ground instead of its head in the clouds. Gregory the Great himself summed this up as *"vagatio mentis erga illicita."*

5. Wenzel rightly notices that Dante in his *Divine Comedy* has widened the concept of acedia to include the temporal order (Wenzel, 135). And in his vision one must give Dante more credit than all the scholastics and Church Fathers put together, for he includes in his fifth circle not only the bacchantes who give *accidia* bites recalling their practice of omophagia, as Wenzel points out (242 n. 12), as well as Homer's words about Bellerophon who devours his soul, but also Ixion's father, Phlegyas. In this sense, then, the seventh circle of the violent with its three rings 1) against the neighbor, 2) against the self, and 3) against God, unmistakably belongs to acedia, and sure enough, it is here that we find the Centaurs, Chiron, Pholus, and Nessus. For a similar reading, see, Kristeva (1989, 9). Dante's greatest insight in this context is shown, perhaps, in his description of "the sect of the wicked, hateful both to God and to His enemies" (*la setta d'i cattivi, a Dio spiacenti e a' nemici sui*) (*Inferno*, III).

6. The division between cognition and affection did not cease with Aquinas, of course. It rose into prominence again with the emphasis on the contrast between human subjectivity and objective scientific thought in the sixteenth and seventeenth centuries, which accordingly contributed the insight that reason represented maleness while passion belonged to the feminine, or the association of reason with the public realm, and passion with the private and domestic, notions which only betray the neurotic and concealed character of their inventors. The European Enlightenment consolidated further these awkward ideas, lending them the semblance of light and clarity. In psychiatry they rise again in the eighteenth and nineteenth century, e.g. with faculty psychology and phrenology,

which, of course, owe their thanks directly to Aquinas. For an overview of their historical development, or more correctly, their static and resilient nature, see Radden (2002, 25-8).

7. See, for example, "Review of a Heresy or A Heretic Review," at www.guerrilaconcepts.com

6.3. ONCOLOGICAL CREATION: THE EARTH SICKNESS

1. Dizionario Etimologico Online (DEO); **cièlo**.

2. See A. P. Ruck (1986) who connects *chattra* "mushroom; parasol" in classical Sanskrit with the Shade-foots and Cover-foots from Greek mythology, figures likely related to an ancient mushroom cult (1864-8). In Albanian this root can be found in *çadra* "umbrella, parasol" and *çatí* "roof." On the other hand, *kutí* "box," another term related to κύτος has entered Albanian by a roundabout way from Turkish *kutu* "box." (Çabej; **kuti**).

3. Çabej, it seems, follows Meyer and Buzuku without question for he does not even dedicate an entry to the word in his *Etymological Studies*, which is only mentioned in passing in **ferr** "hell."

4. The word in that sense would be *kthjell, kthill* "clear, cloudless."

5. The point of contact between the concept of a cell and the sky in Albanian seems to be the palate (*qellzë*) which brings together both the notion of the roof and the notion of a closed space inside the mouth with its horrific grinding gates of teeth rows.

6. A valuable point of convergence is provided by the Kabbalists' discussions of the revelation of the Commandments on Mt. Sinai. Some argue that only the first two Commandments were communicated directly to the people, who were overwhelmed and could no longer endure the divine voice. Rabii Mendel, however, claimed that Israel did not even hear the first two Commandments. "All that Israel heard," Scholem relates, "was the *aleph* with which in the Hebrew text the first Commandment begins, the *aleph* of the word *anokhi*, 'I'." "In Hebrew," he adds, "the consonant *aleph* represents nothing more than the position taken by the larynx when a word begins with a vowel. Thus the *aleph* may be said to denote the source of all articulate sound... To

hear the *aleph* is to hear next to nothing; it is the preparation for all audible language, but in itself conveys no determinate, specific meaning." ([1969] 1974, 30).

7. How it became possible for him to speak is not a challenge that embodied cognition theorists can tackle, since neither the body image nor the body schema constructions can be of any help here. Nor is it a problem that traditional computational theory is in any way in a better position to resolve, since there can be no "inner" mental processes where all is one. Here all logic, all postulations break, and creation becomes alien to itself. The question, again, is how can the eternal balance of noumena be disturbed? (for an answer to this question, see Book I, ch 2).

8. http://www.touchbible.org/index.php

9. John F. Walvoord, in "The Bible Knowledge Commentary: An Exposition of the Scriptures," follows much the same simplistic analysis.

10. Nevertheless, the mere existence of the second version indicates that attempts to reinstate the tablets throughout the centuries by esoteric circles or individuals with some knowledge of their existence have not been lacking. It is believed that the work of Marcion the Heretic may fall into this category, and close parallelisms can be drawn between his doctrine and *The Book of Wars*, e.g. his attempt to reinstate the image of Mother Earth (Gaia), and expose God's Great Wars (the lost book). Within scientific circles, some of the most prominent figures standing out are: Brahmagupta, the man who found zero, without which mathematics could not have advanced (his book, *Brahmasphutasiddhanta*, is the first book in which zero is treated as a number); Fibonacci, the man who spread the knowledge of zero in the West; and even, oddly enough, Bishop Etienne, who played a crucial role in the condemnations of Paris. He considered a heresy the prevailing scientific opinion of the time which stated that perfect vacuum was impossible, arguing that if God wished to create perfect vacuum He could do so. This seemingly simple statement, erroneous as the immediate cancerous growth of the earth demonstrates, nevertheless brought down a great barrier, clearing the way for a radical transformation in the way vacuum was conceptualized, and bringing forth many advances in science and technology.

11. Closely related to *bote* "mud, clay, earthen pot" and "jar, barrel, vessel" as well as "strike," bringing together all the aforementioned meanings, indicating thus the cancer

growth stages of the earth sickness (*bote* "strike, wound" → *bush/mbush* "empty/fill" → *both* (Tosk. *byth*), *bisht*, *bosht* "bottom, tail; axis," in the sense of "that which supports, that on which one sits" → *botë* "globe," in the sense of "swelling, growth"). For "wound," see Book I, ch's 1 and 2."

12. Indef. *pelë*; see also *lopë* "cow" formed by metathesis.

13. *Pjell* (v.) is the old world, now reserved only for animals. As a noun, *pjellë*, is used for humans only in the pejorative sense, e.g. *pjellë e keqe* "bad seed." The modern word is *lind* "to give birth" from *le, lej* "give birth," with a sense of "to leave," etymologically related to English "let." (Çabej; **le, lej**).

14. OED; **dead**; Alb. Gheg, *dek*; Tosk *vdek*. Demeter, as it is known, presided over the cycles of life and death, and her daughter, Persephone was goddess of the underworld, perhaps a different aspect of the same deity, as Graves theorizes, or the atavistic image of Demeter, according to Ruck.

Of some interest in this context may be Wasson's description of a similarly animate mushroom in the Santal villages in Orissa and the Santal Parganas in Bihar; the *putka*, the one mushroom "endowed with a soul." Its name is derived from *pūtika*, the first surrogate for the Soma of the Vedic hymns, the divine entheogen. Etymologically it is related to "putrid," and both species gave off a bad odor in a matter of hours justifying their name. The locals related they believed it had a soul because if it were not consumed quickly, it would stink like a cadaver (Wasson 1980, 42-3, Wasson and al. 1986).

15. In Albanian, there is a multitude of similar examples of interrelated words crisscrossing from the so-called centum to the satem group and vice versa: *dhamb, dhëmb* (n.) "tooth" (cf. Greek γόμφος "peg, pin, nail"); *gjëmb* (n.) "thorn"; *thumb* (n.), *thumboj* (v.) "sting, spike, thorn; to sting." *Thumboj* (v.) "to sting" shares its root with *sëmboj* (v.), *sëmbim* (n.) "prick, prickle, stab, pang" which in turn goes back to *dhemb* (v.), *dhembje* (n.) "ache, pain, smart." It almost seems that *dhëmb* (n.) "tooth" was named after the ache (*dhemb* (v.)) it caused. *Gërmoj* (v.) "to dig"; *dërrmoj* (v.) "crush; smash; destroy"; *thërrmoj* (v.) "crush; mince; crumb, crumble"; *thërrime* (n. pl.) "crumbs"; *ther* (v.) "stab; butcher, slaughter; smart, sting," etc. And lastly, there are also words in which this switch occurs at the end of the word, such as, *lang, lëng* (n.) "juice; broth; liquid"

and *landë, lëndë* (n.) "matter, substance, material," in which the animate-inanimate genders seem more easily discernible; *lëndoj* (v.) "to hurt"; *lëngoj* (v.) "to languish," etc. If these words exhibited only phonological similarities, it would be easy to dismiss them as unrelated. Yet, they show such clear semantic affinities, one wonders how they could have gone unnoticed for so long.

16. Compare this also with the myth of the repopulation of the world after the flood by Deucalion and Pyrrha by throwing behind their back Mother Earth's bones (i.e. rocks), which, depending on whether it was Deucalion or Pyrrha who threw them, upon touching the ground grew into men or women respectively.

17. *Saʿiyr* (s.), *seʿirim* (pl.) "shaggy, he-goat." For a discussion of the *seʿirim* and their relation to the Satyrs, see Isler-Kerényi (2004).

Bibliography

Abbott, Edwin. 1952. *Flatland: A Romance of Many Dimensions*. New York: Dover Publications.

Adorno, Theodor. 1982. *"Cultural Criticism and Society" in Prisms*. Kindle Edition. Translated by Samuel Weber and Sherry Weber. Cambridge, MA: The MIT Press.

Agamben, Giorgio. 1998. *Homo Sacer: Sovereign Power and Bare Life*. Kindle Edition. Translated by Daniel Heller-Roazen. Stanford, CA: Stanford University Press.

Artaud, Antonin. 1958. *The Theatre and Its Double*. New York: Grove Press.

Baral, Lok Raj. 2000. *The Regional Paradox: Essays in Nepali and South Asian Affairs*. Delhi: Adroit Publishers.

Baur, Paul. 1912. *Centaurs in Ancient Art: The Archaic Period*. Berlin: Karl Curtius.

Benjamin, Walter. 1986. *"Critique of Violence" in Reflections: Essays, Aphorisms, Autobiographical Writings*. Translated by Edmund Jephcott. New York: Schocken Books.

Bhaskaracarya. [2001]2015. *Lilavati of Bhaskaracarya: A Treatise of Mathematics of Vedic Tradition*. Private Limited, 4th. ed. Translated by Krishnaji Shankara Patwardhan, Somashekhara Amrita Naimpally and Shyam Lal Singh. Delhi: Motilal Banarsidass Publishers.

Bierling, Neal. 2002. *Philistines: Giving Goliath His Due*. Warren Center: Shangri-La Publications.

Brown, John Pairman. 1995. *Israel and Hellas*. Vol. I. New York: Walter de Gruyter.

Chomsky, Noam. 1970. *Current Issues in Linguistic Theory*. The Hague: Mouton.

Cioran, Emil M, *A Little Theory of Desitny*. 1968. Translated by Richard Howard. Chicago: Quadrangle.

—, *History and Utopia*. [1978]2015. Translated by Richard Howard. New York: Arcade Publishing.

Cochran, Johnnie, and David Fisher. 2003. *A Lawyer's Life*. New York: Thomas

Dunne Books.

Çabej, Eqrem. 2008. *Hyrje në Indoeuropianistikë: Leksionet e Prishtinës, (1971-3)*. Tiranë: Botime Çabej.

—. 1976-2014. *Studime Etimologjike në Fushë të Shqipes*. Vols. I-VII. Tiranë: Akademia e Shkencave: Instituti i Letërsisë dhe i Gjuhësisë.

Dodds, Eric Robertson (trans.) 1987. *Bacchae*. New York: Clarendon Press, 1987).

Dodds, Eric Robertson. 1951. *The Greeks and the Irrational*. Kindle Edition. Berkeley: University of California Press.

Engels, Friedrich. 1908. *The Origin of the Family: Private Property and the State*. Kindle Edition. Chicago: Charles H. Kerr.

Evans, Dylan. 2006. *An Introductory Dictionary of Lacanian Psychoanalysis*. New York: Routledge.

Ferenczi, Sandor. 1968. *Thalassa: A Theory of Genitality*. New York: W. W. Norton.

Fiore, Pasquale. 1918. *International Law Codified and Its Legal Sanction, Or, The Legal Organization of the Society of States*. Edited by Edwin M. Borchard. New York: Baker, Voorhis.

Fox, Leonard (trans). 1989. *Kanuni i Lekë Dukagjinit (The Code of Lekë Dukagjini)*. Albanian Text Collected and Arranged by Shtjefën Gjeçov. New York: Gjonlekaj Publishing Company.

Foucault, Michel. 2003. *"Society Must Be Defended" Lectures at the College de France 1975-76*. Translated by David Macey. New York: Picador.

Frashëri, Naim. 1895. *Gjithsija*. Bucharest: Shpnesa e Shqypnis.

Gonzalez--Wippler, Migene. 1977. *A Kabbalah for the Modern World*. New York: Bantam Books.

Graves, Robert. 1960. *"Centaurs' Food" in Food for Centars: Stories Talks, Critical Studies, Poems by Robert Graves*. New York: Doubleday.

—. 2012. *The Greek Myths*. New York: Penguin Books.

Guterbock, Hans Gustav. 1951. "The Song of Ullikummi: Revised Text of the Hittite Version of a Hurrian Myth." *Journal of Cuneiform Studies* 5 (No. 4): 135-61.

Hall, Edith. 1989. *Inventing the Barbarian: Greek Self-Definition Through Tragedy*.

New York: Clarendon Press.

Hardt, Michael, and Antonio Negri. 2001. *Empire*. Kindle Edition. Cambridge, MA: Harvard University Press.

Hedayat, Sadeq. 1979. "Buried Alive: The Jottings of a Madman" in *Sadeq Hedayat: An Anthology*. Edited and translated by Ehsan Yarshater. Boulder: Westview Press.

Heller-Roazen, Daniel. 2013. *Dark Tongues: The Art of Rogues and Riddlers*. New York: Zone Books.

—. 2009. *The Enemy of All: Piracy and the Law of Nations*. New York: Zone Books .

—. 2011. *The Fifth Hammer: Pythagoras and the Disharmony of the World*. New York: Zone Books.

Taylor, Jerome (ed.) [1961] 1991. *The Didascalicon of Hugh of St. Victor*. New York: Columbia University Press.

Isler-Kerényi, Cornelia. 2004. *Civilizing Violence: Satyrs on 6th-Century Greek Vases*. Translated by Eric Charles de Sena. Fribourg: Academic Press Fribourg.

Jackson, Rosemary. [1981] 2009. *Fantasy: The Literature of Subversion*. Edited by Terrence Hawkes. New York: Routledge.

Jakobson, Roman. 1978. *Six Lectures on Sound and Meaning*. Translated by John Mepham. Cambridge, MA: The MIT Press.

Jane, Cecil (trans). 1960. *The Journal of Christopher Columbus*. New York: Clarkson N. Potter.

Jaynes, Julian. [1976]2000. *The Origin of Consciousness in the Breakdown of the Bicameral Mind*. Boston: First Mariner Books.

Kadare, Ismail. 2011. *Eskili, Ky Humbës i Madh*. Kindle Edition. Tiranë: Onufri.

Kenny, D. Philip. 2003. "Socratic Knowledge and the Daimonion". *Aporia* 13 (No. 1): 26-40.

Knop, Karen. 2002. *Diversity and Self-Determination in International Law*. Cambridge: Cambridge University Press.

Kolbert, C. F. (trans.) 1979. *The Digest of Roman law: Theft, Rapine, Damage, and Insult*. New York: Penguin Books.

Kristeva, Julia. 1989. *Black Sun: Depression and Melancholia*. Translated by Leon S.

Roudiez. New York: Columbia University Press.

Lacan, Jacques. 2006. *"The Instance of the Letter in the Unconscious" in Ecrit: The First Complete Edition in English.* Translated by Bruce Fink. New York: W. W. Norton.

Ligotti, Thomas. 2010. *The Conspiracy Against the Human Race: A Contrivance of Horror.* New York: Hippocampus Press.

Mackie, C. J. 1997. "Achilles' Teachers: Chiron and Phoenix in the Iliad." *Greece & Rome* xliv (1): 1-10.

Magnus, Margaret. 2009. *The Gods of the Word: Archetypes in Consonants.* Kindle Edition. New York: Thomas Jefferson University Press.

Metzinger, Thomas. 2003. *Being No One: The Self-Model Theory of Subjectivity.* Cambridge, MA: The MIT Press.

Meyer, Gustav. 2007. *Fjalor Etimologjik i Gjuhës Shqipe.* Tiranë: Çabej.

Michelet, M. J. 1861. *The Sea.* New York: Rudd & Carlton.

Mohaghegh, Jason Bahbak. 2016. *Insurgent, Poet, Mystic, Sectarian: The Four Masks of an Eastern Postmodernism.* Albany: Sunny Press.

—. 2010. *New Literature and Philosophy of the Middle East: The Chaotic Imagination.* New York: Palgrave Macmillan.

Montesquieu. [1989]2013. *The Spirit of the Laws.* 17th. Edited by Anne M. Cohler, Basia Carolyn Miller and Harold Samuel Stone. New York: Cambridge University Press.

Mossman, Judith. 2012. *"Women's Voices in Sophocles" in Brill's Companion to Sophocles.* Edited by Andreas Marcantonatos. Leiden & Boston.

Mukherjee, Siddharta. 2011. *The Emperor of All Maladies: A Biography of Cancer.* New York: Scribner.

Negarestani, Reza. 2008. *Cyclonopedia: Complicity with Anonymous Materials.* Melbourne: re.press.

Negarestani, Reza. 2011. "Globe of Revolution: An Afterthought on Geophilosophical Realism." *нститутот за општествени и хуманистички истражувања »Евро-Балкан«* (17): 25-54.

Negarestani, Reza. 2010. "Undercover Softness: An Introduction to the Architecture and Politics of Decay." *Collapse* VI: 379-430.

Nietzsche, Friedrich. [1968]2011. *The Will to Power.* New York: Knopf Doubleday.

Orel, Vladimir. 1998. *Albanian Etymological Dictionary.* Leiden: Brill.

Padgett, J. Michael. 2004. *The Centaur's Smile: The Human Animal in Early Greek Art.* Princeton: Princeton University Art Museum.

Ponticus, Evagrius. 1972. *The Praktikos & Chapters on Prayer.* Translated by John Eudes Bamburger. Trappist: Cistercian Publications.

Radden, Jennifer (ed.). 2002. *The Nature of Melancholia: From Aristotle to Kristeva.* New York: Oxford University Press.

Rendich, Franco. 2013. *Dictionary of Classical Indo-European Languages: Indo-European Sanskrit - Greek - Latin.* Kindle Edition. Translated by Gordon Davis. Franco Rendich.

Riedl, Matthias. 2012. ""The Containment of Dionysos: Religion and Politics in the Bacchanalia Affair of 186 BCE"." *International Political Anthropology* 5 (No. 2): 113-33.

Rousseau, Jean-Jacques. 2012. *The Major Political Writings of Jean-Jacques Rousseau: The Two Discourses and The Social Contract.* Translated by John T. Scott. Chicago: The University of Chicago.

Sagan, Carl. 1985. *Cosmos.* New York: Ballantine Books.

Saussure, Ferdinand de. 1983. *Course in General Linguistics.* Kindle Edition. Edited by Charles Bally and Albert Sechehaye. Translated by Roy Harris. Peru, IL: Open Court.

Schmitt, Carl. 2015. *Land and Sea: A World Historical Meditation.* Edited by Rusell A. Berman and Samuel Garrett Zeitlin. Translated by Samuel Garrett Zeitlin. Candor: Telos Press.

—. [1962] 2007. *Theory of the Partisan: Intermediate Commentary on the Concept of the Political.* Translated by G. L. Ulmen. New York: Telos Press Publishing.

Scholem, Gershom. [1969] 1974. *On the Kabbalah and Its Symbolism.* 5th. Translated by Ralph Manheim. New York: Schocken Books.

Sherrat, Susan. 1998. "'Sea Peoples' and the Economic Structure of the Late Second

Millenium in the Eastern Mediterranean,' in Mediterranean Peoples in Transition: Thirteenth to Early Tenth Centuries BCE. Jerusalem: Israel Exploration Society.

Sissa, Giulia. 1990. *Greek Virginity.* Translated by Arthur Goldhammer. Cambridge, MA: Harvard University Press.

Sloterdijk, Peter. 2010. *Rage and Time: A Psychopolitical Investigation.* New York: Columbia University Press.

Smolin, Lee. 1997. *The Life of the Cosmos.* New York: Oxford University Press.

Snell, Bruno. [1953]1982. *The Discovery of the Mind in Greek Philosophy and Literature.* New York: Dover Publications.

Thorup, Mikkel. 2015. *The Total Enemy: Six Chapters of a Violent Idea.* Eugene, OR: Pickwick Publications.

Vattel, Emmerich de. 2014. *The Law of Nations, Or, Principles of the Law of Nature Applied to the Conduct and Affairs of Nations and Sovereigns, with Three Early Essays on the Origin and Nature of Natural Law and on Luxury.* Edited by Béla Kapossy and Richard Whatmore. Indianapolis: Liberty Fund.

Vitoria, Francisco de. 1991. *"On the American Indians" in Political Writings.* Edited by Anthony Padgen and Jeremy Lawrence. Cambridge: Cambridge University Press.

Wasson, R. Gordon. 1980. *The Wondrous Mushroom: Mycolatry in Mesoamerica.* New York: McGraw-Hill.

Wasson, R. Gordon, Carl A. P. Ruck, et al. 1986. *Persephone's Quest: Entheogens and the Origins of Religion.* New Haven: Yale University Press.

Webb, Richard C. 2004. *Sophocles: Plays. Trachiniae.* Edited by P. E. Easterling. Bristol: Bristol Classical Press.

Weissman, Judith. 1993. *Of Two Minds: Poets Who Hear Voices.* Hanover: Wesleyan University Press.

Wenzel, Siegfried. [1960] 2015. *The Sin of Sloth: Acedia in Medieval Thought and Literature.* Chapel Hill: The University of North Carolina Press.

Wharton, W.J.L. (ed.). 1893. *Captain Cook's Journal During his First Voyage Round the World Made in H.M. Bark "Endeavour" 1768-71.* Kindle Edition.

London: Elliot Stock.

Žižek, Slavoj. 1996. *The Indivisible Remainder: An Essay on Schelling and Related Matters*. New York: Verso.

—. 2006. *The Parallax View*. Cambridge, MA: The MIT Press.

Index of Terms

gnOme is a secret press specializing in the publication of anonymous, pseudepigraphical, and apocryphal works from the past, present, and future.

"In our societies, characters dominate our perceptions. Our attention tends to be arrested by the activities of faces that come and go, emerge and disappear.

"...[With anonymity] the effects of the book might land in unexpected places and form shapes that I had never thought of. A name makes reading too easy." (Michel Foucault, "The Masked Philosopher")

gnOme is acephalic. Book sales support the authors.

GNOMEBOOKS.WORDPRESS.COM

Printed in Great Britain
by Amazon

84491873R00159

Written on Water

Written on Water

Five Hundred Poems
from the Man'yōshū

translated by Takashi Kojima

sketches by Midori Toda

CHARLES E. TUTTLE COMPANY
Rutland, Vermont & Tokyo, Japan

Published by the Charles E. Tuttle Company, Inc.
of Rutland, Vermont & Tokyo, Japan
with editorial offices at
2-6 Suido 1-chome, Bunkyo-ku, Tokyo   112

LCC Card No. 95-60248

ISBN 0-8048-2040-6

First edition, 1995

Printed in Japan

Contents

Acknowledgments

The *Man'yōshū*, which consists of twenty volumes, was compiled during the course of 130 years, and its poetry is not systematically arranged or classified. In order to help the reader understand the *Man'yōshū* and appreciate its lyricism and literary merits, I have selected five hundred poems from the total of 4,516 and have divided them into three categories: poetry of known authorship, anonymous poetry, and poetry of envoys and frontier guards.

Without the kind help of many native English speakers, it would have been impossible to complete this work. Any mistakes are solely my responsibility.

Thanks are especially due to Mr. Jimmy Snyder, Dr. Piero Policicchio, and Mr. Lindsay O'Neil, who kindly read the greater part of my manuscript and gave me valuable suggestions.

My gratitude also goes to Mr. James Gardener, Mr. David Spiro, Mr. Gordon Barclay, Mr. William James, Mr. Grant Jennings, Mr. Todd Thacker, and Mr. John Patton.

Sincere thanks are also due to Mr. Yasui Nagafuji, professor of ancient Japanese literature at Meiji University; Mr. Tatsuyuki Gotō, music critic and former professor of musical theory at Kinjō Music Academy, and his daughter, Ms. Takashima, an expert in traditional Japanese music; Mr. Michitaka Takeuchi, professor of Japanese music at Kunitachi Academy of Music; Mr. Takashi Imai, archaeologist; and Mrs. Takashi Imai, scholar of ancient Japanese literature. I also wish to thank Mr. Donald Iwamura, my son-in-law, and his son, Mr. Ken Iwamura; and Mrs. Lindsay Gene O'Neil, my granddaughter.

I wish to dedicate this book to Mr. and Mrs. Umenosuke Bessho, who kindly enabled me to go to college, and last but not least to my late dear wife, Yuki Kojima, who enabled me to devote myself to the accomplishment of this work.

A Note on the Translation

There is a school of thought that claims poetry cannot be translated. There is no way, states this argument, that the meaning, subtlety, depth, beauty, spirit, and essence of the original language can be transmuted into another language. The only possibility with poetry translation is approximation and compromise, and the result is little more than a wan shadow of the original.

Should the result emulate the formal conventions of the original language or should it take on the formal conventions of the new language? In other words, should a Japanese poem in translation try to approximate the sense and feeling of the original language or should it be translated into an English poem? To what degree should the translation hold its own as poetry, or should a rendering of meaning be the main aim?

With something as fluid and alive as language, and with poetry in particular, there is no simple right answer to such questions. Somehow an ideal mode or method of translation must be chosen, but anything attempted can only be partial. Even with poetry as close to contemporary English as that of, say, Rainer Maria Rilke, the translation problems are hardly small, but with a genre of poetry that follows linguistic conventions totally different from any Indo-European language, and one generated in the ancient past by a society that eludes comprehension by the West even today, the problems of translation take on entirely new nuances of the word "difficult."

Impossible? Probably. But even so, should any attempt to translate such poetry be avoided? That would mean that anyone who does not read Japanese and who is not conversant with eighth-century Japanese aristocratic society would be denied any indication of what the poetry of that period is about. Particularly, if the poetry in question is considered among mankind's great artistic legacies, should there not be some means of conveying, however partial and incomplete, an idea of what the original says?

Assuming that the answer is yes, assuming that the intrinsic worth of the *Man'yōshū* makes its translation into English and any other European language an important contribution, how should the translation be done?

Should a scholar, who is not a poet and, with rare exceptions, does not possess the poet's gift of language, attempt to translate poetry of any kind (in the process adding to mankind's burden of footnotes)? Should a language specialist—a translator—who is not a scholar attempt such translation?

How knotty the translation of this material is was made clear when a check of other English *Man'yōshū* translations revealed that other translators' interpretations often were totally different from Mr. Kojima's and from each other's, some poems even being given opposite meanings. This should not be surprising, perhaps, because, as one commentator has pointed out, by the late Heian period, the language in which the *Man'yōshū* was written had already become partially incomprehensible, and the following 800 years or so have complicated the task of interpreting the original poetry.

Without pretension and without scholar's pomp and posing, Mr. Kojima selected 500 poems out of the total of about 4,500 and has given us a charming book. The translator of this little volume undertook a task rather like skiing down Mt. Blanc—there are more reasons for not doing it than for doing it. Ignoring all the obstacles and the arguments for not attempting to translate the poetry of a society that might as well be Martian, he jumped into the task with verve and caring and a lifetime's experience as a translator of Japanese into English. This editor never met the translator, for Mr. Kojima passed away some years before this publication project was initiated. As a result, queries and problems could not be discussed, but had to be handled as English-language problems, and the few translation queries that occurred were given to another linguist to solve. Much gratitude goes to Ruth McCreery for her patient and supportive help on many levels.

Introduction

The *Man'yōshū* is the oldest and yet the freshest and most important collection of Japanese poetry. It surpasses all later poetry collections and, in the quality of pure lyricism, it ranks among the masterpieces of world literature. It comprises, in twenty volumes, 4,516 poems, most of which were composed over a period of 139 years, ending in the middle of the eighth century—a period that some consider to be the golden age of Japanese poetry.

The *Man'yōshū* is a unique anthology, whose poets are people from all walks of life, ranging from members of the imperial family to the humblest level of society. The poems cover a wide range of expression and content, from court poets' highly polished expressions of delicate emotions and subtle sentiments, to anonymous poems that read like folk songs. These poems are a natural outpouring of genuine love and intense emotion and often directly reflect life experiences. Poems of later ages, though elegant and beautifully composed, often read like the product of imagined or fanciful experiences. Thus, one may well say that Man'yō poetry is both ancient and yet among the freshest poetry of any time.

In those days, men and women married for love, and a mother's consent remained important. Over 70 percent of the *Man'yōshū*'s poetry describes aspects of romantic love. Here we find the fire, amazing candor, and eloquent rapture of love known in Western poetry but not found in later Japanese poetry. Most of the poems not concerned with love are expressions of the joys and sorrows of life and of wonder and admiration for the beauty of nature. The poetic expressions of love in all its aspects written in refined yet direct language make delightful reading and have a universal appeal. All these exquisite gems of poetry deeply touch people today, 1,300 years after their composition.

The influence of Chinese literature and poetry spurred the progress of Japanese poetry. The native Japanese oral poetry tradition provided fertile ground for the stimulus of continental modes of expression, and by the beginning of the seventh century, the Japanese were writing refined poetry. It was the invention of the crude Japanese syllabary, called the Man'yō-*gana*, which enabled people to write poetry freely in their mother tongue. During Man'yō times and in the subsequent Heian period (794–1185), composing poetry was one of the indispensable accomplishments of a cultured person, and there were numerous occasions to demonstrate this skill. It was common practice for literate men and women to exchange poems, particularly love poems.

Another notable feature of the *Man'yōshū*, compared to later Japanese court poetry, is that, although poets of the time were well acquainted with classical Chinese literature, their use of Chinese words and their references to Chinese literature are few. In those days, Chinese words were used as devices by intellectuals to express abstract idea; few Chinese words had yet found their way into the everyday Japanese vocabulary. Therefore, they were not vehicles for emotional expression. Poets express subtle emotions and delicate shades of meaning most naturally and powerfully in their own, familiar, native language.

Three Poetical Forms

The nature of the Japanese language makes it necessary that its poetry employ formal devices other than the meter and rhyme familiar to the West. From a very early time, Japanese poetry utilized forms of rhythm or syllabic stress reminiscent of music.

By the time the Japanese language had been given a written form, many forms of poetry had been tried, and by Manyō days, the *tanka*, the 31-syllable poem, had become the most common form. This short poetic form is grouped into five lines of 5-7-5-7-7 syllables.

In the *Man'yōshū* three kinds of poetic forms are employed. The vast majority of the poems, about 93 percent, are *tanka*. Since Man'yō days the *tanka* has been the most common and orthodox poetic form for intense emotional expression.

The *Man'yōshū* contains 262 long poems (*chōka*). These are formed by the indefinite repetition of 5-7-syllable lines, ending with an additional 7-syllable line. This form declined in use after the eighth century.

Sixty-one poems are in the form called *sedoka* ("repetition poem"), which twice repeats triplets of 5-7-7-syllable lines. After the Nara period (710–794) this form was abandoned.

Except for six long poems, the five hundred poems presented in this book are all *tanka*.

Four Periods

A few poems in the anthology are said to date back to the end of the fourth century, but their authenticity is doubtful. The vast majority of the poems were written during a span of 139 years, which may be divided into four periods.

The first period covers about forty years from 629, when Emperor Jomei, the father of emperors Tenji and Temmu, ascended the throne, to 672, when the Jinshin Uprising occurred. Most of the Man'yō poems of this period were composed by members of the imperial family, including emperors Tenji and Temmu.

The second period also covers about forty years, from the Jinshin Uprising of 672 to 710, when the capital was moved to Nara. From the second period on, most of the prominent poets were court poets and officials. The most prominent representative of this period is Kakinomoto-no-Hitomaro, the greatest lyricist in Japanese literature. Among the major poets of the time, Takechi-no-Kurohito and Prince Shiki may be mentioned.

The third period covers roughly twenty years, from 710, when the city of Nara became the first permanent capital of Japan, to about 730. Modeled after Changan, the great capital of the Tang dynasty, Nara was a magnificent city, built on a grid plan on a north-south axis like its prototype. With a population of about 200,000, it was the center of national life and culture. This period saw many gifted poets: Yamabe-no-Akahito, Ōtomo-no-Tabito, Yamanoue-no-Okura, Takahashi Mushimaro, Lady Ōtomo-no-Sakanoue (Ōtomo-no-Tabito's sister), and others.

The fourth period, which saw the gradual decline of Manyō poetry, covers about thirty years, from 730 to 759, when the last poem was added to the *Man'yōshū* by Ōtomo-no-Yakamochi. Yakamochi was the leading poet of this period and the most important compiler of the *Man'yōshū*. During this time, artificial and sentimental poems increased, though there were some passionate love poems written by Lady Kasa and those exchanged between Maiden Sano-no-Chigami and Nakatomi-no-Yakamori.

Most scholars consider that the compilation of the *Man'yōshū* was completed toward the end of the Nara period.

Social Background

By Man'yō days, matriarchy had ended in Japan, and the ruling class was patriarchal and polygamous, but among the populace, social traditions and customs had not yet been influenced much by those of the continent. It was still customary for daughters to inherit from the mother, and men married into their brides' families. Women had greater authority than men in household affairs and in the arrangement of their daughters' marriages. Since the mother was the paramount domestic authority, a young man wishing to marry a girl had to obtain her mother's approval. Yet there was often an indefinite waiting period before he was adopted into her family as her husband. Under such circumstances, not just lovers, but also newly married couples could meet only briefly and in secret. Most trysts were at night, when the suitor or young husband would visit the girl at a late hour and leave her company at dawn. This fact is considered one of the primary reasons why the *Man'yōshū* has so many love poems. Particularly numerous are poems about a young man's impatience to meet his lover, poems expressing a girl's longing for her young man, and poems about newly married couples who are able to spend only a few brief hours together in the deep of night.

In Man'yō days men and women had no inhibitions about the open expression of emotion—a very different situation from the later feudal period, when, in public at least, expression of emotion was not condoned. The equal status of men and women provided a favorable milieu for the manifestation of love and genuine emotion. Love marriages were the rule, and even married men and women were not inhibited from exchanging love poems for pleasure.

On Language and Translation

The formal conventions of Japanese poetry are very different from those of poetry in European languages, because the Japanese language does not have the same reliance on stress and meter and rhyme as the languages of Europe. Further, the rhythm is also quite different.

Japanese poetry finds its origins in poetry sung to quadruple-time music, and the *tanka* retains the traits of an elegant quadruple-time song. The five 5-7-5-7-7-syllable lines are equal in duration both when read and sung. This is the basis of the euphony of Japanese poetry. In the 7-syllable line, one syllable is sustained for two beats. In order to make the 5-syllable line and 7-syllable line equal in length, three syllables in the shorter line must be lengthened. In reading, all five lines are lengthened to the same eight-beat duration. This formality of poetry recitation results in the 5-syllable lines sounding rather drawn out, while the 7-syllable line sounds somewhat breezy. It is this contrast that contributes to the emotionality of sung or recited Japanese poetry.

A notable feature of pure Japanese language is that all words end in a short unaccented vowel. So rhyme is ineffective and is not used.

When a quadruple-time song is sung, the primary stress falls on the first note and the secondary stress on the third note. However, in traditional Japanese music, it is generally said that no stress is used except for emphasis. I wished to ascertain whether or not any stress falls on the first and third notes when Japanese poetry is read. I took some Man'yō and other poems read by various specialists to the Technical College of Meiji University. Dr. Kamada Hiroyuki kindly tested them in a speech trainer, an instrument used to measure the intensity of stress. The results of these tests indicated that, although generally unperceived, some primary stress very often falls on the first note and the second stress often falls on the third note. This accounts for the fact that alliteration is occasionally found in Japanese poetry, although no rhyme is used.

Accordingly, it may not be wrong to say that any meter in Japanese poetry approaches something resembling trochaic meter rather than iambic, although it does not matter much which meter is used in translating Japanese poetry into English.

Because of its brevity, Japanese poetry is full of suggestion and implication. It is the reader's job and pleasure to perceive and appreciate this. In the case of the *Man'yōshū,* however, too much time and social change and cultural difference separate us from the ambience and intent of the original. Unfortunately, a great deal of unstated and implied content of the original has been totally lost in the chasm of time. In my translation, I have mainly directed my endeavors to the reproduction of the artistic merit of the original poetry, for literal translation often fails to reproduce poetic essence.

In this book, the Japanese practice of giving a person's surname first, followed by his or her given name, has been followed, except in the Acknowledgments.

The number in parentheses following a poem is the poem's number in the original text.

PART ONE

Poetry of Known Authorship

Members of the Imperial Family

China was to Japan what Greece and Rome were to Europe. Under the edifying influence and impact of continental literature and poetry, the Japanese aristocrats, bureaucrats, and members of the imperial family learned to write refined poetry, and their learning and culture spread from the capital to the provinces. During the first period of the *Man'yōshū*, most of the poets whose poems appear in the anthology were members of the imperial family.

Empress Iwa-no-Hime

1

I would rather go
To a lofty mountain top
On a rock to die
Than remain at home and suffer
On the painful rack of love.[⊛]

(86)

⊛ This poem is traditionally ascribed to Empress Iwa-no-Hime and is said to express her ardent love for her consort, Emperor Nintoku. However, critics say that it was composed by a later poet.

Emperor Nintoku reigned during the second half of the fourth century. During his reign, the influence of the Yamato state, extending over most parts of Japan, reached the zenith of its power. Emperor Nintoku's enormous burial mound, which was built as a symbol of national unity and power, covers an area of eighty acres and is said to be the largest tumulus in the world.

2

As the morning mist
Hangs o'er autumn paddy fields,
So my yearning
Hangs o'er my heavy heart.
When will it dissipate?

(88)

Princess Yata

3

For but a day
I await his return.
How can I bear
This weary, endless wait
Which will bring me to my grave?❽

(484)

Crown Prince Naka-no-Ōe (later Emperor Tenji)

Crown Prince Naka-no-Ōe was the thirty-sixth sovereign of Japan. In 646 he overthrew the Soga family, which had threatened to usurp imperial sovereignty. Becoming crown prince in 646, he promulgated a reform edict known as the Taika (Great Reform) and assiduously strove to lay the foundation for a centralized bureaucratic monarchy on the model of China's Tang dynasty. After the expedition that he sent to Korea in aid of the Kingdom of Paekche was defeated by the combined forces of Tang and Silla in 663, he moved the palace to Ōtsu and ascended the throne in 667. Recruiting frontier guards (*sakimori*) from across the country, he consolidated Japan's defenses against possible continental invasions.

He was an enthusiastic student of Chinese literature and culture and invited continental scholars as instructors. He was the patron of the imperial poetry salon.

---

❽ This poem is traditionally ascribed to Princess Yata and expresses her ardent love for Emperor Nintoku, her half brother by a different mother. Later she became Empress Nintoku after the death of his consort, Iwa-no-Hime. Critics also say that this poem is the work of a later poet.

In ancient days marriage between half brother and sister was permitted if their mothers were different.

4

> All the sky is aflame
> With resplendent evening clouds
> Glowing above the sea.
> Bright and clear the moon will shine
> O'er the glassy sea this night.

(15)

Crown Prince Ōama (later Emperor Temmu) and Princess Nukata

In 668 Emperor Tenji hosted a hunting party on the royal hunting preserve. Among those present were Crown Prince Ōama, who was Emperor Tenji's younger brother and who later became Emperor Temmu, and Princess Nukata, who was an eminent poet highly endowed with beauty and talent. Princess Nukata was formerly a favorite of Crown Prince Ōama and bore him Princess Tōchi. But Emperor Tenji took her from his younger brother and made her one of his consorts. This affair embittered their relationship but was not the primary cause of the later Jinshin Uprising of 672 between Crown Prince Ōama and Emperor Kōbun, Emperor Tenji's son.

Crown Prince Ōama had poetic talent and fostered learning and poetry. His reign as Emperor Temmu (673–686) and the subsequent reign of his consort, Empress Jitō (687–702), saw the greatest number of preeminent poets and was the golden period of Man'yō poetry.

Princess Nukata

5

> Riding hither and yon
> In the royal hunting fields
> Spread with red and violet tints,
> Wide you wave your arms at me.
> Will not the watchman notice?[a]

(20)

[a] The "watchman" alludes to Emperor Tenji.

In the Japanese of No. 6, the beauty of the princess is compared to a gromwell plant (*murasaki-gusa*), from which a violet dye is obtained. In the translation, it is replaced by the more familiar rose.

Some say that Nos. 5 and 6 were introduced as an entertainment at a dinner party given after the hunting was over. Others say that they were privately exchanged between Prince Ōama and Princess Nukata.

Crown Prince Ōama

6

You're as sweet and fair
As a lovely rose in June.
Wedded as you are,
Were you not next to my heart,
Why would I long for you?

(21)

Princess Nukata

Princess Nukata's fine aesthetic sentiment and sophisticated phraseol-
ogy rank her among the leading Man'yō poets. She was a favorite
figure in the imperial poetry salon.

7

At Nigitatsu
We've waited to board ship.
The moon has risen now,
And the tide is on the ebb—
Let us be away!ⓐ

(8)

When Emperor Tenji gave a poetry party on the subject of judging
between the brilliance of myriads of cherry blossoms on the spring
mountains and the glory of tinted leaves on the autumn mountains,
Princess Nukata submitted the following poem and won a prize. This
poem, which shows the sophisticated technique of antithetical phrases
in the Chinese poetic style, is not exactly lyric, but is given here to
illustrate how Emperor Tenji and later sovereigns were patrons of the
imperial poetry salon.

ⓐ In 663 an expedition was sent to Korea to aid the Kingdom of Paekche. It mus-
tered its forces at Nigitatsu, on Shikoku island facing the Seto Inland Sea. At the
headquarters were Empress Saimei, Crown Prince Naka-no-Ōe, the de facto su-
preme commander, and his consort, Princess Nukata, together with Prince Ōama
and his consort, Princess Ōta. Princess Nukata is presumed to have been performing
the duty of expressing the sovereign's command and intentions in poetry. The expedition sustained a total defeat by the combined fleets of Tang and Silla.

In ancient times it was believed that a god could enter into a woman but not into
a man, and a woman was regarded as a mysterious being capable of deriving divine
inspiration and of supplicating divine protection. In the event of war, a woman of
high birth accompanied a warship.

8

When spring comes,
Freed from winter's frigid bonds,
Birds which have been mute
Return with merry songs.
Flowers which were dead
Come alive in brilliant tints,
But luxuriant growth
Puts the blossoms beyond our
 reach,
Rank weeds in the fields
Bar our access to the blossoms fair.
Tinted leaves on autumn's hills
We can pick and delight in.
And wish the green leaves
Were tinted as well.
'Tis our sole regret.
We prefer the autumn hills.[footnote]

(16)

The following poem was composed for Emperor Tenji.

9

Longing for my lord,
I start up, anxious,
When an autumn breeze
Blows and sways the bamboo blind
Hanging at my bower door.

(488)

Princess Kagami

It is said that Princess Kagami was either the elder sister or the mother of Princess Nukata.

The following poem is her reply to a poem given her by Emperor Tenji, who loved her as well as Princess Nukata.

[footnote] This poem has been regarded as difficult to appreciate. The merits of spring and autumn were frequently compared at poetry contests.

10

My deep love for you
Is a stream pure and clear
Flowing under tinted growth
Down an autumn mountain
And is deeper than your love for me.

(92)

The following poem refers to Princess Nukata's poem No. 9 in this book.

11

How I envy you!
Even a gentle breeze
Makes your heart rejoice and leap.
Could my heart await
Even the coming of a breeze,
What on earth would I ever rue?

(489)

12

Lovely cuckoo blithe
In the woods of Iware,
Stop your silver air!
Your loud songs
Add to the ardor of my love.

(1419)

Princess Kagami and Fujiwara-no-Kamatari

Princess Kagami composed the following poem when visited by Fujiwara-no-Kamatari, who was lord keeper of the privy seal at that time.

Princess Kagami

13

Should you leave after dawn,
Trusting we can cover up our tryst
Just as easily as we cover up my comb
    casket,
Our affair would come to light
And I'd fall in disgrace,
Though your name remains intact.

(93)

Fujiwara-no-Kamatari (614–669)

Fujiwara-no-Kamatari rendered such distinguished services to Emperor Tenji that he was granted the special privilege of being allowed to pay court to a princess. Later he rose to premiership and became the founder of the Fujiwara family, which controlled power at court for the subsequent four centuries.

The following is a reply to the preceding poem.

14

I'm a sleeping vine
On sacred Mt. Mimuro.
Pray, pray, sleep with me,
As the troth of your love,
Else I'll be overcome by longing.🐝

(94)

Prince Ōtsu (663–686) and Lady Ishikawa

Prince Ōtsu was the son of Emperor Temmu. His mother, Princess Ōta, the daughter of Emperor Tenji, died when he was a very young child. He had a magnanimous character and extraordinary intellectual and literary endowments. His Chinese poems included in the *Kaifūsō*, the first collection of Chinese poetry written by Japanese poets, are among the best in the collection. He was greatly loved by his father, Emperor Temmu, was given the highest court office next to the crown

---

🐝 This poem contains a play on words with reference to *sanekazura* (here translated as "sleeping vine"), which is a climbing plant of the genus *Magnolia*.

prince, and was allowed to take part in the affairs of state. When Emperor Temmu died in 686, his consort ascended the throne as Empress Jitō. Her son, Prince Kusakabe, was heir apparent to the throne, but he was in delicate health, so the highly gifted and popular Prince Ōtsu was a formidable rival for the throne. The prince must have been aware that he was in a difficult situation. The *Kaifūsō* says: "A Korean astrologer and fortuneteller, seeing his physiognomy, told him that he had a noble, kingly countenance and that he would have to be a sovereign or he would perish." Presumably these words motivated Prince Ōtsu to plan to seize the throne. The *Kaifūsō* also says that he confided this scheme to a close friend, who later turned informer, and the prince was executed.

From statements made about him in the *Man'yōshū*, the *Chronicles of Japan (Nihon-shoki)* and the *Kaifūsō*, some commentators gather that on the advice of her close councilor, Fujiwara-no-Fuhito, Empress Jitō may possibly have devised a scheme to induce the prince to revolt against the throne. On the discovery of his treason, he was executed only twenty days after the death of Emperor Temmu. His early death was greatly regretted.

When he was executed, his young consort, Princess Yamanoue, the daughter of Emperor Tenji, rushed to her husband's side, barefoot and with her hair disheveled, and shared his fate. All those present were brought to tears at the tragic sight.

It is likely that Prince Ōtsu was too young to have the statesmanship to handle his precarious situation, as his father, Emperor Temmu, had.

The following is a poem that he wrote to a court lady, Ishikawa, a talented beauty who was a favorite of Prince Kusakabe. Her reply poem follows. Nos. 15 and 16 are a pair.

Prince Ōtsu

15

On the yonder hill,
Taking shelter in a cave,
I awaited you.
Meanwhile dewdrops, falling,
Made my garments wet and cold.

(107)

Lady Ishikawa

16

O that I had been
The mountain dew, which falling,
Made your garments wet and cold,
While you awaited me,
Taking shelter in a cave.[☺]

(108)

Prince Ōtsu

Prince Ōtsu composed the following poem on the eve of his execution.

17

This will be the last
I shall see of mallards
On Iware Pond,
For tomorrow I shall be
Hidden behind the clouds.[☙]

(416)

Princess Oku

Princess Oku was the daughter of Emperor Temmu and elder sister of Prince Ōtsu. On the eve of his execution, possibly to bid him farewell, Princess Oku, who was at that time Chief Priestess of the Grand Shrine of Ise, visited Prince Ōtsu. She composed the following three poems when she saw him off at daybreak.

18

My dear brother left
For Yamato when still dark,
Never to return,
Seeing him off, long I stood,
Till my feet were drenched with dew.

(105)

☺ Some days after exchanging the above poems, the pair had a tryst.

☙ Being "hidden behind the clouds" was a euphemism for death in the Man'yō days.
His tragic death, the pathos of his elegy, and the dirges his sister composed (Nos. 18 to 20) left deep impressions on the minds of his contemporaries and later generations.

19

How can he alone
Cross the autumn mountains,
Which are difficult to cross
Even when
We together go?

(106)

20

Left alone in the world,
From tomorrow I shall look on
    Mt. Futagami,
Where my brother is interred,
As my very brother dear.

(165)

Empress Jitō (d. 703)

Empress Jitō was the forty-first sovereign and the second daughter of Emperor Tenji. After the death of Emperor Temmu, she succeeded to the throne. She was a woman of talent and dignity tinged with sternness. During the Jinshin War (672) and during the reign of Emperor Temmu (673–686), she constantly assisted him. During her reign (687–696) and later regency (697–702) for her very young grandson, Emperor Mommu, she assiduously administered the affairs of state.

She was a talented poet. Kakinomoto-no-Hitomaro and other eminent poets were very active during her reign. Her poem below is also included in the popular *Hyakunin-isshu* ("One Hundred Poems by One Hundred Poets") anthology and is very well known to the Japanese.

21

Spring has passed.
Summer seems to be here now.
Rows of white garments air
In the sun upon the slopes
Of graceful Mt. Kagu.

(28)

Emperor Shōmu (701–756)

Emperor Shōmu was the forty-fifth sovereign. He was a fervent Buddhist and built the vast Tōdaiji temple, which houses the famed bronze Great Buddha image. Its construction laid a heavy burden on the national coffers.

22

In your poem you say
That when I met you on the road with a
    smile,
You were so smitten
That you felt as if you'd fade away
Like a flake of falling snow.
Far beyond words you are sweet.

(624)

Empress Kōmyō (701–760)

Empress Kōmyō was the highly intelligent and benevolent consort of Emperor Shōmu. She was the daughter of Fujiwara-no-Fuhito and the granddaughter of Fujiwara-no-Kamatari. After the death of Emperor Shōmu, she donated his treasures to the Tōdaiji temple, including precious works of art not only of Japan but also from China, India, and Persia. They are preserved in the Shōsōin Repository in Nara.

She presented the following poem to her consort, Emperor Shōmu.

23

Snow is falling thick,
Blossoming upon the trees.
Were you here with me
To share this loveliness,
How joyful I would be!

(1658)

29

Prince Atsumi

The prince was a government official.

24

Yamabuki blossoms—
Their golden petals mirrored
In the crystal stream
Of the river
Where frogs in chorus sing.

(1435)

Princess Hirokawa

Princess Hirokawa was the granddaughter of Emperor Temmu.

25

Stricken heavily
With the painful burden of love,
I am just like one
Straining to pull uphill
Seven heavy-laden carts.

(694)

Princess Kamo

Princess Kamo was the granddaughter of Emperor Temmu. She sent
this poem to a member of the Ōtomo family.

26

In the moonlit night
I met you, to my joy.
But never will I breathe
Anything of our tryst,
Nor even that I know you by sight.

(565)

Prince Kashiwade

Prince Kashiwade was vice-governor general of the *Dazaifu* (government and defense headquarters of Kyushu).

27

> I am envious
> Of the wild geese, which forage for food
> On the beach at morn
> And in the evening wing their way
> Toward Yamato, my home.
>
> (954)

Prince Nagata

28

> Sadness comes over me,
> Freezing my heart and soul,
> When chilly rain,
> Gathering in heavy clouds,
> Streams down from a sullen sky.
>
> (82)

Prince Shiki

Prince Shiki was the seventh son of Emperor Tenji and a distinguished poet. He composed the following poem after Emperor Temmu's Kiyomigahara Palace at Asuka was supplanted by Empress Jitō's Fujiwara Palace.

29

> Winds once fluttered
> The elegant sleeves
> Of the ladies fair.
> Now the Asuka Court is gone,
> Sigh and mourn the winds through the
>   ruins.
>
> (51)

30

> Above the rocky wall
> Down which water softly flows,
> Clumps of bracken
> Fan out in tender green.
> Spring has arrived.
>
> (1418)

Princess Tajima

Princess Tajima was a granddaughter of Emperor Temmu. She fell in love with Prince Hozumi, her cousin, the grandson of Emperor Temmu, and their meeting was the subject of gossip.

31

> Tortured by sharp tongues,
> At the early break of day,
> My dear love to meet,
> I wade to the far shore of the river,
> Which I've never dared to cross.

(116)

Princess Takada

Princess Takada was a great-granddaughter of Emperor Temmu. The following poem was written to Prince Imaki.

32

> If you let me know
> That you mean to marry me,
> I will meet you,
> However sharp
> People's tongues may be.

(539)

Princess Yamaguchi

The following two poems are among the five poems that Princess Yamaguchi wrote to Ōtomo-no-Yakamochi.

33

> As the flood tide comes,
> Flowing up the reedy shore,
> So my yearning for you,
> Surging within me,
> Ever overflows my heart.

(617)

34

As drops of dew,
Sparkling on the autumn grass,
Scatter like pearls
With a gentle breath of air,
So my tears never cease to fall.

(1617)

Prince Yuge

Prince Yuge was the sixth son of Emperor Temmu.

35

Moored at a wharf,
Ships roll at the mercy of waves;
So my heart is never at rest,
Pining, wasting for my love,
Who is now another's bride.

(122)

Prince Yuhara and a Maiden

Prince Yuhara was the son of Prince Shiki and a grandson of Emperor
Tenji. This and the following four poems were an exchange with a
maiden.

36

The lady of my heart
Is the laurel in the moon.
She is in my sight,
But is beyond my reach.
Whatever should I do?[*]

(632)

[*] The Japanese word translated here as "laurel" is *katsura* (Judas tree). The Japanese
phrase meaning "*katsura* tree in the moon" originates from a Chinese proverb and is
used in allusion to something precious that is visible but unobtainable.

Maiden

37

How I envy your good wife!
You see her always at home,
Yet you never tire of her sight.
Even when you travel,
She is in your company.

(634)

Prince Yuhara

38

I present you
This robe as a keepsake.
Wear it close to you
When you sleep at night,
And you'll be in my embrace.

(636)

Maiden

39

Silent as it is,
I shall look upon your robe
As your very self.
I will wear it close to me,
And I'll ever be with you.@

(637)

Prince Yuhara

A poem describing the sentiment of a woman waiting for her lover's coming.

40

In the glorious light
Flowing from the lunar orb,
Let my lover come,
For he dwells not far,
Just beyond yonder hill.

(670)

@ A faithful translation of the fifth line reads: "Though it does not speak to me."

Ten Poets

Ten poets are selected here as being of major importance. It is their poetry that immortalizes the *Man'yōshū*. These ten poets are divided into two groups; the five poets of the first group are the best known and most important.

Five Preeminent Poets
>   Kakinomoto-no-Hitomaro
>   Yamabe-no-Akahito
>   Ōtomo-no-Tabito
>   Yamanoue-no-Okura
>   Ōtomo-no-Yakamochi

Five Major Poets
>   Takechi-no-Kurohito
>   Takahashi Mushimaro
>   Lady Ōtomo-no-Sakanoue
>   Maiden Sano-no-Chigami
>   Lady Kasa

Five Preeminent Poets

Kakinomoto-no-Hitomaro

Kakinomoto-no-Hitomaro was a court poet during Empress Jitō's reign (686–702). His superb poetry may be divided into two types: ceremonial and lyric. His ceremonial poetry is unsurpassed. He must have enjoyed immense popularity in the imperial salon. When the empress or members of the imperial family made trips for pleasure, hunting, and the like, he was in their retinue and composed peerless eulogies, extolling the glory of the imperial reign. When a member of the imperial family passed away, he composed elegies in incomparable rhetoric. These poems comprise his ceremonial poetry.

But it is in his lyric poetry, in both quality and quantity, that he stands out as the prince of poets, not only during the Man'yō days but throughout the entire history of Japanese literature. His lyricism is so beautiful, so deep in feeling, and so felicitously expressive of the genuine love and subtle feelings of men and women that he has been venerated as a "Saint of Poetry" (*kasei*). The best of his lyric poems are presented in this collection.

The *Man'yōshū* contains a total of eighty-four poems of his genuine composition, sixty-six of which are short and eighteen are long poems. The *Man'yōshū* also includes 365 anonymous poems taken from the Hitomaro Collection. It is thought that some of the poems in the Hitomaro Collection are his, and the remaining are those that he selected from contemporary poems and folk songs, some of which he is supposed to have touched or improved.

Hitomaro was one of many *toneri,* a lower official who attended a sovereign or a member of the imperial family, handling miscellaneous jobs. Hitomaro first entered the service of Crown Prince Kusakabe. In 689, when the crown prince died, he was transferred to the service of First Minister Prince Takechi, who was a highly popular man of distinguished ability, but in 696 Takechi died suddenly, and Hitomaro took office at Empress Jitō's court.

In ancient days all higher offices were monopolized by members of the imperial family and the higher nobility. The way was open for the sons of officials and people of position to enter government service by means of an examination system, but it was practically impossible for those who did not come of a noble family to rise to a higher office. Officials of the sixth and lower court ranks were classed as "lower officials."

Poems written by the members of the imperial family and

higher officials were accepted for the *Man'yōshū*, and these were accompanied by biographical sketches and brief notes. Poetry by officials of lower rank and by commoners is included in the *Man'yōshū*, but not accompanied by biographical sketches or notes. Hitomaro's poems in the *Man'yōshū* have no accompanying biographical sketch or notes, and he is thus presumed to have been a lower-ranking official. Accordingly, his life and activities have to be surmised from his poetry.

After First Minister Prince Takechi died unexpectedly, the late Crown Prince Kusakabe's young son was enthroned as Emperor Mommu in 697 under the regency of Empress Jitō, his grandmother.

Emperor Temmu's absolute sovereignty had been secure. Empress Jitō was a woman of talent and dignity, but many princes and powerful lords were disgruntled with her arbitrary rule. As a boy, Hitomaro witnessed the tragic Jinshin War of 672, and he must have known that her reign was not altogether stable or secure. In his ceremonial poetry, he is said to incorporate his generation's adulatory ideal of imperial rule. After Empress Jitō died in 702, real political power passed to the hands of Fujiwara Fuhito, young Emperor Mommu's father-in-law. (Fuhito's daughter was Emperor Mommu's consort.) Hitomaro must have been disappointed. He no longer composed poetry glorifying the imperial reign or eulogizing the newly risen Fujiwara family. He was transferred to the government office of remote Iwami Province (present-day Shimane prefecture). There he married his beloved second wife, Yusami, also a poet, an educated woman and daughter of a country squire.[●] In 707, when he was ordered to return to the capital, he had to leave her behind. The long elegiac poem below (No. 42) with two short epilogues, which describes his parting sentiment, is considered one of his masterpieces. After his service in Iwami Province, nothing is known about his life. He is supposed to have died sometime before 710, when the capital was transferred to Nara.

Hitomaro composed the following poem while on an overnight hunt in the retinue of Prince Karu (later Emperor Mommu).

41

Over the eastern fields
Pours the mellow golden light
Of the rising sun.
In the western sky, the moon
Declines behind the hills.

(48)

[●] In those days most government officials who were ordered to serve at provincial offices could not afford to take their wives and families to their posts. Thus an official in provincial service often became intimate with a country girl and married her.

37

42

'Tis often said,
That the Tsuno Coast
Of the Sea of Iwami
Has no sandy shore
Nor a good lagoon.
Even though there is no good bay
Nor lagoon,
Whales abound off the coast.
And green sleek seaweed
Grows abundant in the sea.
Wings of winds at dawn
Wings of foamy waves at eve
Bring green smooth seaweed
To the pebbly strand.

The poet, leaving his wife behind, starts for the capital.

Sorely was I grieved
When I had to leave my wife,
Who oft twined round me
Smooth and tender as seaweed,
Which with wind and wave,
Drifts upon the sea.

The poet now climbs a mountain on his way to the capital.

As I look back
Toward my darling's home,
At each turn of the road
Over this mountain,
Lower and lower falls the town,
Higher and higher the mountains rise.
O you Mountain which I climb,
Become flat!
Let me once glimpse
My lovely wife,
Downcast
As the wilting summer grass,
Pining after me.

(131)

This long poem is followed by the following two.

43

Through the trees,
Can my darling wife at home
See me wave my arms,
Bidding her my last farewell,
From the top of Mt. Takatsuno.

(132)

44

At the top of the hill
Overgrown with bamboo grass
Rustling in the wind,
How I yearn for my dear wife
Left alone at home.

(133)

The following two poems are the envoys of a long poem that is not included here.

45

Rapidly
My gray horse has carried me
To the mountaintop,
To the height of floating clouds
Far past my sweet one's abode.

(136)

46

O you tinted leaves!
Cease your swirling about.
Through the vista of trees,
Pray, let me have a glimpse
Of my darling love at home.

(137)

The following elegy indicates that Hitomaro had a wife in the capital whom he had some reason to hide from others' knowledge. From his two long poems, he is presumed to have had two wives.

47

Karu is the town
Where my fair, sweet darling dwells.
Should I often visit her,
Our intimacy would be revealed.
Harboring my love
Hidden deep in my heart
As in the depths of a pool
Girt round by cliffs,
I felt secure
As riding a large ship,
Confident
That we would meet anon.
One day word was brought.
As the orb of day
Fades away at eventide,
As the bright full moon
Hides behind murky clouds,
So my darling wife,
Whose embrace was
Smooth as green seaweed,
Had fallen, like an autumn leaf.

At the news of her death,
I did not know
What to say or do.
Hoping to allay
Even a thousandth part
Of my grief,
I betook myself in tears
To the market of Karu,
Where my wife was wont to go.
There I watched and listened.
But no trace of her voice was there,
Not even the birds
In the nearby hills were heard.
No face
Resembled hers.
Nothing could I do
But call her name
And wave my arms in vain.

(207)

The following lyric is one of two envoys to the preceding long poem.

48

The hillsides are ablaze
With glorious tints of red and gold,
So dense that
I've strayed from the path
To the grassy grave
Of my beloved wife.

(208)

The following two short elegies (Nos. 49 and 50) are the envoys of a long elegy on his late wife, which is not included here.

49

Full bright shines the moon,
As it did this night last year.
Distant has become the day
When my late dear wife and I
Shared the joy of watching the moon.

(211)

41

50

Burying the corpse
Of my darling wife
In a dreary mountain grave,
In deep grief,
Like one dead, I came down the trail.

(212)

51

My beloved wife
Must await my coming home,
Little knowing that I lie
Pillowed amidst the crags
Of wild Mt. Kamo.[@]

(223)

52

Our great lord of lords,
Gracious holy god,
Dwells above the rainy clouds,
Where the thunder rolls and peals
Amid flashes of lightning.[※]

(235)

53

Plovers' plaintive cries,
Sweeping o'er the evening waves
Of Lake Biwa,
Overwhelm our hearts,
With yearnings for sweet bygone days.[☙]

(266)

@ A poem that Hitomaro composed on the eve of his death. The location of Mt. Kamo has not been ascertained.

※ Hitomaro composed this poem when Empress Jitō ascended Ikazuchi-no-Oka ("Hill of Thunder") and offered prayers.

☙ Hitomaro composed this poem when he accompanied Empress Jitō on her visit to the ruins of Ōmi Palace at Ōtsu. This palace was built by Emperor Tenji in 667 by the western shore of Lake Biwa, only to be destroyed in the Jinshin Uprising five years later.

54

Men of yore as well,
Pining after their sweet loves,
Must needs have passed
Many painful sleepless nights,
Just as have I.

(497)

55

Swept away
By the haste of departure,
I left without a gentle word
With my dear wife.
Fathomless is my yearning.[註]

(503)

56

In the ocean of the skies,
Waves of clouds rise and fall—
Fair and clear the lunar boat,
Passing in and out of clouds,
Floats amid the sea of stars.

(1068)

57

Far above the roar
Of the rapids of the stream,
About the peak
Of graceful Mt. Yutsuki,
Hover heavy clouds.

(1088)

[註] See note to No. 110.

58

We are like foam,
Always coming, going
On the stream
Rushing down the vale
Of Mt. Makimuku.

(1269)

59

For my dear one's attire,
I have put my heart
Into weaving this white cloth.
When spring comes,
What color shall I dye the robe?

(1281)

60

The year has worn away;
Now in the dead of night
Wild geese cry
Across starry skies
Where sails the bright full moon.[@]

(1701)

61

Never can I see the beach
Where I passed a happy moment
With my dear wife
But I'm overwhelmed with grief.
Last autumn, she passed away,
Like an autumn leaf.

(1796)

[@] This is regarded as a poignant evocation of an autumn scene.

44

62

Sorrow fills my heart
As I come to this strand,
This lovely seashore,
Which I once enjoyed with my dear wife,
Years ago, when she lived.

(1798)

63

In the vernal fields
Warblers sweetly sing and part,
While we sadly weep and part.
As you return home,
Keep me in your heart.[⊛]

(1890)

64

With the coming of spring,
The lovely soul of my dear girl,
Fair and pliable
As a willow leaf,
Has now taken hold of me.[⚘]

(1896)

65

Every time I see her
With her pink cheeks
Fair as the Weaver Maiden,
I yearn for her,
Wed to another though she is.

(1999)

[⊛] This poem was written from a woman's point of view.

[⚘] The literal translation of the fifth line reads: "Has now entered into me [or my soul]."

66

How brief
Our ardor,
After our long-pent love.
Too short,
Our time together,
Yet you ask me for your sash.[@]

(2023)

67

What is there to regret,
If I could but hear the voice
Of my darling love,
Sweet as the songs of birds
In the tinted autumn hills?[*]

(2239)

68

The girl for whom I long—
Let her die. What do I care?
Many say that
However long I live,
She'll never give her heart to me.

(2355)

69

At daybreak you rise
And through the dewy field go,
With your robe hem wet with dew,
I will also rise betimes,
With my hem wet with dew.[*]

(2357)

[@] In this poem, a woman sulks, wishing to keep her lover with her.

[*] A poem of a man's sorrow over a long separation from his love.

[*] This poem was written from a woman's point of view.

70

What would it avail
Should I live to old age?
Even should I live long,
'Tis well nigh impossible
For me to meet my love.[a]

(2358)

71

Shunning the public eye,
Seldom do I meet him,
Who is my love and life.
Were I a breeze,
I could sport about him.

(2359)

72

Never, since I left
My mother's tender care,
Has my plight
Been so sad and dire.
I am entirely lost.

(2368)

73

I never sleep about
As all other women do,
And I pass sad, sleepless nights,
Dying for a sight of you,
Who are everything to me.

(2369)

[a] This theme occurs a number of times in the *Man'yōshū*. See No. 164 and compare Nos. 287, 315, 331, and 345.

74

"Let her die from love
If she will. What should I care
If her heart breaks?"
That must be what he thinks.
Not a word he writes to me.

(2370)

75

There's no time of the day
When I don't think of you.
But at eventide,
So intense becomes my love
That I know not what to do.[*]

(2373)

76

I so hope
That those who see
The light of day after me
Stray not away from the beaten path
Into the thorny path of love.

(2375)

77

So lost in love
Night and day
Gone is my sense
Of life
Worthy of a stalwart man.

(2376)

[*] This poem was written from a woman's point of view.

48

78

No more do I care to live
On the painful rack
Of unrequited love.
How I wish I'd died
Ere I lost my heart to her!🖾

(2377)

79

I know well enough
That he'll never come to me,
And my love is all in vain.
Yet I wonder how it is
That I keep loving him.

(2378)

80

Walking back and forth,
Looking toward the ferry,
Anxiously I await
The dear beloved of my heart,
Coming for our tryst.

(2379)

81

So ardent
Is my desire to meet you—
For the two nights past
I have pined away
As if for a thousand years.

(2381)

🖾 Poems Nos. 79 to 84 portray women's longings for their lovers or husbands, who come to visit them only at intervals and leave them at daybreak. In Man'yō days, many men and women had to live apart for an indefinite time even after their marriage.

82

Crowds pass along
The royal city's roads,
Dazzling in the sun.
But among them only one
Is the lover of my heart.

(2382)

83

Were you to visit me
Every night,
Our love would be revealed.
How I wish this happy night
Was a thousand years long!

(2387)

84

O that this sweet night
Would never pass away—
After you are gone,
I will be in agony
Till you return to me in the depths of
   darkness.

(2389)

85

It was but last night
That I glimpsed her.
But beyond all help,
This morn I am consumed
By flaming love.

(2391)

86

Since I've known my love,
All the dearer has she grown.
I long for her
Far more than when I
But saw her at a distance.[*]

(2392)

87

Merely a single glimpse,
And gone—
That instant
Has left me worn away,
Thin as a morning shadow.[**]

(2394)

[*] The viewpoint here could be that of a man or a woman, so "she" and "her" can be replaced by "he" and "him."

[**] This is considered one of Kakinomoto-no-Hitomaro's most exquisite poems, expressing a young man's ardent love for a beauty he had seen momentarily, just once.

88

In all my days,
Never have I seen a girl
Of such lovely grace.
O that I could please my eyes
With another sight of her!

(2396)

89

There goes my love,
Casting not a glance at me,
Seeming to say,
"Let him die from love. Who cares?"
Looking prim, she passes my gate.

(2401)

90

Now the year is at an end.
And my life is at an end.
But I'll never forget
My sweet one, with whom, when young,
I pledged my troth of love.

(2410)

91

My underclothes
Somehow have come loose.
Never shall I disclose our love
Till I see him face to face
And confirm his love for me.[a]

(2413)

92

As the sky we see
And the earth on which we live
Have no bounds or end,
So our passion is endless.
We'll never cease to meet and love.

(2419)

93

Gazing at the moon—
It shines the same everywhere.
So our love is e'er the same,
Though lofty mountains
Keep my wife and me apart.

(2420)

[a] The poet implies that her sensual state is due to her lover's desire for her; she wishes to keep their love secret till she meets him and confirms his commitment to her.

94

To be sure, I have a horse,
But to meet you secretly,
I have come on foot
Across the hills and vales,
Driven by my love for you.

(2425)

95

In vain is my life,
Like a word written on water.
Praying to the gods,
I have vowed
That I'll meet my darling love.

(2433)

96

Though she lives
At the end of the earth
Where heaven meets the firmament
And clouds are born and rise,
Yet with whom should I lie
But the darling of my heart?

(2451)

97

Gazing at the moon,
My distant love
Must think of me.
Let no speck of cloud
Dim the lunar brilliance.

(2460)

98

I am lost in love for my dear one,
And melancholy rules me.
In my tear-filled eyes,
Even the grass by my abode
Droops and withers.[8]

(2465)

99

As a snowbell fair
Heavy laden with clear dew
Bends its head,
So I hang my head,
Heavy laden with deep love.

(2469)

100

As you bind
Stout sedge on the hills,
If you bind me
To a pledge of love,
Then I will tryst with you.[*]

(2477)

101

Would that I could see
My dear love, who remains hidden
At home,
Like the silkworms in cocoons,
Which her mother rears.[*]

(2495)

---

[8] A poem writen from a woman's standpoint.

[*] A poem from a woman to a man who is wishy-washy in his courtship of her.

[*] A poem complaining about a mother's protective care of her daughters, especially her oldest.

102

Every morn and eve,
Even if I could see your face
Clearly in my hand mirror
Which I hold before me,
I'd never tire of gazing at you.

(2502)

103

O that I had gazed
Longer at the face
Of the dear lover of my heart
When he left in the early morn.
All this day long I'll pine for him.[a]

(2841)

104

How can I e'er see
My sweet one with indifference,
Just as other people do?
I never see my love
But I wish to rest my head
On her tender silken arm.

(2843)

A more modern young man might express the last two lines in some other way, e.g.,

But I wish to kiss
Her cheeks and rosy lips.

[a] Maybe this was her lover's first visit, and since it was still a little dark when he left, she was too shy to gaze at his face.

105

Longing for him,
While I tie my sash,
Visible to all,
Many a time I untie
The unseen inner cord.[@]

(2851)

106

Rumors spreading wide,
Now I dare not meet her.
Were she undergarments,
With the rumor everywhere,
I would wear her close.

(2852)

107

My consuming passion
Robbed me of restful sleep.
O morning breeze!
If you brushed my sweet love,
Come and touch me as well.

(2858)

108

Cherry blossoms fair
Only too soon fall and scatter.
Such is the way of life.
Crowds come and go,
Meet and scatter in a moment.

(3129)

[@] The person is probably a woman. Again, the image of a loosened inner sash (which fastens the underclothes) occurs. On the most immediate level, the image is an anticipation of a love tryst and the events that will occur then.

109

'Tis a thousand years
Since I met you last.
I must be bemused.
Anticipating seeing you—
So many years have passed, it seems.

(3470)

110

Swept up
In the haste of departure,
I came away without speaking
To my beloved wife.
Fathomless is my regret.[@]

(3481)

Yamabe-no-Akahito

Next to Kakinomoto-no-Hitomaro, Yamabe-no-Akahito stands out as the greatest poet in the history of Japanese poetry. His genius lies especially in the realm of short poems, and his nature poems are particularly inspired. The short poems introduced here are his loveliest. His masterpieces (Nos. 112 and 113) are the two envoys of a long poem portraying a view of the Yoshino mountains, which he composed when he accompanied Emperor Shōmu on a trip to Yoshino.

The dates of his birth and death are uncertain. He was a contemporary of Ōtomo-no-Tabito and was most active in the middle of the Nara period. The Nara period was different from the preceding period, when Kakinomoto-no-Hitomaro lived, for the real power had shifted to the hands of the Fujiwara family, and the emperor no longer had absolute power. In his poetry, instead of eulogizing the divine glory of the imperial reign, Akahito laid emphasis on the aesthetic appreciation of natural beauty.

[@] This may possibly be a poem composed by a man sent to be a frontier guard. No. 55 is almost identical.

The following poem is the envoy of a long poem.

111

On the Tago coast,
The graceful form of Mt. Fuji
Appears in clear view,
Its sky-high peak
Thickly clad in white snow.

(318)

112

In the treetops
On the slopes of Mt. Kisa,
Flocks of singing birds
Fill the dense woods
With their joyous songs.

(924)

113

As the night wears on
By the banks of a clear stream
Overgrown with bushes,
Plovers in the thicket
Send up their cry.

(925)

114

Should my travels leave me spent,
Like clothes worn to tatters,
Would I forget
My captivating love
For a single day?

(947)

115

Violet gathering,
Into the vernal fields I went.
So beautiful were the fields
That I slept the night
In the open air.

(1424)

116

Leaving their abodes
And flying over hills
Into the vernal fields,
Warblers sing
Among the trees in bloom.

(3915)

Ōtomo-no-Tabito (665–731)

Ōtomo-no-Tabito was born of an illustrious family renowned for its military exploits. The once illustrious Ōtomo military clan, of which he was the leader, was in steady decline, eclipsed by the rising influence of the Fujiwara family. He was well acquainted with Chinese literature, Buddhism, and Taoism. He rose to assume a good ministerial post at court. In 727, when he was a little past sixty years of age, he was appointed governor general of the *Dazaifu* (the headquarters of the government and defense of Kyushu). He must have felt frustrated, for he had to leave the central political arena in Nara.

He had a bright, sociable character, and he formed a poetry circle at the *Dazaifu*, which was as prestigious as the one in Nara.

Earlier he had lost his first wife. While he was on his way to Kyushu, he shared the joy of viewing noted sights and scenic spots in company with his second wife. However, shortly after their arrival in Kyushu, his second wife died. In poetry he sought consolation for his grief over her death and frustration in life. His noted poems in praise of sake are considered to have been written in part to drown his grief over the death of his beloved wife and in part to express his feelings of frustration in politics. Two of his sake poems (Nos. 117 and 118) are included in this book. His short, touching poems about his late wife (Nos. 121 to 127) are treasured as exquisite gems of poetry.

In 730 he was recalled to court service to assume the high office of chief councilor. He died a year later.

The following two poems are in praise of sake.

117

'Tis no easy task
To become a man of worth.
Fain I'd be a jug
For holding fine sake,
In which I'd steep myself.

(343)

118

Not a precious stone
Nor a priceless brilliant gem
Nothing whatsoe'er
Has so much worth to me
As a cup of raw sake.

(345)

119

If I can enjoy myself
While I'm in this mundane world
What should I care,
If I were born a bird
Or an insect in my next life?

(348)

120

All that live on earth
Will be shortly dead and gone.
So while we're alive,
In this mundane world, why not
Let our life be sweet and gay?◉

(349)

121

How should I e'er let
Anyone, however fair,
Rest her head upon my arm,
Whereupon my late beloved wife
Used to pillow her lovely head?✿

(438)

122

Now the time has come
To return to my old home
In the capital
But no fair one shall I find
On whose arm to rest my head.

(439)

◉ In the following seven poems (Nos. 121 to 127), Ōtomo-no-Tabito expresses his deep yearning for his late wife and the immense solitude of a man bereft.

✿ To sleep or rest with one's head on someone's arm was a euphemism for having sex.

123

Now my wife is no more.
Far more trying it will be
For me to abide alone
At my lonely residence
In the royal city of Nara
Than to travel in the wilds,
Sleeping on a bed of grass.

(440)

124

Juniper tree
With your roots fast spread o'er a crag!
I once saw you with my wife.
Should I ask you where she is,
Could you tell me her whereabouts?[*]

(448)

125

The Cape of Minume,
Which gave great delight
To my wife and me,
Blinds my eyes with bitter tears
On my solitary return home.

(449)

126

O this scenic cape,
Which delighted us
During our travel,
Is not worth a glance to me
On my lonely return.

(450)

[*] The juniper (*muro no ki*) was looked upon as a sacred tree in ancient times. The poet and his wife might possibly have prayed to the tree for their well-being on their way to Kyushu.

127

I can never see
The plum tree which my late wife
Planted in the garden
But I am overcome with grief,
And my eyes blur with bitter tears.

(464)

128

When I confront
The world's emptiness,
All the more I feel
The futility and the grief
Of our mortal life.

(793)

129

Plum petals
Fluttering in my garden—
Could they be flakes of snow
Falling from the azure sky,
Dancing in the air?

(822)

When Ōtomo-no-Tabito was transferred from the governor generalship to a high post in the central government, many people gave him a send-off as far as the *mizuki* (a moated castle). Among them was a courtesan. She presented him with the following poem, singing it while dancing in tears. He was deeply moved and composed No. 131.

130

You are going home to Yamato,
Far beyond the clouds.
Pray don't think me gauche
If I wave my arms,
Bidding you farewell.

(966)

64

131
Warrior as I am,
I could not repress my tears
On the bank of the castle moat
At the tender farewell song
Of the maid who saw me off.

(968)

Yamanoue-no-Okura (660–733)

Yamanoue-no-Okura was born in the Korean Kingdom of Paekche. At that time, the Korean peniusula was in turmoil. The peninsula was divided into three kingdoms—Koguryo, Paekche, and Silla—which often were at war with one another. In 660, when Okura was born, Silla, in alliance with Tang China, conquered Paekche. In 663 Japan sent an expedition in aid of Paekche, but it suffered a crushing defeat by the combined forces of Silla and Tang. At this time, many people from Paekche took refuge in Japan, and numbers of competent officials and skilled people of Paekche served at the Japanese court.

In 663, when Okura was three years old, he was brought to Japan by his father, a physician, who became a physician-in-ordinary to Emperor Temmu. Okura served at court as a lower-rank official. In 703, when he was forty-three years old, he was selected as a clerk for an embassy to the Tang court, in recognition of his great knowledge of Confucianism and Buddhism. After returning to Japan, he was promoted to tutor to the crown prince, who later became Emperor Shōmu. When he was sixty years of age, he was appointed governor of a province in Kyushu and served under Ōtomo-no-Tabito, governor general of Kyushu. For five years, he was a prominent member of Ōtomo-no-Tabito's poetry circle. During this time he composed most of his good poetry. While most other poets of the *Man'yōshū* dealt with the theme of love, his best works are on the themes of poverty and misery and parental love for children.

Upon leaving a banquet earlier than the other guests, Okura humorously gave his loving care for his children as the reason.

132

Ladies and gentlemen,
Let me retire
From this banquet now.
My young children may be crying,
While their mother, careworn,
Awaits my return home.

(337)

133

Ne'er a melon do I eat
But my children I recall.
Ne'er a chestnut do I taste
But I wish to give them some.
From whence did they come?
Always there in my thoughts
Floating ever before my eyes,
They disturb my restful sleep.

(802)

134

More to be desired
Than fine silver and bright gold
Are my children dear.
Far more highly than vast wealth
My children do I prize.[a]

(803)

[a] This poem is proverbial in Japan and is the best known of Okura's poems.

A Dialogue on Poverty

Around 732, when Okura composed this poem, the country, which was groaning under heavy taxes, was visited by a series of disasters—drought, famine, severe earthquakes, and a country-wide plague of smallpox—that took a heavy toll of life. The people were in great distress. Being governor of a province, he was well acquainted with the people's miseries.

The poem is in the form of a dialogue between two men in poverty and is divided into two parts. The first part is a monologue of a man who may possibly be an official of very low rank or an influential personage in his village. He thinks of himself as a man of consequence, though he is pinched with poverty and cold, and wonders how still poorer people sustain their lives. The second part gives a vivid portrayal of a man and his family in dire poverty. The second part forms a reply to the first part.

In Okura's day, no one could hazard frank political criticism with impunity. This moving dialogue between poverty-stricken people may well have had a more effective reformatory influence than any blatant criticism of politics and life. Poems portraying poverty and suffering are rare in the *Man'yōshū*. This poem is considered among the most important poetical works of the anthology.

A question by a poor villager
135

> On chilly nights
> When the wind howls and rain pelts
>   down;
> On bleak, cold nights
> When sleet turns to snow,
> I am numb and frozen,
> And I know not what to do.
> Nibbling raw salt,
> Sipping gruel of sake lees,
> Sniffling, my nose cold,
> Loud I cough and clear my throat.
> Yet I proudly think,
> Stroking my meager mustache,
> No one in the world
> Is as worthy as I am,
> Yet so cold is the night
> That I wrap myself

In my tattered hempen quilt,
Piling on all my clothes.
How does a poorer man fare?
Parents, freezing, must starve.
His poor wife and little ones
Beg for food with bitter tears.

A reply by a man in destitute poverty

136

Sky and earth are large.
But for me they have shrunk.
Sun and moon are bright.
But for me they do not shine.
Is this my sole fate?
Or do others fare the same?
I was born a man,
And I work my hardest on the farm.
I wear unlined rags,
Which, tattered like seaweed,
Dangle from my shoulders.
Lowly is my hut,
And nearly fallen in.
On the ground is spread mere straw,
Whereon we all sleep.
My old parents crouch near my head.
My poor wife and children
Huddle near my feet.
We but groan,
And the children cry piteously.
In the sunken hearth
There is no spark of fire.
The cooking pot
Has so long been out of use
That it is draped with spiders' webs.
We never dream of cooking rice.

****

Their voices
Were feeble, like night birds,
When to crown their ills,
Came as far as their bedside
Came the loud shouts
Of the village headman, whip in hand,

Dunning for their tax.
Is this a way of life?
Wretched beyond help?

(892)

137

Too hard is my life,
Far beyond all help and succor.
How I wish to escape
From this world of misery!
But the sight of my children halts me.

(903)

This elegy with two envoys has no author's name, but from its content and style, it is believed to be Okura's work. It is not known whether he lost his own child or not, but many commentators say that he did. This elegy and its envoys are rated among his best works.

138

What do I care for
Gold, or silver?
We were blessed with a child
Worth more than his weight in gold.
Before dawn,
When the morning star rose,
Our child, Furuhi,
Would not leave our bedside,
Frolicking with us,
Boisterous or quiet.
While at dusk,
When the evening star appeared,
Saying, "Now let's go to sleep,"
He would lead us to our beds.
"Father, Mother, don't leave me,
I will sleep between you."
Lovely beyond words,
He was our immense delight,
Though we could never know
What would occur.
Suddenly,
Came an evil blight.
He was struck with plague,
Growing worse every day.

Mirror in hand,
Fervently we prayed to the gods,
Lifting our faces
To the gods of the heavens;
Prostrating ourselves
To the gods of the earth.
"Cure him,
If that is your will," we prayed.
But never did he mend,
For even a moment.
Each day
Weaker and feebler he became,
Fewer and fainter his words,
Till at last he breathed his last.
In dismay and grief,
Down we lay on the floor in tears.
We had lost our pearl,
Our darling child.
In despair we beat our breasts.
Thus is the way of the world.

(904)

Envoy

139

My dying child
Is too young to know the way.
I will reward you,
O you who show the way to the world
  below.
Please bear him on your back.

(905 & 906)

140

One who is born a man,
Lives to no purpose
If he makes no name
Worth being handed down
For a myriad of years.[a]

(978)

---

[a] When Yamanoue-no-Okura fell seriously ill, the chief councilor of state sent a messenger to inquire after his well-being. After expressing his thanks, he composed this poem.

Ōtomo-no-Yakamochi (718–785)

Ōtomo-no-Yakamochi, a preeminent poet and the most important compiler of the *Man'yōshū*, was born the eldest son of Ōtomo-no-Tabito. During his boyhood, when he was in Kyushu with his father, he was under the edifying influence of his father's poetry circle. At the age of thirteen, he lost his father. Thereafter, he was under the tutelage of his aunt Sakanoue-no-Iratsume, who was a distinguished poet. When he was twenty years old, he entered court service. The next year he lost his first wife. Being a refined noble of a celebrated family, he was a favorite with young ladies in the capital, and he exchanged love poems with more than a dozen ladies, many of which he included in the *Man'yōshū*. Later after exchanging love poems with his cousin, Sakanoue-no-Ōiratsume, he married her. She was a daughter of his aunt Sakanoue-no-Iratsume and was also a talented poet.

In 746, when he was twenty-eight years old, he was appointed vice-minister in the Department of the Imperial Household and he was able to participate in the compilation of a large collection of poetry, which the Imperial Bureau of Poetry had just commenced. In the same year he was appointed governor of the large province of Etchū (present-day Toyama prefecture). Being away from the arena of political strife for the five years of his governorship, he composed many of his finest poems. In 751 he was recalled to the capital as vice-minister of the Ministry of Military Affairs.

141

Transient is life.
But we have lived free of care,
My wife and I,
As though we might live
A thousand years.

(470)

142

A brilliant flower,
So radiant that even
The mountains shone,
Faded all too soon—
Our glorious crown prince.

(477)

143

Could I be cured of
The agony of love,
Fain would I be turned
Into a tree or a stone
With no feeling, dead to my heart.

(722)

144

None can be born
Into this world again.
How can I forego
The pleasure of your company
And sleep alone?

(733)

145

Meeting in a dream
Is a painful disappointment.
Waking in delight,
I reached for you
With both hands, but in vain.

(741)

146

I can see the image of my love,
Tearful, wistful, forlorn,
Loath to part
When I left her house
At the break of day.

(754)

147

While it was still dark,
Oft I took leave of my love.
Never did I leave her home
But I felt my heart in flame,
Pierced to the core.

(755)

148

I say I am going
To see your hedge,
Now in lovely bloom.
But what I desire
Is to look at you.

(778)

149

I never see a crescent moon
In the evening sky
But I recall
The lovely brows
Of a beauty I once glimpsed.[@]

(994)

150

Going to the sea,
I shall be a watery corpse.
Going to the meadows,
I shall be a grass-grown corpse.
As long as I die
By the side of the sovereign
What do I care?[※]

(excerpt of a long poem; 4094)

[@] Yakamochi composed this poem when he was about sixteen years old.

[※] A poem expressing the spirit of loyalty of the Ōtomo clan, which had been the imperial guard for centuries.

151

      Amid the vernal fields,
      Where the blossoming peach trees
      Spread ruby tints,
      Stands a winsome lady
      In the fragrant floral shade.

                    (4139)

152

      Many maidens fair
      Draw fresh water with roped pails
      At the temple well,
      Where abundant lilies white
      Are in fragrant bloom.

                    (4143)

The following three poems are thought to be the best works of
Yakamochi.

153

      This fair spring day
      The hills are veiled in gauzy haze,
      Blithe with warblers' songs
      In the mellow evening light,
      While I am veiled in sorrow.

                    (4290)

154

      As the autumn breeze
      Softly blows past my abode,
      Faintly from the yard comes
      The rustling of bamboo leaves,
      With the deepening of dusk.

                    (4291)

155

      This balmy spring day—
      Fields bathe in mellow light,
      With ascending larks
      Pouring forth a flood of bright song,
      While thought weighs down my soul.

                    (4292)

Five Major Poets

Takechi-no-Kurohito

Takechi-no-Kurohito was a leading court poet and a contemporary of Kakinomoto-no-Hitomaro. He was a tireless traveler and excelled in the graphic portrayal of the landscapes of the places that he visited.

156

> Where'er shall I lodge
> Should nightfall envelop me
> In the desolate fields
> Of Takashima[⊕]
> Out of sight and sound of man?

(275)

157

> Coming to the fork in the road,
> Being of one mind,
> My dear love and I
> Found it hard to part,
> Each going one way.

(276)

Takahashi Mushimaro

Takahashi Mushimaro was an outstanding romantic poet contemporary with Ōtomo-no-Tabito. Many of his poems are based on legendary stories. His poetry excels in the graphic description of nature and is rich in imagination. While he was an official in East Japan, he visited Mt. Tsukuba and wrote a long, important poem, which is introduced here.

[⊕] Takashima is on the west shore of Lake Biwa.

158

At the waters of Mohakitsu
On Mt. Tsukuba, where eagles dwell,
Men and women gather.
Joining hands, they dance away,
Singing lustily.
I will lie with others' wives,
And let men here
Come and woo my wife at will.
'Tis our festival,
Which of old the guardian god
Of the mountain
Has never banned.
Today let's be free
And celebrate.[@]

(1759)

159

Envoy

Even if clouds rise
Around the lofty peak,
And if showers drench us,
How can we leave,
Giving up this festival?

(1760)

Lady Ōtomo-no-Sakanoue

Ōtomo-no-Sakanoue, the half sister of Ōtomo-no-Tabito by a different mother, was an accomplished lyricist who combined talent and beauty. Her poetry is noted for a refined delicacy, as distinguished from the poetry of the early period of the *Man'yōshū*, which is marked by simplicity and vigor.

  Her mother was Lady Ishikawa, a talented poet whose re-

[@] In ancient days there was an observance characterized by singing, dancing, and sexual freedom. This observance remained in some parts of Japan until the recent past. The foregoing folk song is regarded as a significant source of information about ancient customs in Japan. Mt. Tsukuba is a solitary peak rising above the plain of the Kantō district of East Japan and is a well-known mountain in Japan, appearing in many poems and folk songs.

ply poem to the poem (No. 15) by Prince Ōtsu, Emperor Temmu's son, is included (No. 16) in this book. When young, Sakanoue was the greatly cherished favorite of Prince Hozumi, Emperor Tenji's son. After the prince died, she was loved by Fujiwara Maro, the son of Fujiwara Fuhito, who was the most powerful statesman in those days. Later she married her half brother by a different mother, Ōtomo-no-Sukunamaro, and bore him Lady Ōtomo-no-Ōiratsume, who married Ōtomo-no-Yakamochi. After Ōtomo-no-Tabito died, she became the guardian of the Ōtomo clan and a good tutor to her nephew, Ōtomo-no-Yakamochi. She was amorous in nature and enjoyed love for love's sake.

160

As ripples ever gleam
On the Saho River
Where the plovers cry,
So my longing for you,
Knows no rest.

(526)

161

Now that I have placed
My jewel, my daughter dear,
In her husband's hands,
I will rest my head on the pillow,
Whereupon her head once rested.⊛

(652)

162

Aware
That it is no use
Pining away,
Yet and yet, I find myself
Lost in my love of you.

(658)

⊛ A poem describing the feelings of the mother who married off her daughter to her nephew, Ōtomo-no-Yakamochi.

163

After years
Of our ardent love,
We meet today.
Speak endearing words to me
That our love may be unending.

(661)

164

Now I think I'll die.
No more do I care to live.
For so long as I live,
'Tis beyond hope
That I'll win my dear one's heart.

(684)

165

Do not give me
Such sweet smiles.
As drifting white clouds
Hide the mountains,
So let our love be hidden.

(688)

166

O agony is love.
Walking along the shore,
Should I find shells of forgetfulness,
I would gather them
To soothe my pain.

(964)

A poem composed at a social event given by the Ōtomo clan.

167

        Let's be merry over cups
        And enjoy our fill tonight.
        See the trees and grass,
        How they grow and bloom in spring,
        And in autumn wither and fade.

(995)

168

        Spring has arrived.
        Mists blur hills and fields,
        The earth has come to life.
        The fires of love
        Quicken and trouble my heart.

(1450)

169

        Deep in my heart
        Love's star lily blooms,
        Blushing unseen,
        In summer's verdure.
        Painful is love, unrequited.

(1500)

170

        Thinking of me,
        Weep alone.
        Never appear sad or melancholy,
        Heaving heavy sighs,
        Lest they see you're sick with love.

(2604)

Maiden Sano-no-Chigami and Nakatomi-no-Yakamori

Maiden Sano-no-Chigami was a low-grade clerk in the office of the Grand Shrine of Ise. No one was permitted to marry a woman serving this shrine. Nakatomi-no-Yakamori, who was a court official, fell in love with her. On the charge of acting against this ordinance, he was banished to Echizen Province, about sixty kilometers north of the capital. While he was in banishment, he was able to exchange love letters and poems with her on four occasions. Their sixty-three poems are preserved in the *Man'yōshū*. On the whole, the ardent love poems by the lady, who gave her heart to Yakamori, have greater pathos and appeal than the love poems that he sent to her.

Years later Yakamori was pardoned and was able to return home, but none of the poems that they might have written after his return is included in the *Man'yōshū*.

The following series of poems expressing her intense grief over their separation and her pure love for him ranks her among the foremost women poets in the *Man'yōshū*.

171

I anguish that
You must labor over
The rugged mountain pass
To the place of your banishment.
My mind knows no rest or peace.

(3723)

172

How I wish I had
Heaven's fire
To destroy
The long mountain road
Along which you must travel.

(3724)

173

Never yield to death.
Worry not about me,
Nor pine away.
So long as we are alive,
We may meet again.

(3745)

80

174

Gazing at the pine of my abode
Every day I wait for you.
Hasten back home
That I may not die
Of my consuming love for you.[a]

(3747)

175

Search everywhere—
The corners of the earth,
The starry skies.
There is no more ardent passion
Than my love for you.

(3750)

176

Always wear this close to you,
This white silken underrobe,
Till the day arrives
When you are back safe
And we can live together.

(3751)

177

Here's a silken robe
Which a tender maid has sewn
In distress and grief,
For her husband dear to wear
On the day he returns home.

(3753)

[a] In the original poem, there is play on the word *matsu*, which means both "pine tree" and "wait."

178

Morning and evening
My soul holds communion
With yours,
Yet my heart aches with
My passionate love for you.

(3767)

179

Much to my delight
You were at my side last night.
But on waking,
I was alone in bed,
And my heart filled with grief.

(3768)

180

Secretly,
You came only in the dark of night,
Leaving before the gray of dawn.
Never could I see you well,
To my infinite regret.[a]

(3769)

181

When I heard a voice
Saying that some had returned
From banishment,
I felt all but dead,
Hoping you might be among them.[b]

(3772)

[a] Since their tryst was unlawful, they took great care to keep its secrecy. Probably this poem refers to a tryst before Yakamori's banishment.

[b] In 740 there was a general amnesty, and she hoped that Yakamori might be among the returnees. Yakamori was pardoned some time after 740.

Nakatomi-no-Yakamori

Yakamori composed the following poems in banishment.

182

Insignificant I am,
And I find no worth
In myself. Nonetheless,
She longs for me.
She is far too sweet for words.

(3727)

183

In the brightness of day
I am sunk in melancholy,
Longing for you.
In the utter darkness of night,
I am drowned in bitter tears.

(3732)

184

Had I not the robe
Which my darling gave me,
How could I
Stay alive
In this place of banishment?

(3733)

185

So often
I weep in vain.
Helpless and forlorn
Distracted with despair,
I fall into a deathlike sleep.

(3759)

186

Today, were I
In the city of Nara,
I would tarry outside the stableyard
On the west of the court
Anxious for a tryst with you.[e]

(3776)

Lady Kasa

Lady Kasa was a highly gifted poet. There is no information about her
life except for the twenty-nine short poems of ardent love that she
wrote to Ōtomo-no-Yakamochi during the course of some years around
755. Her intimacy with Yakamochi did not last long before they separated, so most of her love poems here express spite or grief. She wrote
all her poems to him to no purpose. Finally, she sent him a desperate
poem (No. 194) in which she reviled him, and she left the capital of
Nara for good. The beautiful, heart-breaking pathos of the best of her
love poems has touched readers for over twelve hundred years.

Yakamochi incorporated into the *Man'yōshū* the love poems that Lady Kasa and many other ladies had written to him.

During the thirty years of the fourth period of the *Man'yōshū*, refined poems expressing sentimental love increased, but Lady
Kasa and Maiden Sano-no-Chigami wrote poems overflowing with
real passion.

187

Overwhelmed with love
For you, I am lost.
Beneath a pine
On the side of Mt. Nara,
I stand in despair.

(593)

[e] Probably Yakamori had a tryst with Chigami, his love, at the place mentioned in
this poem.

84

188

So faint with love,
I feel I'll fade away
Like a drop of dew
On the night-blooming flowers
In my garden.

(594)

189

As long as breath is left in me,
I am yours.
Daily grows my love for you,
Till it will be
More than I can bear.

(595)

190

From afar I had
But a glimpse of you
As if through morning mist.
Yet I'm so consumed with love
That I will die of longing.

(599)

191

Evening never falls
But my ardor blazes—
The image of my dear one,
Who once spoke to me,
Floats before my eyes.

(602)

192

If love
Always brings a painful death,
A thousand times
I would have died in pain
For the dear one of my heart.

(603)

193

Now the temple bell
Tolls the time
For the night's repose.
But my ardent love for you
Keeps me awake the night through.

(604)

194

I might as well
Worship a hungry demon,
Prostrating myself to his back,
As conceive love for a man
Who does not return my love.

(608)

195

Living near you,
Though I did not see you oft,
Some ease of heart I had.
Living far away from you
Will soon lead me to my grave.

(610)

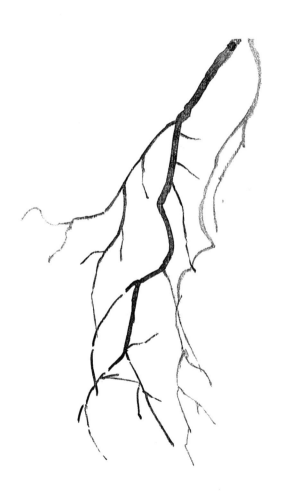

Minor Poets

The poets included in this chapter were skilled, but their poems in the *Man'yōshū* are few in number, and their names are not as well known as those of the major poets.

Abe-no-Asomi Mushimaro

Abe-no-Asomi Mushimaro was a court poet. The following poem was written for his cousin, Lady Ōtomo-no-Sakanoue.

196

> When I sit with you
> Face to face, I am spellbound
> And I am unable to rise and depart.
> Never do I tire,
> However long I gaze at you.
>
> (665)

Lady Abe

Although little is known about her life, she was a talented poet. The following three poems express her devoted love for her husband.

197

> I can think of nothing else
> But my dearest.
> All my love and all my soul
> I offer as your own.
> My heart has turned to you.
>
> (505)

198

> Be at ease, my lover.
> Should your life be ever at risk,
> I will be with you,
> Ready to confront
> Fire and water for your sake.[@]
>
> (506)

[@] Man'yō women poets were more daring than later poets to express fiery love.

199

Into every seam
Of the robe which I have sewn
For my husband,
I have stitched
My love and my heart.

(514)

Ato-no-Sukune Toshitari

Nothing definite is known about his life.

200

How dear is my love.
Her voice is as sweet
As the songs of singing birds,
Which across the nearby hills
Come fly to my abode in spring!

(663)

Fujiwara-no-Kamatari

Fujiwara-no-Kamatari rendered distinguished service to Emperor Tenji. He rose to premiership and became the founder of the Fujiwara family, which held predominant power at court for the subsequent four centuries.

201

I have won Yasumiko,
The fairest of the ladies at court,
Whom all people know
Is impossible to win.
I have won the fairest one.

(95)

In those days beautiful girls were picked to be ladies-in-waiting to the emperor and the empress. They were known as *uneme,* and were not permitted to be courted or to marry. The girl called Yasumiko was the fairest of them. In recognition of Kamatari's illustrious service, Emperor Tenji granted him this girl as his mistress. Out of his joy, he composed this poem. His legal wife was Princess Kagami.

On the whole, the *Man'yōshū*'s emotional poetry reflects sorrow and disappointment rather than good fortune or the happy fulfillment of expectations. Its jubilant mood may be one of the reasons why this poem has been valued.

Fujiwara-no-Asomi Maro

Fujiwara-no-Asomi Maro wrote this poem to Lady Ōtomo-no-Sakanoue, whom he later married. He was a statesman of great influence.

202

> Though I sleep
> Under thick quilts
> And on soft mats,
> Yet I am cold
> If I do not sleep with my dear love.

(524)

Priest of the Gangōji Temple

Though highly erudite and widely informed, the priest lived in obscurity and was treated with contempt. This poem expresses his response to his social status.

203

> My exquisite pearl,
> Even if it remains unrevealed
> What should I care—
> I know its worth,
> And I treasure it.

(1018)

Lady Heguriuji

The following are three of the twelve poems that she wrote to Ōtomo-no-Yakamochi.

204

With my heart afire,
I am consumed with burning love,
Pungent as the salt
Made by boiling water of the sea
By the men on the shore.

(3932)

205

Gazing at my hand,
I recall how overjoyed I was
When he came round and said,
"You will ever be my love,"
Giving me a gentle stroke
On the backs of my hands.[@]

(3940)

206

The bloom of the pine
Is never noticed.
I'm a pine flower, too plain
To be seen by the eyes
Of lords who pass by.

(3942)

[@] Probably some misunderstanding between her and Yakamochi was clarified, and she composed this poem.

The literal translation of lines 4 and 5 reads: "When you gave me a pinch on the back of my hand." This act was occasionally done as a sign of friendship, but was considered too weak to be a sign of reconciliation of two lovers. Kissing was not customary in Japan until this century.

Ise-no-Ōmitomo

207

> Not an islet can be seen
> On the vast expanse of the sea,
> Far as the eye can reach.
> O'er the boundless cobalt blue,
> White clouds float in the azure sky.

(1089)

Lady Ishikawa

208

> Now that old age
> Has reduced me to a crone,
> How could I fall
> Into helpless love
> As a maiden in the bloom of youth?[⊗]

(129)

Maiden Kamunagibe-no-Maso

Nothing is known about Kamunagibe-no-Maso except the love poems that she sent to Ōtomo-no-Yakamochi.

209

> Ever since the day
> I met you, my love,
> My sleeves have never been dry
> Of the tears
> Which fill my eyes.

(703)

[⊗] She was a lady-in-waiting at court and was loved by Crown Prince Kusakabe and Prince Ōtsu. She was a talented poet, and her reply poem to Prince Ōtsu's poem is No. 16 of this book.

Kasa-no-Asomi Kanamura

Kasa-no-Asomi Kanamura was a courtier of lower rank.

210

All the fields
Are adorned with bush clover
In such gorgeous bloom
That those who pass through
Will be saturated with their scent.

(1532)

Maiden Kafuchi-no-Momoe

Nothing is known about Kafuchi-no-Momoe's life except the two love poems that she wrote to Ōtomo-no-Yakamochi.

211

With delight
I remember the moonlit night
Of our tryst.
I have cherished that sweet time
Ceaselessly to this day.

(702)

Lady Ki-no-Ojika

Lady Ki-no-Ojika was once the love of Ōtomo-no-Yakamochi, but he later broke with her. The following two poems air her feelings.

212

Sunk in black despair,
Now I have no choice
But to let you have
Your way—you whom I've loved
As my very life.

(664)

213

The day draws near
When I must part from you,
To whom I've oft pledged my troth.
I am drowned in bitter tears,
My heart rent with grief.

(645)

214

Bright and clear tonight
Shines the moon in the starry sky.
Within my heart
Blooms a fragrant plum blossom
Which reminds me of your noble grace.[*]

(1661)

Mikata-no-Sami

Shortly after marrying a girl, Mikata-no-Sami fell sick and could not go and see her for some time. Instead, he sent her this poem. One source says that he was once a Buddhist priest but later was given a good post in recognition of his erudition.

215

Her glossy locks
If tied up, dangle down,
If not tied up, are too long.
I have not seen her for some time—
She may have dressed her hair in a
    bun.[**]

(123)

[*] The blossom is that of the *ume,* which botanically is a variety of apricot but is customarily translated as "plum."

[**] In those days a very young girl had her hair bobbed. When she grew up, she wore it long, and when she reached marriageable age, she either put it up or let it hang down.

The following reply poem by his young wife is charming.

216

They all say to me,
"Now your hair has grown too long.
Why not put it up?"
Tangled as it is,
I will keep it as it was
When it won your praise and caresses.

(124)

Lady Nakatomi

Lady Nakatomi was one of the many women who wrote love poems to Ōtomo-no-Yakamochi.

217

Not till I see you eye to eye,
Resting in your arms,
Will I find ease
From the ardor of this love,
For which I'd give my life.

(678)

218

Do not feign love.
If you have no love for me,
I shall never demand it,
Even though I'm torn
With longing for you.

(579)

A literal translation of the last two lines is:

Even though I'm distraught with love
Like the intertwined roots of a sedge.

Nukike-no-Ōbito

Nukike-no-Ōbito was a government official. This poem he sent to his love, whom he later married.

219

My mind and soul
Are exhausted night and day
With longing for you.
No more can I exist with the pain
Of my poignant love for you.

(1769)

Lady Ōtomo-no-Sakanoue-no-Ōiratsume

Ōtomo-no-Sakanoue-no-Ōiratsume was the eldest daughter of Lady Ōtomo-no-Sakanoue. She married Ōtomo-no-Yakamochi, her cousin.

The poems given here are two of the ones that she exchanged with him before they married.

220

Mighty warrior
'Tis fine how you love women,
But far deeper is
A maiden's tender ardor
For her lover.

(582)

221

The path of love is the path of thorns
Sharper far than needles,
Sharper far than I can bear.
Better to die and have no pain
Than to walk upon the thorns of love.

(738)

A more literal translation reads:

> Hard and trying is life.
> Suffering the acute
> And poignant pain of love,
> I'm afraid that I shall die.

Ōtomo-no-Sukune Ikenushi

Ōtomo-no-Sukune Ikenushi was a close friend of Ōtomo-no-Yakamochi, particularly when the latter was governor of Echizen Province. They exchanged poems and letters.

222

> With the cherry trees in bloom
> People rejoice and say
> The world is bright.
> But you are not here with me—
> I'm alone in the dark.

(4074)

Ōtomo-no-Sukune Sukunamaro

Ōtomo-no-Sukune Sukunamaro was the younger brother of Ōtomo-no-Tabito and the father of Sakanoue-no-Ōiratsume. Probably he composed the following poem while he was a provincial governor.

223

> The girl hopes to serve
> At the royal court.
> But she's everything to me.
> It will pain my heart to keep her here.
> It will break my heart to let her go.

(532)

Ōtomo-no-Yotsuna

Ōtomo-no-Yotsuna, the deputy commander of the *Daizaifu* (see page 171), composed this poem at a farewell party in honor of Ōtomo-no-Tabito.

224
> Brightly shines the moon.
> Sweetly runs the crystal stream.
> Let those leaving here
> And those who remain behind
> Enjoy this merry eve.

(571)

Maiden Ōyake

The following poem denotes a girl's genuine love and wish to stay with her sweetheart.

225
> It is hard to find the way
> In the dark. Await the rise
> Of the moon, then depart.
> In the meantime, I'll treasure
> Your sweet company.

(709)

Sami Mansei

Sami Mansei was a Buddhist priest.

226
> Life here may well be
> Likened to a fishing boat
> Which at break of day
> Puts out upon the sea,
> Leaving no trace behind.

(351)

Tabe-no-Imiki Ichihiko

Tabe-no-Imiki Ichihiko composed this poem when he was appointed to service at the *Dazaifu* in Kyushu, putting himself in the place of his love or wife, who was left behind.

227

> Mark my words, my dear!
> When I'm left behind,
> I'll have none on whom to lean
> And shall be more grieved
> Than a child, crying and
> Clinging to its mother's sleeves.

(492)

Tachibana-no-Sukune Fuminari

Tachibana-no-Sukune Fuminari was a court official.

228

> The day before yesterday,
> Yesterday, and today again
> We could meet.
> Yet tomorrow all the more
> I shall wish to meet you.

(1014)

Lady Yosami (Wife of Kakinomoto-no-Hitomaro)

229

> Do not grieve, you say.
> If I could foretell the day
> When you will return
> Or how soon we'll meet again
> I would never pine or grieve.[⊛]

(140)

[⊛] When Kakinomoto-no-Hitomaro was an official at the government office of Iwami Province, he married the daughter of a country squire. When he left for the central government, she composed this poem. See page 37.

PART TWO

Anonymous Poetry

West Japan

The *Man'yōshū* has roughly 2,300 anonymous poems, half the anthology. Most of the anonymous poems deal with the theme of love, and many show excellent work. The direct expression of intense emotion, the subtle workings of sentiment, and the diverse aspects of love claim a universal appeal. There are numerous reasons why so many poems in the *Man'yōshū* are anonymous. The compilers of the *Man'yōshū* sought good poems, drawing on various sources, which included earlier collections of anonymous poems.

As was explained in the introduction to the life of Kakinomoto-no-Hitomaro (page 37), good poems by lower-ranking officials and by commoners were included in the *Man'yōshū*, but generally with no record of their names or biographical data. This is the main reason for the anonymity of so many of the Man'yō poems.

Because court poets were eager to collect provincial poetry and folk songs as sources of poetic ideas, it is highly probable that provincial government offices submitted their own collections of poetry and folk songs to the Imperial Bureau of Poetry.

A Court Lady of Suruga

230

Bitter tears flowed down
My pillow onto the floor,
Till I dreamed I was afloat
On a great river of tears.
So ardent is my love.

(507)

A Maiden of Hitachi Province

A poem presented by a maiden to a provincial governor who had been ordered to court service. Hitachi is a province in the East.

231

Remember always
There's a maiden in the East,
Reaping, drying, bleaching hemp
In the yard, while in her heart
She pines for her lord.

(521)

232

I never sit before
My old koto to play
But grief consumes me.
I know that my late dear wife
Dwells therein.[⊗]

(1129)

233

'Tis already daybreak,
Warn the ravens,
And I leave my love's abode,
Yet o'er the treetops of the hill,
Reigns the deathly still of night.

(1263)

234

Clad in hempen attire
Young frontier guards
Go their long weary way.
Should their shoulder seams come
    unsewn,
Who would mend or stitch them?

(1265)

235

Happy is the man,
Greatly blessed and enviable,
Who can live to hear
The voice of his beloved wife
Till his jet-black hair turns gray!

(1411)

⊗ In ancient times a human soul was considered to dwell in the hollow of the body of the koto.

236

Little did I dream
My dear husband would soon die.
Now how I regret
Sleeping with my back to him
Like bamboo split and turned around.

(1412)

237

If my dear late love,
With whom I long shared the bed,
Were here with me now,
I would deeply grudge
How short the night seems.

(1414)

238

The crystal stream,
Falling headlong down the cliff
To boulders below,
Forms a glassy pool,
Mirroring the moon's brightness.

(1714)

A Maiden of Harima

239

When you're gone,
Little will I care
For gowns, nor for
My precious boxwood comb
To dress my hair.

(1777)

240

If the dreary fields
Where the mission has to lodge
Should be rimed with frost,
May a flock of sky-bound cranes
Warm my son under their wings!⊛

(1791)

241

If I could be sure
That we'll later meet again,
Though we part today,
Never would I pine,
With my heart rent asunder.

(1805)

242

You are no more seen
Than a shrike which
Passes through the grass,
However often toward your house
I turn my eyes.

(1897)

243

I am so lost in love
For a lovely girl
With rosy cheeks
That the mellow sky of spring
Seems shadowed by dark clouds.

(1911)

⊛ A poem expressing a mother's concern for her son, who was a member of a Japanese mission sent to the court of the Tang dynasty in 733.

244

Lovely as the spring haze
Softening verdant hills and fields
On a sunny day
Is your graceful figure,
Which I constantly adore.[@]

(1913)

245

Dazed with love for my dear one,
I did not know where to turn.
Not till I had walked
Far from home was I aware of
The drizzling rain.

(1915)

[@] Spring in Japan is a time of hazy vistas.

246

How I wish I'd seen you clearly
When you left my home at dawn.
All this long spring day
My soul yearns for you,
And my heart is consumed with love.

(1925)

From a man

247

May the wisteria
Blossom once again
For our sweet delight of love,
If it does not bring forth fruit
Ripening into marriage.

(1928)

The woman's reply

248

As for the wisteria,
It's already borne its fruit
And is past its blossom time.
Should a gentle spring rain fall,
No more blossoms can it bear.[●]

(1929)

249

Evening cicadas
Sing only at dusk.
What else can a woman do
Whose love remains unrequited
But weep from morn to eve?

(1982)

● No. 247 was sent by a man to a married woman, inviting her to renew their affair. No. 248 is a reply poem by the woman, saying that since she is already married, she can no longer afford to take pleasure in sportive love.

In the original, the plant is the *akebi*, not wisteria. The *akebi* is a vine that bears light purple blossoms and succulent pods containing sweet, juicy flesh.

250

Let the rumor spread
Fast and wide like summer weeds.
But so long as I can lie
With my love,
What should I care?

(1983)

251

As a daisy blooms,
Quiet, modest,
Unremarked and unnoticed,
So my love in silence blooms,
Unrequited, in my heart.@

(1989)

252

In the spring the earth
Is adorned with flowers fair.
In the summer 'tis clad in green.
In the autumn the mountains wear
Glorious tints of red and gold.

(2177)

253

Never do I see
Dewdrops sparkling pure and fair
On a bush-clover spray
But I recall
Your dear image with noble grace.❧

(2259)

@ The Japanese refers to a deutzia, not a daisy.

❧ Probably a poem by a woman.

254

Would my darling were
A soft undergarment.
When the autumn wind
Sends a chill up my spine,
I would wear it next to me.

(2260)

255

Though I writhe with passion and
Die of the agony of love,
Yet ne'er I will let my ardor
Show forth in my face,
Clear as a morning-glory's hue.

(2305)

256

Even while traveling,
With the gentle sex I lie.
These long autumn nights
All alone I sleep at home
That annoying rumors may not spread.

(2505)

257

Weak and faint
With the gnawing pain of love—
I feel I'll fade away
Like a pearl of dew
On a spray of plum blossoms.

(2335

258

When you aren't with me,
Evening never falls
But that I am cold and alone,
Though no mountain wind
Chills my spine.

(2350)

259

Come in, my dear one,
Through the opening in the blinds.
Should my mother ask,
"Who has come in?" I will reply
"It's just the wind."

(2364)

260

Such is my agony—
A wedded lady fair
Seen but once
On the royal thoroughfare.
Now my nights are often sleepless.

(2365)

261

Even now I see
The image of my beloved wife
Crying her heart out,
Till her sleeves were soaked with tears
On the day she saw me off.●

(2518)

● Possibly a poem by a frontier guard.

262

Though I sleep
Only on thin mats of
Newly mown straw,
I'm not cold,
As long as I sleep with you.

(2520)

263

I have lost my heart
To one who is not inclined
To return my love.
I feel more dead than alive.
No more do I care to live.⊛

(2525)

264

With eagerness
She must be awaiting me—
I will hasten
So that I may see a charming smile
On her lovely face.

(2526)

265

Through the opening of her bamboo
  fence,
If I could but glimpse
My lovely girl
For a moment now and then,
How could I ever be melancholy?

(2530)

⊛ The poet may be of either sex, but this poem probably is written from a woman's
standpoint.

266

For whom and why
Should I ever free my hair,
Rich and ebony black,
To flow and ripple in the air,
But to be admired and stroked
By the dear love of my heart?◉

(2532)

267

I have kept my love for you
Hidden even from my dear mother.
I am yours—
All my heart and all my soul
I offer as your own.

(2537)

268

'Tis a thousand years
Since our last tryst.
No, that cannot be.
Just waiting to see you again,
It seems an age has passed.

(2539)

269

As soft and tender
As young grass
Is my sweet young wife.
How can I ever for even a night
Miss my darling?

(2542)

◉ See note to No. 215, page 94.

270

Thinking of a sudden visit
To my love—
I can see
How her lovely smile
Will brighten her face.

(2546)

271

Little did I think
She was everything to me.
Now how I regret
That it was not every night
I laid my head upon her arm.

(2547)

272

The image of the girl
Who, in crimson gown,
Left here days ago,
Is still vivid in my eyes,
Night and day, awake or asleep.

(2550)

273

In the agony of love,
Muddled,
All I could do
Was wander from my house,
And go past her gate.

(2551)

274

At the sight of you,
So shy,
I hide my face.
But even with face hidden,
How I wish to gaze at you!

(2554)

275

Should I ever tell my mother
What is going on
Twixt you and me,
We would have no chance to meet
Till we reach a ripe old age.

(2557)

276

You are leaving me
In this drear village
Falling into ruin.
Take pity on me;
I shall die of melancholy.

(2560)

277

With her jet-black hair
Unbound about her head,
My sweet love
Must now be in her lone bed
Anxiously awaiting me.🅐

(2564)

🅐 By a man late in visiting his love.

278

Longing for a girl of whom
But a glimpse I caught
Through a hedge of reeds,
I heave a thousand melancholy sighs
Each day.

(2565)

279

"Meeting the girl you love,
Eases the pangs of longing,"
'Tis what many say.
Nevertheless, after meeting the girl,
All the more to pine for her.

(2567)

280

I shall die
If I go on longing for you,
So I've let my mother know
That we are lovers.
Come see me whenever you will.[*]

(2570)

281

Carousing with friends—
Men may well sport
And amuse themselves,
But I have to bear
The gnawing pain of love.

(2571)

---

[*] In Man'yō days, generally the mother had the greatest authority at home. The girl in the poem has won her mother's consent and urges her lover to visit her freely.

282

Are you dying from love of me?
You should lie more plausibly.
From days of old,
Who ever has perished for the love of
    one
Whom he has never seen?[a]

(2572)

283

All night long my hair
Rested on his sturdy arm
And his fond caressing hand.
Though it is snarled this morn,
I will keep it as it is.

(2578)

284

Worthless fellow that I am—
If I could remove
Her fair charms
From the depths of my heart,
Why should I ever long for her?

(2580)

285

Should I tell you of my love,
Commonplace my words would sound,
And too dull my speech.
Too full is my heart for words.
Too deep is my love for speech.[b]

(2581)

[a] A reply poem by a woman to a man who claimed he was dying from love of her.

[b] Probably a man's poem to a woman who told him that his courtship lacked sincerity.

286

What a shameful act!
What a sheer absurdity
That at this age
I should lose my heart in love
As young men are wont to do!

(2582)

287

Nothing shall I gain
If I should be so lovelorn
As to die.
So long as I am alive
I can hope to meet my love.[a]

(2592)

288

I'm distraught with love
For a lady to no avail.
For when evening comes,
It is in her husband's arms
That she comfortably lies.

(2599)

289

Ever since I knew my love,
With my flesh touching his,
My consuming love for him,
Ever growing in my breast,
Gives me no rest or peace.

(2612)

In the original, the second line is more euphemistically expressed as:

With my sleeves in touch with his.

[a] This seems to be a common theme in Man'yō poetry. See Nos. 315, 331, and 345 and compare Nos. 70 and 164.

290

When I tapped on the gate
Of my dear love
In the mountain depths,
It echoed so loudly
That I slept in the frost outside.

(2616)

291

On our wedding night
My young bride of tender age,
Twixt innocent sweet smiles
And sullen angry looks,
Slowly untied her sash.

(2627)

292

Her head resting on her arms
And her glossy raven hair
Spread around her neck,
My sweet love must anxiously
Be waiting for me this night.

(2631)

293

Before my eyes
Floats the image of a girl
In the glow of lamplight,
Her lovely face
Brightened in a smile.

(2642)

294

Humble as a hut
Stained with smoke and soot,
Worn with age and cares,
Is my wife. But for all that,
She's ever the loveliest to me.

(2651)

295

Never do I hear
The clopping of a horse's hoofs
But I go to watch
From behind the pine trees,
Hoping that it might be you.[a]

(2653)

296

Slanders and abuses
Do not please the gods.
Whatever they may say of us,
I will not deny or mind.
You, upon people's lips,
Are the lover of my heart.[b]

(2659)

[a] A woman is expecting her lover will come on horseback.

[b] Probably the poet is glad at heart that her love affair with a well-known man is gossiped about.

297

Not a day goes by
But I visit holy shrines,
Praying to the gods
That the lover of my heart
Each night may visit me.

(2660)

298

Full bright was the moonlight.
I was sure
Dawn was yet far,
Yet my love and I overslept.
Our affair has been revealed.

(2665)

299

Straightening the bed,
Brushing it with my sleeves,
Anxiously I awaited you.
In the meantime, the moon
Sank low in the western sky.

(2667)

300

'Tis a fine robe
That I've sewn with all my heart
For my dear one.
All this rainy day,
I've been anxious for his call.◉

(2682)

◉ A poem expressing a woman's impatience for a visit from her lover, who is not likely to come.

301

The downpour has just passed,
Starting leaks inside the walls
Of the hut in the fields.
Even the matted floor is wet.
Lie tight against me, my dear.

(2683)

302

Passing near the gate
Of my sweet one,
How I wish it would begin to rain—
A good excuse
For calling at her house!

(2685)

303

All the weeds
In the hemp fields
Are wet with dew.
You'd better leave after dawn,
Even if mother discovers our tryst.

(2687)

304

'Twas so cold last night
That the ground is white with frost.
Day is dawning now.
Walk with care,
Lest your footprints reveal our tryst.

(2692)

305

If I have to pine away
Daily in love's agony,
Fain I'd be a clod of earth,
Which she walks upon
In her garden morn and eve.

(2693)

306

As a pheasant flies
O'er a lofty mountaintop
Straight to his mate,
So straightway should I fall in love
With a girl whom I've just glimpsed?

(2710)

307

As a mountain stream
Rushing down a rugged cliff
Dashes against rocks and breaks,
So my heart in pieces breaks
On nights when I can't meet my love.

(2716)

308

Fain I'd be an isle
Dashed against by raging waves
Breaking into foam,
If I could e'er be released
From the gnawing pains of love.

(2733)

309

If I could be free
From the deadly pain of love,
Fain I'd be a grain of sand,
Drifting with the tide
Up and down the briny shore.

(2734)

310

Where the ospreys fly,
Waves rise and fall.
Never can I tell
Where my love for her will wend
Any more than where the waves will go.

(2739)

311

There must be a lull
In the billows which arise
In the mighty deep.
But the billows of my love for you,
Ever raging, know no lull.

(2741)

312

Could I be freed
From my gnawing love for him,
Fain a diver I would be
Gathering seaweed and shells
In the nearby bay.

(2743)

313

I'm a river barge
Heavily laden with reeds.
Since I met my love,
She has boarded me,
Heavy on my heart.

(2748)

314

When we chance to meet,
Only cast a smile at me.
That should be all.
See that no one ever suspects
That we are lovers.

(2762)

315

I am so distraught with love
That I feel I shall die.
But I'll try to keep alive,
For death leaves no hope
For me ever to meet my love.◉

(2764)

◉ See note to No. 287.

316

Tell my love
That I've waited for her,
Stamping my feet
Till the rank weeds by the road
Are as dead as winter grass.

(2776)

317

Little do I care
With whom I may lie,
But as seaweed sways to the tide,
So my heart has swayed to you.
Now I wait for your sweet will.⊗

(2782)

318

Flowers, coming into bloom,
Pass away in time.
But my ardent love,
Ever flaming in my heart,
Knows no time to rest or cease.

(2785)

319

In my nightly dream
Appears my sweet love,
Fresh and beautiful
As a fragrant rose in pink attire,
With a smile upon her face.

(2786)

⊗ A reply poem by a woman to her lover's poem inquiring if she has a new lover. She wonders why he has not visited her for a long time.

320

When I turn my eyes
Toward where my love dwells,
I feel our love
Will continue always,
To where the earth meets the sky.

(2787)

321

As a string is cut,
So I've broken with him.
If I'm still distraught
By my love for him,
There's no choice for me but to die.

(2789)

322

Day is dawning now.
Cocks crow in the yard.
Let them crow on loudly.
What do I care for dawn?
I sleep alone.[a]

(2800)

323

When I sleep alone,
Missing my darling love,
How long is the night?
Long as a mountain pheasant's tail
Trailing on the ground.

(2802)

[a] Her lover did not appear that night.

324

I wish to sleep more
On the pillow of your arm.
But the plovers cry,
Telling us that day has dawned,
When my husband of one night
Has to rise and go away.[@]

(2807)

325

I will await my love,
Patient far into the night,
Even till the moon
Now rising, descends low
Into the western sky.

(2820)

326

As you reap sedge
That you do not mean to plait
Into useful things,
So you dally with my love
With no mind to marry me.

(2837)

327

Would that I could float
Like a spray of leaves
Drifting downstream
To the shallows of the brook
Where a maiden fair stands.

(2838)

[@] This poem is substantially a folk song.

328

I awaited him,
Hoping he might come at any time—
While the night wore away,
My long anxious vigil
Gave way to bitter tears and grief.

(2864)

329

If I had a love
To share my bed,
The longer the cold night lasts,
The happier
I would be.

(2865)

330

Who is it that is
Talking to a wedded woman?
Untie my sash for him?
Is that what he means? Oh, no.
Who is it that talks like that?[⊕]

(2866)

331

In the throes of love,
I'm ready to fade away,
But I'll try to stay alive,
For my death will dash my hope of
Ever again meeting my love.[※]

(2868)

[⊕] A coquettish woman replying to an amorous advance.

[※] See note to No. 287.

332

People's talk of us
Has wounded you—
You said you hated
To encounter me
Even in the street.

(2871)

333

For long I have not seen my love,
And I am in anguish.
A rumor going round
All the louder strikes my ears
And the sharper stings my heart.

(2872)

334

Once I thought myself
Nearly equal
To heaven and earth.
Captive now to female charms,
Where is my bravado?

(2875)

335

Even since the night
When I threw myself in my lover's arms,
The white heat of love
Into shreds has torn my heart,
Leaving me no peace of mind.

(2878)

336

Could my late wife
Return to life for even a day!
In my dreams I sleep with her,
But 'tis of little solace,
For I know she's no more.

(2880)

337

Could I even catch
A distant glimpse of you,
The agony of my love
Would abate—
Else I'll die of longing.

(2883)

338

I am all but dead
With the pain of love.
I may live today,
But from tomorrow
How shall I keep alive?

(2884)

339

Leaving home at morn,
You return home at eve.
Yet, all the time
You are away,
For you I long.[⊛]

(2893)

340

Captivated now
By enthralling female charms,
I'm entirely bereft
Of all sense and wit—
I shall die a slave to love.

(2907)

341

Were you not so dear to me,
My heart and soul
And even my life,
Why should I long for you,
Who are now another's wife?

(2909)

342

Say, was it not you
Who proposed to meet me?
And yet when we meet,
Bashfully behind your hands,
You conceal your lovely face.

(2916)

[⊛] A poem by a woman whose husband lives in a separate home and visits her at night.
This kind of marriage was not uncommon in Man'yō days.

343

> Was it in my dream
> That my darling was here
> Or did she really come?
> So bemused by love,
> I'm puzzled which it was.

(2917)

344

> Till the day we meet again
> I will never undo the knot
> She tied in my inner sash,
> While I tied a knot in hers
> As our mutual pledge of love.[a]

(2919)

345

> Mortal as I am,
> If I die, I do not care.
> What most concerns me
> Is that if I die,
> Nor more can I see my love.[b]

(2920)

The following is a woman's reply poem.

346

> Maiden as I am,
> Devoted and strong
> Is my love for you.
> What most concerns me
> Is to see you always.

(2921)

[a] The image of tieing a knot in the inner sash that fastened underclothes occurs frequently in Man'yō poetry, as does the sensual image of loosened undergarments. There was a belief that if lovers tied a knot in each other's inner sashes, they would be able to meet again, when the knots would be untied. When a married man left on a long journey, his wife often tied a knot in his sash or in the cord used to tuck up his sleeves. See Nos. 91 and 105.

[b] See note to No. 287.

347

Eventide brings
The lover of my heart to me.
Doubtless, this is why
When evening comes,
My heart throbs and pounds with joy.

(2922)

The following two poems were composed by a woman as gibes at a much younger man who wooed her, proposing marriage.

348

Nurses are for babes.
Do you seek a nurse for a babe?
O I am surprised.
Are you still suckling at the breast?
Do you woo me as a nurse?

(2925)

349

Deeply I regret
That I have grown too old to be
Your beloved nurse.
Else I'd gladly
Attend to your wants and needs.

(2926)

350

The agony grows
As I sit and wait for him.
When dark night arrives,
If he's late coming here,
Forthwith will I go to him.

(2931)

351

Living not far off,
Time and again we meet.
How trying it is!
You're a lady of high birth;
We never have a friendly talk.

(2934)

352

Now I fear I'll die.
So consumed
With ardent love for you,
My heart is never at rest
For a single night or day.

(2936)

353

Mischievous wild talk,
Idle and unfounded and spread about,
Irritates us.
So I see him with my eyes,
But never do I meet him.

(2938)

354

I'm so lost in love
That I cannot tell
When 'tis morn and when 'tis eve.
Better to die
That my mind may be at ease.

(2940)

355

Now I'm weak with age,
I never see this old white robe
But it brings memories of sweet days
    past.
Clad in this long-sleeved robe,
I pledged the troth of love
With my dear sweet one.

(2952)

356

"You are my dear love,"
Say you. These are hackneyed words.
And yet for all that,
Your repeated assurances
Make me think it is true.

(2961)

357

I never see these seams
But that I am moved to tears.
Handing me this robe, she said,
"Look at this and think of me,
If for years you cannot return."®

(2967)

358

Could I clearly see your face
As I do mine in the mirror,
It might calm
My blazing love for you,
Which consumes my body and soul.

(2979)

® A poem probably composed by a frontier guard, by a man who lost his wife, or
by a man away from home on a journey.

359

It is many months now
Since I have seen
My darling love, of whom
Never do I tire or become sated.
Now I feel as good as dead.

(2980)

360

Since our souls commune,
I may meet and sleep with her.
But her mother
Keeps careful guard,
As with deer and boar
That ravage the farms.

(3000)

361

"I await the moon
Rising above the hills,"
Said I to a man nearby.
But in fact it was my love
That I had long awaited.

(3002)

362

How I long and pine
For a lovely lady
Whom I vaguely glimpsed
In the darkness of early dawn
When a crescent moon had just set.[@]

(3003)

[@] When a crescent moon goes down before dawn, the sky becomes suddenly dark.

363

Not until the orb of night,
Shining over sky and earth,
Loses its bright light
Will my blazing love
Lose its heat and die away.

(3004)

364

As the glassy stream
Of the Saho flows softly,
So I wish to stay in your arms
In this calm, happy peace
Till we bathe in morrow's light.[@]

(3010)

365

Hot was my breast
With flaming love
For my darling girl—
As I opened the door at dawn,
The world was filled with fog.

(3034)

366

"Let us fall and fade
Together like dewdrops
Sparkling on the grass at morn,"
He would say to me.
What could have become of him?

(3041)

@ The Saho is a river near the city of Nara.

367

As sleek seaweed
Drifts in the sea intertwined,
So let us lie entwined.
Come to see me, my dear one,
To end my painful wait.

(3079)

368

Oft I am rebuked
Like a horse that steals feed
From another manger.
But my heart so longs for him
That I can never sever our ties.[⊕]

(3096)

369

At dawn
You hurry away.
By the river
Stop your horse and let him drink.
There I'll have a good look at you.[✿]

(3097)

[⊕] A girl is sharply rebuked by her mother, but is unable to give up her lover.

[✿] After visiting his love at night, a young man hurries away on horseback. In the dark of night, she could not obtain a good look at him.

The following poem is a proposal of marriage or courtship from a man. In her reply poem, the woman politely declines his proposal.

The proposal

370

As camellia ash is added
To make purple dye,
Who are you that
I glimpsed at the camellia fair
Where all the world crossed paths?[@]

(3101)

The reply

371

Fain I'd let you know
The name my mother calls me,
But I have yet to learn
Who you are. You're a passerby
Who has but chanced to speak to me.[※]

(3102)

From a man

372

From tomorrow
I shall travel far away,
Greatly missing you.
Early come to bed tonight,
And untie your sash, my sweet.

(3119)

[@] Purple was a noble color used for dyeing the attire of the three highest court ranks. What seems like a forced allusion today is meant to convey the fact that a woman of beauty and worth becomes particularly noticeable when she mixes with the general public.

[※] Her decline of the proposal in No. 370 is demure. If a girl revealed her name to a stranger offering a proposal of this sort, she indicated her acceptance of it.

His wife's reply

373

'Tis no time to sleep.
Let us spend the night in talk.
Hence never fail
To appear in my nightly dreams,
That we may renew
The joy of our wedding night.

(3120)

374

It has begun raining now,
And the night has worn away.
'Tis too late for you to go.
Why not bide here
And undo your sash?

(3124)

375

Being far away,
I can't see her lovely grace.
And yet night and day
My dear girl's smiling face
Floats before my eyes.

(3137)

376

I see my beloved wife
Reduced to a shadow
Of what she once was,
Hoping that I might return
By the time the year is out.

(3138)

377

Now that you are gone
On your travels far away
How forlorn and helpless I feel!
I now know
How deep is my love for you.

(3140)

378

Could I have foreseen
How I long for,
How I miss my love,
I'd have striven to win her heart.
Bitterly I rue the day.

(3143)

379

I cannot know
What is in store for me,
But you are so dear to me
That I have followed you
Up the hills and down the vales.[@]

(3149)

380

Let me tie a knot
In your inner sash,
While you do the same on mine.
We will never undo our knots
Till the day we meet again.

(3181)

@ This poem reads like a folk song.
See note to No. 344.

381

You'll be long away
On your travels.
After you are gone,
Even glorious moonlit nights
Will be the darkest black for me.

(3208)

382

Morning after morning
Toward Tsukushi I face,
Sunk in bitter grief,
Praying to the gods
For the welfare of my love.

(3218)

383

Crossing the hill,
I come in view of Lake Biwa,
Where waves
Rise and break in foamy crests
As white flowers in bloom.

(3238)

384

Could I find
A replica of you
In the Land of Yamato,
There would be no cause
For my deep longing.⊛

(3249)

⊛ Yamato refers not only to the region of that name (present-day Nara prefecture) but also to the whole of Japan.

385

Bitter jealousy
Which inflames me
Is the work of my heart.
My sweet love for you
Is also the work of my heart.

(3271)

386

My mind is dazed
With impassioned love for her.
Try as hard as I may,
I cannot even count the nights
When I must sleep alone.

(3275)

387

Even from my dear mother
I have hidden my love for you.
But now, for all that,
I have placed at your sweet will
All my heart and all my love.

(3285)

388

O would it be every night
That the jet-black horse came,
With my gallant one astride,
Dashing over the stony sands
Along the shallows of the stream.[B]

(3313)

[B] This is substantially a folk song.

In the following long poem with its envoy, a woman expresses her concern for her husband's traveling on foot and urges him to buy a horse. Her husband's reply poem follows.

Wife

389

Going down the Yamashiro Road,
Other husbands ride horseback.
I never see my husband dear
Go on foot his weary way
But my heart cries in pain.
Gladly will I sell
My precious mirror
And my gossamer silken hood
Left me by my mother
So that you may buy a horse.

(3314)

Envoy

390

What is the use
Of my precious mirror,
If my husband
Has to walk his weary way?
Go, husband, sell my mirror
And buy a horse.

(3316)

Husband

391

Should I buy a horse,
Still, we cannot ride together.
Though I stumble on stones,
I will walk along with you.

(3317)

392

You are now all young,
But in time you will be old
With snow-white hair,
And you'll be the butts of children's
  jests,
Just as you make fun of me.

(3793)

393

Should my parents
Discover our affair,
Fain I'd be interred with you
In a stone-walled tomb
Atop Mt. Hatsuse.[⊛]

(3806)

394

In the grove
Where the mandarin oranges grow,
Once, with a sweet girl I lay.
With her hair set high,
She now must be fully grown.[✻]

(3823)

395

Hark! Around the gate
Plovers cry.
Wake up. Rise and go,
My dear husband of one night,
Lest they find you here.[✿]

⊛ Mt. Hatsuse was dreaded as a place for interring the dead.

✻ See note to No. 215, page 94.

✿ Generally women's poems express sorrow or regret at parting from a sweetheart.
This folk-song-like poem is exceptional.

East Japan

A total of 231 anonymous poems of East Japan are collected in volume 14 of the *Man'yōshū*. These poems are divided into two groups: those whose original provinces are known, and those whose original provinces are unknown. In this book, sixty-five of the finest have been selected, regardless of their origins.

East Japan was completely subjugated by the central Yamato regime in the fifth century. Thereafter, the provincial governments of East Japan made a point of manifesting obedience and loyalty to the central government and accorded courtesy and hospitality to governors and officials sent by the court. As a result, though the East was relatively remote from the capital, the region was under the cultural sway of the imperial court.

Provincial government offices in the East are presumed to have offered local poetry and folk songs, as a testimony of their loyalty and allegiance, to the Imperial Bureau of Poetry.

Before the fifth century, when the Japanese language was first given written form, poetry was mostly composed for singing. The word *uta* meant both song and poetry, and song and poetry were one and the same thing. From the sixth century, poetry came to be composed not only to be sung but also as a literary accomplishment.

In Man'yō days, composing poetry was a major pastime of the educated and cultured. Even married couples exchanged love poems for pleasure and diversion. Folk songs remained a source of inspiration for anyone who dabbled in poetry.

Some of the anonymous poems in the *Man'yōshū*, especially in the poetry of East Japan, read like folk songs, either songs accompanying dances or work songs.

On occasions such as welcome and farewell events for high officials and also at parties, poems resembling folk songs were read, and troupes of professional entertainers performed dances accompanied by folk songs.

The controversy continues regarding the extent to which folk-song material and forms are present in the *Man'yōshū*.

396

I don't care a straw
For my gorgeous robe
Woven of new silk.
What I desire to don
Are the clothes you wear.

(3350)

397

How I wish to sleep
In my beloved's bed,
As smooth and soft
As a noble's bed
With thick, downy quilts.

(3354)

398

Long and arduous
Is the road around the foot
Of lofty Mt. Fuji.
In my eagerness to see my love,
I have halved the traveling time.

(3356)

399

As a vine by the shore
Clings fast to a rock,
So you have
All my trust,
Despite my mother's wishes.

(3359)

148

400

Snares and traps were set
On Mt. Ashikaga.
While folk were off to collect the
 game
With the clanging of cymbals,
Secretly I lay with my dear love.

(3361)

401

As we ignore familiar Mt. Sagami,
So I tried to forget my dearest,
Not looking back.
However, turning on the mountain road,
I wept when her name escaped my lips.

(3362)

402

I am on the way
To sleep with my love.
The River Minase,
Which I have to cross,
May soon be in flood.

(3366)

403

Why do you rest your head
On a pillow of sedge
Growing on the hill?
Come, my sweet love, why not
Make a pillow of my arm?

(3369)

404

Are you a doll bride
Made of ferns
From the Hakone Hills,
Coming to bed
With your sash so tightly knotted?[@]

(3370)

405

Who can behold
The maiden
Bleaching cloth
In the crystal Tama waters
And not be smitten?[🐝]

(3373)

406

To what shall I compare
My dear lover?
He's a graceful aster bloom,
Which, like the stars of the sky, adorns
The boundless Musashi Plain all the
    year.[🌸]

(3379)

[@] On their wedding night, a man chides his beautiful young bride.

[🐝] This is considered one of the loveliest poems of the *Man'yōshū*, portraying a maiden's magnetic beauty.

[🌸] The plant in the original poem is a perennial of the chrysanthemum family bearing white or light pink flowers, which bloom in autumn for a long time.

407

Would I had a horse
That could run without sound.
I'd ride across
The bridge of cleft boards
And oft visit my sweet love.

(3387)

408

Heaving great sighs,
He can no more pass by your house
Than mist avoid a mountaintop.
Hey, lass, why not let him in,
Lie with him, and let him go.[●]

(3388)

409

I will wave
To the darling of my heart,
Till the gate of her house
Disappears from view
Behind the hill.[❀]

(3389)

410

As Mt. Tsukuba
Is always in view
So I'm under the constant gaze
Of my mother's wary eyes.
For all that, our souls met.[❦]

(3393)

● This playful poem is a folk song in substance. This kind of song might well have been sung in chorus by men and women as banter at, say, an older man who sponsored a party or gathering.

❀ A poem by a man departing on a journey.

❦ In ancient days there was the belief that if lovers' souls meet in their dreams, their love will be fulfilled.

152

411

As water plummets
Down the sheer cliff
Of Mt. Tsukuba,
Roaring and foaming,
So wild is my love.

(3392)

412

Like seeing birds
Flying through the trees
Of Mt. Tsukuba,
So I see you pass,
Though once we lay together.

(3396)

413

Even if everyone
Reviled me,
What should I care,
So long as my darling
Holds me dear and writes to me?

(3398)

414

The Shinano Highway
Is a newly opened road,
Stony and rough.
Wear good, new straw sandals,
Lest you stumble.

(3399)

415

Even pebbles
In the River Chikuma
Which you tred upon
Are precious to me.
Gladly I would gather them.

(3400)

416

When my husband crossed Usui Pass,
I saw him against
The evening sun,
Waving both arms—
His heartfelt goodbye.

(3402)

417

How sweet is my darling.
Nightly lost in love,
In my arms I clasp her tight,
Yet I never tire.
Is there a better way
I can show my love?

(3404)

418

Try hard as I may
No more can I bring the lovely girl
Closer to me
Than I can pull Mt. Tago
To me with a rope.

(3411)

419

Heedless of finding a ford,
Once I crossed a river wide
And I came upon a rapid stream.
Likewise unawares I found myself
In your tender, sturdy arms.[@]

(3413)

420

Could I but sleep with my dear love,
Locked close in each other's arms,
Till a rainbow rises high
O'er the dike of Ikaho,
I would have no worry.

(3414)

421

As if in a dream,
Flying over the stones
Of the riverbed,
I have come to see you now.
Tell me if you love me, dear.

(3425)

❋ The last two lines, literally translated, read: "So unawares I encountered you." But some annotators say that this poem may be interpreted as in the translation given here.

❋ Until a young man could obtain the permission of his love's mother, he had to visit his love by stealth at night and leave her by dawn. This poem, substantially a folk song, expresses many lovers' desire to sleep long into the day.

422

My dear girl in the East
Made a knot in my inner sash.
Coming to Kyushu,
I have had the knot untied
By a charming maiden.

(3427)

423

O pray, lovely maiden,
At the post house,
With horses' bells ringing,
Let me drink at the spring
From your fair cupped hands.[*]

(3439)

The following poem is interpreted in two ways. Many scholars consider that it portrays a young man bantering with a girl for fun (version A), using euphemisms for the genital organs, while some scholars consider it a dialogue between two women (version B) arranging their children's marriage.

424 A

Hey, hey, pretty girl
Washing greens in this clear stream!
You have got a little girl in you,
I have got a little boy in me.
They are of an age, well matched.
Would you give your girl to my boy?

424 B

There is a lovely girl
Washing greens in this clear stream.
I, too, have a son.
They are of an age, well matched.
Would you give her for his wife?

(3440)

[*] Travelers' thirst and imagination are thought to have produced this beautiful poem, substantially a folk song.

Woman

425

> "On the fresh green fields
> Near the wooded hill
> I am gathering herbs,
> But my basket is not full."

Her acquaintance

> "Why not go picking with your dear
> love?"

(3444)

426

> If you long for me,
> Come, come.
> I'll watch for you,
> Pruning willows at the hedge
> Till not a twig remains.

(3455)

427

> While you serve at court
> You will sleep upon the knees
> Of a lady fair.
> Then remember me in the East,
> Who thinks of you.[*]

(3457)

428

> O my husband dear!
> When you're lost to sight
> Past the bend in the road,
> My heart is stricken,
> And I weep by the gate.

(3458)

---

[*] A poem written by a woman in the East to her lover who has probably been ordered to go to the capital on some official duty. This may well have been a folk song.

429

When I open
The heavy gate of cypress wood
Brought from the mountain depths,
Come in quickly, silently,
So we may share the bed.

(3467)

430

"I am married,"
Oft you say to me.
But when in need,
Who does not borrow fine garments
From a neighbor?⊛

(3472)

431

Again tonight,
My young lord
Will gently take my hands,
Roughened from pounding rice,
And be grieved.🦋

(3459)

432

Rumors spread
If I lie with my darling.
But if I do not,
Heavy is my heart
Consumed with love.

(3466)

⊛ A poem by a man whose attentions to a married woman have been repulsed.

🦋 A maid, lamenting her roughened hands, modestly airs her joy in her love affair.
It is presumed that this kind of folk song was widely popular in East Japan.

433

Having mown the grass,
We made a place for love
At the foot of a hill.
How sweet and lovely is she
Who demurs from our pledge of love.⊛

(3479)

434

The sash of my undergarment
Which won't come undone by day
Comes undone with ease at night.
Does this mean
My lover will come?✻

(3483)

435

The tub is full of yarn
You have spun.
Yet tomorrow you cannot wear
Your new nice robe.
Come and rest next to me, my dear.

(3484)

436

As hemp is coiled
Fast around the grip of a bow,
So with both my arms,
I will clasp my love in bed
Far more tightly than my rival would.

(3486)

⊛ A young woman sulks at the last moment, when the couple is to fulfill the final pledge of love. The young man thinks her all the lovelier on account of such behavior.

✻ In Man'yō days there was a common belief that the cord of one's undergarment coming undone easily foretold that one's love would be fulfilled.

437

Fain I'd lie with you
Till the fresh green maple leaves
Turn to autumn tints.
What say you
To that, my dear?

(3494)

438

"No more shall I leave you
Than the snow-white clouds
Move away in the eve
From the distant hills."
So vowed my darling girl.

(3513)

439

You're a lofty peak
Girt round by clouds.
O that I could rise
To those lofty heights
And be at your side.

(3514)

440

Should you lose
The memory of my face,
Just behold the clouds
Over the mountain
And my image will be brought to mind.

(3515)

441

Severely rebuked
By your mother, now I go.
But before I depart, my dear,
Please appear, quickly, like a patch of
 blue
In a cloudy sky.

(3519)

442

It was but last night
That I lay with my sweet love.
But it seems as distant
As a crane
Flying above the clouds.

(3522)

443

With my heart too full to speak,
Hurriedly I had to go,
Leaving her,
Like a wild bird
On a lonely pond.

(3527)

444

Departing in haste,
As waterfowl take wing,
How I rue the day
That I found no time to talk
To my dear wife before I left.

(3528)

445

Like a stag concealed
In trees and brush,
She remains unseen,
And yet I never pass her gate
But my heart thrills with joy.

(3530)

446

When I touch my horse,
Feeding him a bit of wheat
Across a wooden stable bar,
How I yearn after that girl,
Whose smooth skin I have enjoyed but
  once.

(3537)

447

'Tis as great a risk
To approach another's wife
As to tie a horse
To the edge of a crumbling cliff.
Yet as ever do I breathe,
I'm smitten with her charms.
I shall risk my life for her.

(3541)

448

Little did I know
That you are the River Asuka,
With a mud-roiled stream.
O how I rue the night
When I gave myself to you!

(3544)

449

Setting my pail aside
At the public well
Shadowed by green willow trees,
Anxiously I wait for you,
Wearing a path in the ground.

(3546)

450

'Tis a delight
To yield to you.
But last night you came not.
As a rice plant in the wind,
I tossed about in bed.

(3550)

A literal translation of the first two lines reads:

I would never say no
To the pounding of rice.

The pounding of rice in a mortar with a pestle is an obvious sexual image.

451

Never shall I forsake my love
And untie my sash for another,
As breakers on the shore
Gape wide
And collapse in floral foam.

(3551)

452

Would that I could be
Water flowing among rocks,
That I may flow through
The chamber where she sleeps
And enjoy a night with her.

(3554)

453

Though married,
She'll never fade from my mind,
As a fishing boat
Disappears over the horizon.
Daily grows my aching love.

(3557)

454

As green weed in the sea
Waves with the tides,
So the lithe body of my love
Must toss about in bed
In her anxious wait for me.

(3562)

455

In the eulalia fields
The moon now sinks behind the hills.
The night has worn away.
She has not come yet.
Gone is the chance for a night of love.

(3565)

Frontier guard

456

> Leaving you at home,
> I shall miss you constantly.
> O that you were the grip
> Of my bow, so I could always
> Grasp you closely.

(3567)

His wife's reply

457

> While I stay here
> I shall pine for you.
> Would I were the bow
> Which you hold in your hand
> When you go on morning hunts!

(3568)

The following three poems (Nos. 458 to 460) were composed by frontier guards.

458

> When I left at morn
> For the frontier as a guard,
> My young darling wife
> Cried her heart out
> And would not let go of my hands.

(3569)

459

On a dusky eve
When cold mist hangs
O'er swamp reeds,
And wild geese cry in the sky,
I shall yearn for you.

(3570)

460

Again and again turning my eyes
Toward the village
Where I left my wife,
Till it was lost to sight,
I have come all this weary way.

(3571)

PART THREE

Poetry of Envoys and Frontier Guards

Diplomatic Mission to Silla

In 736 Japan dispatched a diplomatic mission to the Kingdom of Silla in Korea. In those days the sea journey was perilous, and all the more poignant were parting and the travelers' longing for home. The *Man'yōshū* includes 156 poems composed by members of this mission. Among these poems are those exchanged by the envoys during their journey. All the poems of the mission express love for dear ones, not patriotic sentiment or determination to fulfill the mission. The majority of the poems are anonymous. Of these poems, three have been selected for this book.

Usually a farewell poem is written first by the one who will remain behind and a farewell poem in reply is written by the one who is departing. No. 461 is a poem written by a wife to her husband, who was leaving for Silla. No. 462 is a reply poem by the husband.

Wife of Hatano Mushimaro

461

> You have cared for me
> As a hen enfolds her brood
> Under her warm wings.
> Being far from you,
> I shall pine away until I die.

(3578)

Hatano Mushimaro

462

> Could I take my wife
> On our ship,
> I would take tender care of her,
> As a hen, assembling her brood,
> Holds them under her warm wings.

(3579)

169

The following poem is anonymous.

463

Should a mist arise
About an inn where you will stay
On your travels overseas,
Think of it as the white breath
Of the sighs I heave at home.

(3580)

Frontier Guards

The *Dazaifu*, the government and defense headquarters of Kyushu (then known as Tsukushi), was established in northern Kyushu in 670 to defend against possible attacks from the continent and also to suppress local uprisings. For these purposes, frontier guards were recruited from military divisions under the supervision of provincial governors and were sent to Kyushu for a garrison posting of three years under the command of the governor general of the *Dazaifu*.

A greater part of the guards was recruited from the eastern part of Japan, because the people in East Japan, which was remote from the capital, were brave and trustworthy and obedient to their commander.

To the people of East Japan, Kyushu was a region distant beyond imagination, and the trip there was fraught with dangers. Those ordered to serve as frontier guards left home hardly expecting to return alive. Since the provisions and equipment provided by the government for frontier guards were insufficient, the guards' families had to make heavy outlays with great sacrifice and suffered many hardships. The number of frontier guards stationed at the Dazaifu was approximately three thousand. They eked out a living by farming.

Ōtomo-no-Yakamochi, the preeminent poet who was undersecretary of war, was in the position to supervise the affairs of frontier guards. He was sympathetic with the hardships of these men, and he invited each frontier guard to submit one poem of his own composition on the subject of his choice. Thus, in 755 Yakamochi obtained a small collection of frontier guards' poems. Discarding awkward ones, he included ninety-eight of them in the *Man'yōshū*. Of these, eighty-four give the poets' names.

In ancient times, lettered people were rare. Nearly all the frontier guards' poems are thought to have been improved or rewritten by poetically minded people before they were presented to Ōtomo-no-Yakamochi, who, presumably, further improved the poems before including them in the *Man'yōshū*.

The notable feature of this group of frontier guards' poems is that there is not a single war song, and very few of them express patriotic or martial spirit. The men of East Japan were known as the bravest of soldiers, but in Man'yō days, the exhibition of love, grief, and strong emotion was not inhibited, and the vast majority of their poems are lyrics that lay bare what was uppermost in their minds—their intense love and longing for loved ones. Poems that give vent to love for wives are greatest in number, followed by those that express love for sweethearts, children, and parents. The poems of wives and lovers are outspoken in their grief at parting and expressions of tender love for husbands and lovers who are far away from home. The unique literary merit of the frontier guards' poems lies in the amazingly frank outpouring of genuine, intense love—the finest and strongest of all human emotions—which makes a treasury of literary gems that never fails in its powerful appeal to all ages and peoples.

Monobe-no-Akimochi

464

In obedience to
The emperor's command,
From tomorrow
I shall sleep on a bed of grass,
Missing my beloved wife.

(4321)

Wakayamatobe-no-Mimaro

465

My beloved wife
Must long for me.
Even in the water which I drink,
Her dear image appears.
She is always with me.

(4322)

466

All the year round
Flowers bloom.
But never in my life
Have I seen a flower as fair
As my mother whom I love.

(4324)

Motonobe-no-Komaro

467

O that I had time
To draw a picture of my wife.
It would ease
And comfort me
On travel's weary way.

(4327)

Tamatsukuribe-no-Hirome

468

Frontier guard as I am,
Hardship I can endure.
But the weight upon my mind
Is the hardship of my wife
Caring for our children.

(4343)

Aki-no-Osa-no-Obitomaro

469

O'er hills and fields
I have traveled,
Yet my parents
Are always in my mind.

(4344)

Hasebe-no-Inamaro

470

How can I forget
My parents,
Stroking me upon the head—
"Come back safe and sound.
Good luck to you!"[*]

(4346)

Father of Kusakabe-no-Omiminaka

471

How I wish I were
Your bright sword,
To be with you
And to fight in your defense
Rather than to miss you so at home.

(4347)

Tamatsukuribe-no-Kunioshi

472

Far away from home,
On my travels sometimes
I sleep under seven quilts.
Yet without my darling wife,
Cold and cheerless is my bed.

(4351)

Hasebe-no-Tori

473

Now I must set out,
Leaving you who tenderly
Cling and clasp me tight,
As a vine entwines itself
Fast around a roadside briar.

(4352)

[*] The poet is supposed to have been a boy of twenty or less who had lived under his parents' loving care.

Hasebe-no-Yoromaro

474

Never shall I forget
The tender glances of love
From my darling,
Amid such flurried haste
As a flock of waterfowl makes
Taking flight from a pond.[e]

(4354)

Mononobe-no-Otora

475

On the day I left
Bitterly my mother wept.
Fast she held my hands,
Burying her face in my sleeves.
I'll never forget.

(4356)

Osakabe-no-Chikuni

476

In my mind I see
My darling wife
Crying bitterly
Behind the garden hedge,
Her sleeves wet with tears.

(4357)

---

[e] Those who were ordered to serve as frontier guards had to leave home immediately.

Mononobe-no-Tatsu

477

When I left home
At the lord's command,
My darling wife,
Clinging to me,
Cried her heart out in bitter tears.

(4358)

Ōtomobe-no-Chifumi

478

How sweet is my love.
Lovely as a lily
Growing on a hill.
I am rapt in love for her by day.
I am lost in love for her by night.

(4369)

479

Praying to the god
Of the Kashima Shrine,[*]
Where hail falls thick and fast,
I have come as a frontier guard
Of the Kyushu Defense Garrison.

(4370)

Imamatsuribe-no-Yosofu

480

I depart this day,
With no regard for myself,
As a humble shield
Of the sovereign
Against a hail of arrows and swords.

(4373)

---

[*] The Kashima Shrine is dedicated to a war god and is one of the largest shrines in Japan.

Mononobe-no-Mashima

481

I never see pine trees
In a row
But I recall
How my family
Formed a line to see me off.

(4375)

Tsumori-Shukkune-Ogurosu

482

I wish
That my mother were a pearl
Or a jewel bright!
Then I'd wear it
In my tightly dressed hair.[a]

(4377)

Otabe-no-Tarihito

483

My sweet lovely girl
Budding into womanhood,
She afforded me ecstasy.
How could I
Tear myself from her?

(4387)

[a] In ancient times, a jewel was believed to have protective power and was carried on the person. This youth wished to have his mother's spiritual protection.

Oshinobe-no-Ihomaro

484

How dear is my wife,
Whom I see, with my mind's eye,
Praying for my sake
To the gods at many shrines,
Making pious offerings.

(4391)

Ōtomobe-no-Mayosa

485

To what god of sky and earth
Should I pray
To once more see
My mother dear,
Who is a thousand leagues away?

(4392)

Osata-no-Toneri Ōshima

486

When I left them,
My motherless children,
Clung to the hem
Of my robe,
Crying their hearts out.

(4401)

Asakura-no-Masahito

487

"Look at this, and think of me,"
Said my wife and made a knot
In my inner sash.
Even though it wears thin and frays,
It shall never be untied.

(4405)

The following two poems are a pair. A husband's poem is followed by his wife's.

Mononobe-no-Toshitoko

488

As we hold a pearl
And gaze on its pure beauty,
So I wish to behold my love
Intently, closely,
Her sweet beauty to enjoy.

(4415)

Kurahashibe-no-Tojime (Wife of Mononobe-no-Toshitoko)

489

Since my husband sleeps
On a bed of grass
On his travel to the front,
I will go to bed at home,
With my sash tightly tied.

(4416)

Mononobe-no-Hirotari

490

O you dear camellia fair
In full glory by the gate!
You'll have fallen, I'm afraid,
Without my touching you
By the time I return home.

(4418)

179

The following two poems were written by a frontier guard and his wife.

Mononobe-no-Mane

491

Though the hearth smokes badly,
Yet how good and comfortable
Is my cottage
Away in Kyushu.
How dear it is to me!

(4419)

Wife of Mononobe-no-Mane

492

Far away from home
Under stars you'll sleep
On a bed of grass.
If your clothes become torn,
With this needle stitch them up.

(4420)

Hatoribe-no-Asame

493

Now my husband is
Away in Kyushu,
All the dearer he is to me.
I go to bed
With my sash tightly tied.

(4422)

The following two poems composed by a couple are also a pair.

Fujiwarabe-no-Tomomaro

494

Standing at the top
Of Ashigara Pass,
If I wave my arms
Will my wife at home
See me clearly?

(4423)

Wife of Fujiwarabe-no-Tomomaro

495

Would I'd deeper dyed
My husband's garments.
All the clearer I'd see him
Till the mountaintop,
Where he'll wave his last farewell.

(4424)

The following four poems are anonymous.

496

"There go frontier guards.
Whose husbands could they be?"
Someone nearby asks.
How I envy her,
Who can ask without concern!

(4425)

497

My dear wife at home
Would have followed me
As a horse which sallies forth,
Breaking its tether,
Not to be left behind.

(4429)

498

On a frosty night
When bamboo grass soughs and sighs,
How much better than
Seven wadded quilts
Is the skin of my dear wife.

(4431)

499

As I embarked into darkness,
Clinging fast to me,
My dear wife asked,
"When will you return?"
In my ears still rings her voice.

(4436)

This, the last poem that Ōtomo-no-Yakamochi added to the *Man'yōshū*, closes the anthology. When he was governor of Inaba Province, he celebrated the snowy New Year's Day of the year 759 with other officials and composed this poem.

Ōtomo-no-Yakamochi

500

> As snow falls
> Thick this New Year's Day,
> So may the grace of the gods
> Fall thick and fast
> And cover us generously.

(4516)

183